T0327075

IPv6 Address Planning

Tom Coffeen

Beijing · Cambridge · Farnham · Köln · Sebastopol · Tokyo

IPv6 Address Planning

by Tom Coffeen

Copyright © 2015 Tom Coffeen. All rights reserved.

Published by O'Reilly Media, Inc., 1005 Gravenstein Highway North, Sebastopol, CA 95472.

O'Reilly books may be purchased for educational, business, or sales promotional use. Online editions are also available for most titles (*http://safaribooksonline.com*). For more information, contact our corporate/institutional sales department: 800-998-9938 or *corporate@oreilly.com*.

Editor: Brian Anderson	**Cover Designer:** Ellie Volckhausen
Production Editor: Nicole Shelby	**Interior Designer:** David Futato
Proofreader: Marta Justak	**Illustrator:** Rebecca Demarest
Indexer: WordCo Indexing Services	

November 2014:   First Edition

Revision History for the First Edition:

2014-11-05:   First release

See *http://oreilly.com/catalog/errata.csp?isbn=9781491902769* for release details.

The O'Reilly logo is a registered trademark of O'Reilly Media, Inc. *IPv6 Address Planning*, the cover image, and related trade dress are trademarks of O'Reilly Media, Inc.

Many of the designations used by manufacturers and sellers to distinguish their products are claimed as trademarks. Where those designations appear in this book, and O'Reilly Media, Inc. was aware of a trademark claim, the designations have been printed in caps or initial caps.

While the publisher and the author have used good faith efforts to ensure that the information and instructions contained in this work are accurate, the publisher and the author disclaim all responsibility for errors or omissions, including without limitation responsibility for damages resulting from the use of or reliance on this work. Use of the information and instructions contained in this work is at your own risk. If any code samples or other technology this work contains or describes is subject to open source licenses or the intellectual property rights of others, it is your responsibility to ensure that your use thereof complies with such licenses and/or rights.

ISBN: 978-1-491-90276-9

[LSI]

This book is dedicated to the memory of my father, Clifford Glenn Coffeen.

Table of Contents

Part III. Maintenance

Foreword

If you've picked up this book and are reading the foreword, of all things, then I'm going to assume you don't need to be persuaded that IPv6 is important. Vitally important, in fact. Downright critical.

In fact, it's so important that even though you're already convinced, I'm going to take a few sentences to try to really galvanize that conviction.

Most of the world is effectively out of IPv4 addresses. Of the five Regional Internet Registries that cover the world's population, only one, AFRINIC, still has any substantial stock of IPv4 addresses. That means that the rest of the world's population, about 85% of us, are going to have to get by without. And this couldn't have come at a worse time, when movements such as cloud computing, Bring Your Own Device, and the Internet of Things are consuming IP addresses faster and faster. Why, Asia alone is home to about 60% of the world's population, or over four billion people, and Internet penetration there is estimated at only about 25%! That leaves three billion people without IP addresses—and poor IPv4 only had 4.3 billion to start with.

Luckily, prescient Internet engineers knew this day was coming and designed a successor to your father's version of the Internet Protocol. This protocol, IP version 6, replaces its predecessor's 32-bit addresses with 128-bit IP addresses, for an address space that is about 8×10^{28} times bigger. A standard IPv6 subnet can contain more IP addresses than the entire IPv4 Internet—squared!

What can you do with all that space? Lots of things. You can forget about trying to allocate subnets that are just big enough to accommodate the hosts on a LAN. You can devote groups of bits in the address to signify important attributes of your networks, like region, country, city, and department. You can design your address space so that it makes route summarization and access controls easier. That's a lot to look forward to.

But you can't just apply the principles you've learned in IPv4 to designing your IPv6 address plan. IPv6's enormous address space is so large that it requires an entirely different way of thinking, dispensing with the practice of trying to allocate subnets just large enough to accommodate the expected population of hosts. But who can lead us out of IPv4's Valley of Despair, with its scarcity and guesstimating and gut-churning doubt? Well, I know a guy.

Tom Coffeen cut his teeth on Limelight Networks' IPv6 rollout, and he's been talking about the protocol ever since, even when we begged him for a break. At Infoblox, he's advised dozens of our customers on IPv6 address planning. And he's whip-smart, a nonpareil wordsmith, and always ready with an amusing-but-relevant quote.

For all those reasons, I think you'll really enjoy this.

—Cricket Liu
Chief Infrastructure Officer, Infoblox

Preface

It's an exciting and somewhat daunting time to be a network engineer. We're living and working through an era of challenging but essential change in our chosen field. Think of the traditional protocols and operational practices that many of us cut our professional teeth on. They've helped deliver the Internet and sustained its initial period of unprecedented growth and success. But now they're rapidly approaching the limits of their ability to enable the next critical stage of Internet and network evolution.

Virtualization, cloud computing, SDN, mobile devices, the Internet of Things—all of these trends are laying bare the weaknesses of traditional networking technology. Such trends would seem to simultaneously promise and demand limitless network scale *and* unprecedented business agility, but from the same old tubes and wires and the quaint rules that bind them together. You can almost hear Scotty inveighing, "She canna' take anymore, Captain!"

Unless you're Rip (or, perhaps, *rIP*) Van Winkle, none of these weaknesses is as familiar as the limited and rapidly dwindling supply of IPv4 addresses. Likely just as familiar is the remedy for this shortage, IPv6.

Who Should Read This Book

I've written this book with network architects, engineers and administrators for enterprises in mind. For practical examples, I've tried to stick with scenarios and network designs that will be familiar to enterprise IT personnel. However, much of the material presented should be suitable to anyone who needs to learn about network address planning using IPv6. The addressing plan concepts we'll explore should be relevant and extensible to IP networks of any purpose or size.

The content of this book is based on the assumption that the reader has a working grasp of both the theory and practice of designing and operating computer networks. Universally deployed protocols like TCP/IP, and Ethernet and WAN and LAN architectures should already be very familiar to the reader, while a general knowledge of more recent trends in data-center virtualization, cloud computing, mobile networks, SDN, and the IoT may be helpful as we discuss how IPv6 addressing plan design is likely to be impacted by (and impact) these rapidly evolving technologies.

I've aspired to make *IPv6 Address Planning* durably useful to network architects and engineers, whether they are:

- Getting started with IPv6 adoption
- Ramping up their IPv6 adoption efforts
- Iterating or improving their existing IPv6 addressing plans
- Adding IPv6 to an existing IPv4 network
- Designing and implementing a "green-field" IPv6 network

Whatever your particular situation, this book aims to help you design an addressing plan that will prove effective for years to come. To do that, you'll need best-practice design concepts, principles, and practical examples. This book was conceived and written to help provide them.

Why I Wrote This Book

Begining in 2008, I was tasked with deploying IPv6 on a large service provider network. At the time, there was already a decent amount of technical literature on IPv6—at least enough to make a substantial, if not entirely confident, start. (And whatever might have been lacking in terms of documented architectural and operational practices, we at least knew we'd need some IPv6 addresses!)

Since we had customers and infrastructure around the world, it made sense at the time to obtain IPv6 allocations from each of the Regional Internet Registries (RIRs). As a service provider, we were used to regularly requesting and obtaining IPv4 addresses, and it turned out to be remarkably easy to get three IPv6 allocations, one each from ARIN, APNIC, and RIPE (for North America, Asia Pacific, and Europe respectively).

Based on documentation we submitted, each RIR assigned us an allocation (still) fairly typical for a service provider request: one /32 of IPv6 address space (or 7.9×10^{28} addresses). Suddenly, after years of designing, deploying, and operating networks where every IPv4 subnet had to be carefully constrained to preserve a limited quantity of addresses for host assignment (along with the mostly futile attempt to preserve the ability to aggregate prefixes), I had the reverse problem on an astronomical scale: how the heck was I going to logically carve up a total of 3 times 7.9×10^{28} IPv6 addresses to number the network? What I needed was a comprehensive resource to walk me through how to design and manage an IPv6 addressing plan. But whatever task-specific information existed seemed to be scattered, very uncomprehensively, across many documents and sources.

This is, of course, not a particularly new kind of problem for any networking engineer. Arguably, it's a perennial condition of our profession that hopefully keeps us challenged and engaged throughout our careers. Still, there's no point in struggling needlessly. The right book at the right time can go a long way toward maximizing our effectiveness and satisfaction as network engineers and architects. More bluntly, if a book can help you avoid dumb and costly mistakes or having to reinvent operational and architectural practice from scratch, that's probably a book worth reading and keeping handy.

And if you're getting the idea that my own efforts in IPv6 address planning were thus afflicted by the lack of such a book, you're absolutely right! My first IPv6 addressing plan design quickly became my second (and third, and fourth) as I struggled to shed habits of mind and practical experiences from IPv4 that were now, if not entirely useless, then greatly limiting.

Thus, as countless tech authors before me have similarly asserted, this is the book I wish I'd had when I started my first IPv6 addressing plan. I sincerely hope and believe you will find it useful.

Navigating This Book

Part I, Preparation

Chapter 1, *Where We've Been, Where We're Going*

This chapter introduces readers to the astronomical abundance of IPv6 addressing. The historical origins of IPv6 are explored while highlighting some of the protocol's fundamental characteristics. We also look at IP addressing methods in the early Internet and the resulting dilemma of scale that led to the development of IPv6. The recent history of IPv6 deployment along with IPv4 exhaustion is covered. We conclude with the outlook for IPv6 along with the importance of IPv6 address planning.

Chapter 2, *What You Need to Know About IPv6 Addressing*

Chapter 2 reviews the basics of IPv6 addressing in the context of IPv6 address planning, including address representation, structure, and types. Improvements to the protocol are covered, as well as the significance of a 64-bit host address portion. We'll briefly cover some of the issues with NAT and conclude with a real-world production loopback address example.

Chapter 3, *Planning Your IPv6 Deployment*

The necessary elements of a successful overall IPv6 adoption effort are covered in this chapter. We look at the challenge surrounding recognizing a business case for IPv6 deployment and how the cross-functional nature of the undertaking introduces unique organizational requirements and challenges. The phases of IPv6 adoption are explored with special attention on phase 1 tasks that entail the lowest risk and cost to the existing production network operation.

Chapter 4, *IPv6 Subnetting*

Chapter 4 explores the methods and concepts of IPv6 subnetting in the context of address planning (and in contrast to legacy practices in IPv4). Nibble-boundary subnetting and its benefits are introduced along with hierarchical subnet grouping. Additional subnetting methods are reviewed, and numerous examples provide an opportunity for the reader to become more comfortable working with hexadecimal.

Part II, Design

Chapter 5, *IPv6 Address Planning Concepts*

The principles and techniques that will guide the reader's IPv6 address planning efforts are covered in Chapter 5. These include the various allocation methods, as well as planning frameworks that have proven the most useful for other IPv6 adoption initiatives. The key idea of site definition is covered as is the method of assigning subnets by location and function. These and other foundational concepts aim to assist the reader in designing an IPv6 address plan that is both immediately effective, as well as long lasting.

Chapter 6, *Getting IPv6 Addresses*

IPv6 addresses are readily available through ISPs or Regional Internet Registries. In this chapter, readers will learn typical IPv6 allocation types and sizes. The standards and administrative policies guiding these allocations will be explored. Using the information provided in the previous chapters, the reader will scope their IPv6 address plan to determine the appropriate size and type of IPv6 allocation required.

Chapter 7, *Creating an IPv6 Addressing Plan*

This chapter brings together the concepts and methods of the previous chapters to walk the reader through IPv6 address planning examples. Techniques such as consistent hierarchical subnetting using nibble boundaries and the encoding of functional and geographical significance into allocated subnet prefixes will be applied. These examples will help demonstrate how the abundant address space available with most IPv6 allocations provides new opportunities for building an operationally efficient address plan.

Part III, Maintenance

Chapter 8, *Working with IPAM and DDI*

DDI (DNS, DHCP, and IP Address Management) products and features are helping network administrators and IT managers effectively run their networks. Chapter 8

---

introduces DDI and reviews how aspects of IPv6 (e.g., the 32-character hexadecimal format of the IPv6 address) create new operational challenges for managing and monitoring change. Auto-addressing via DHCPv6 and DDNS (Dynamic DNS) offer more scalable and flexible methods for deploying and tracking hosts. Readers will learn the key features of DDI, as well as some of its IPv6 capabilities.

Chapter 9, *Managing Growth and Change*

Networks are organic entities that change and grow (or shrink!) over time. In this chapter, we review methods for IPv6 renumbering that, combined with abundant addressing, will allow for easier network scale and integration. In addition, we'll take a look at some of the next-generation network technologies likely to create new integration and address planning challenges—technologies like cloud and the Internet of Things (IoT), which are rapidly becoming part of the networking landscape for enterprises.

Chapter 10, *Keeping Your IPv6 Addresses Reachable*

In Chapter 10, we'll learn some of what we need to know to help keep our IPv6 addresses reachable. IPv6 routing protocols will be reviewed along with the pros and cons of adopting each. We'll examine some of the ways in which particular protocols have been optimized to increase resiliency or conserve router resources when running both IPv4 and IPv6 (dual-stack). We'll also look at the impact of IPv6 packet and prefix size on routing table limits. Finally, securing the global IPv6 routing table will be discussed along with the associated ACL creation and maintenance best-practices.

Conventions Used in This Book

The following typographical conventions are used in this book:

Italic
> Indicates new terms, URLs, email addresses, filenames, and file extensions.

`Constant width`
> Used for program listings, as well as within paragraphs to refer to program elements such as variable or function names, databases, data types, environment variables, statements, and keywords.

`Constant width bold`
> Shows commands or other text that should be typed literally by the user.

`Constant width italic`
> Shows text that should be replaced with user-supplied values or by values determined by context.

This icon signifies a tip, suggestion, or general note.

 This icon indicates a warning or caution.

Safari® Books Online

 *Safari Books Online* is an on-demand digital library that delivers expert content in both book and video form from the world's leading authors in technology and business.

Technology professionals, software developers, web designers, and business and creative professionals use Safari Books Online as their primary resource for research, problem solving, learning, and certification training.

Safari Books Online offers a range of plans and pricing for enterprise, government, education, and individuals.

Members have access to thousands of books, training videos, and prepublication manuscripts in one fully searchable database from publishers like O'Reilly Media, Prentice Hall Professional, Addison-Wesley Professional, Microsoft Press, Sams, Que, Peachpit Press, Focal Press, Cisco Press, John Wiley & Sons, Syngress, Morgan Kaufmann, IBM Redbooks, Packt, Adobe Press, FT Press, Apress, Manning, New Riders, McGraw-Hill, Jones & Bartlett, Course Technology, and hundreds more. For more information about Safari Books Online, please visit us online.

How to Contact Us

Please address comments and questions concerning this book to the publisher:

O'Reilly Media, Inc.
1005 Gravenstein Highway North
Sebastopol, CA 95472
800-998-9938 (in the United States or Canada)
707-829-0515 (international or local)
707-829-0104 (fax)

We have a web page for this book, where we list errata, examples, and any additional information. You can access this page at *http://bit.ly/ipv6_address_plan*.

To comment or ask technical questions about this book, send email to *bookques tions@oreilly.com*.

For more information about our books, courses, conferences, and news, see our website at *http://www.oreilly.com*.

Find us on Facebook: *http://facebook.com/oreilly*

Follow us on Twitter: *http://twitter.com/oreillymedia*

Watch us on YouTube: *http://www.youtube.com/oreillymedia*

Technical Reviewers

Silvia Hagen

Silvia Hagen is the author of the successful books *IPv6 Essentials* and *IPv6 Planning*, both published by O'Reilly. She is owner and CEO of the Swiss Consulting and Education company Sunny Connection, which specializes in IPv6 and network and application performance troubleshooting. She has worked with IPv6 for more than 10 years by writing, teaching, and consulting enterprises in Europe and the United States for the integration of IPv6. She is the president of the Swiss IPv6 Council, which is a non-profit platform to support the integration of IPv6 in Switzerland. As a result of these activities, Switzerland was the first country to reach a double-digit user adoption rate (10% in April 2013) and has therefore received the Jim Bound Award of the International IPv6 Forum for IPv6 World Leadership. In her private time, Silvia likes to read, enjoys music and going to concerts, meets friends, goes on nature walks with her dog, and gardens. For more details and contact information, visit her website at *www.sunny.ch*.

Ed Horley

Ed Horley is the author of *Practical IPv6 for Windows Administrators* from Apress. He's also the Practice Manager, Cloud Solutions and Practice Lead, IPv6 at Groupware Technology in the San Francisco Bay Area. Ed is actively involved in IPv6, serving as the co-chair of the California IPv6 Task Force (*http://www.cav6tf.org/*), as well as volunteering with the North American IPv6 Task Force (*http://www.nav6tf.org/*). He has presented at the Rocky Mountain IPv6 Summit, the North American IPv6 Summit, and the Texas IPv6 Summit in addition to co-chairing and presenting at the annual gogoNETLive IPv6 conference in Silicon Valley. Ed has also presented on IPv6 at Microsoft TechEd North America and Europe, Cisco Live in North America and Europe, TechMentor, and Interop. He is a former Microsoft MVP (10 years from 2004 to 2013) and has spent the last 18-plus years working in networking as an IT professional. When Ed isn't playing around on IPv6 networks, he enjoys being a women's lacrosse umpire. Ed covers technical topics he's interested in on his blog at *www.howfunky.com*. His Twitter handle is @ehorley.

Cricket Liu

Cricket Liu is the author of several O'Reilly titles, including *DNS and Bind on IPv6*. He graduated from the University of California, Berkeley, that great bastion of free speech, unencumbered UNIX, and cheap pizza. He joined Hewlett-Packard after graduation and worked for HP for nine years. Cricket began managing the hp.com zone after the Loma Prieta earthquake forcibly transferred the zone's management from HP Labs to HP's Corporate Offices (by cracking a sprinkler main and flooding a Labs computer room). Cricket was hostmaster at hp.com for over three years, and then joined HP's Professional Services Organization to co-found HP's Internet Consulting Program. Cricket left HP in 1997 to form Acme Byte & Wire, a DNS consulting and training company, with his friend Matt Larson. Network Solutions acquired Acme in June 2000, and later the same day merged with VeriSign. Cricket worked for a year as Director of DNS Product Management for VeriSign Global Registry Services. Cricket joined Infoblox in March, 2003. He is currently their Chief Infrastructure Officer.

Acknowledgments

We've all forced ourselves to read enough acknowledgement sections to read time and again that "book writing is a collaborative effort." Boy, is that the truth!

First, big thanks to my esteemed technical reviewers Silvia Hagen, Ed Horley, and Cricket Liu for helping make the book so much better than I could have made it on my own. And thanks to Jeff Carrell for providing his expert IPv6 auto-addressing configuration guidance.

Thanks to everyone at O'Reilly, especially Mike Loukides for running with the idea in the first place and to my editor, Brian Anderson, for providing feedback and encouragement.

Much gratitude to everyone at Limelight Networks (AS22822) who helped make the IPv6 project a success, beginning with Denver Maddux who assigned the project in the first place (and removed many barriers to help it move forward). Next, the network engineering team members: Guy Tal, Akito Kurokawa, Ken Penttinen, Brent Van Dussen, Gabe Snook, Elisa Jasinska, and Aaron Selenak. Thanks for your invaluable collaboration on IPv6 (all while helping keep the IPv4 network growing and running smoothly). And big thanks to Colin Rasor, without whose efforts our effective demonstration and rollout of IPv6 as a CDN production service, as well as our participation in World IPv6 Day, might not have been possible.

Thanks to members of the IPv6 adoption community who went out of their way to help inspire and guide my initial efforts at adopting IPv6 on a large network, especially John Jason Brzozowski, Erik Kline, and Phil Roberts.

Thanks to all of my coworkers and colleagues at Infoblox, present and past—especially Paul Ebersman, whose abundant knowledge, generosity, and cultivation were a pleasure to work with and Dave Funk, who intrepidly tackled in-house IPv6 adoption with both aplomb and good humor.

Many blessings to the memory of Erwin Schulhoff (1894-1942), whose exquisite and precociously modern piano music was a constant companion during my writing sessions.

It's not hyperbole to say that without Ed Horley's initial encouragement (nagging, really), I would have never believed I could write this book or even gotten started on it. So remember: If this book annoys you for any reason, Ed is at least partially to blame. Of course, his motives were somewhat selfish as he related more than once how weary he was of being asked for a title on IPv6 address planning. And now that he has one, I expect many more sales as a result. On a more serious note, Ed was a tireless advocate, a bottomless wealth of bulletproof professional expertise and wisdom, and a living example of the dictum that knowledge is meant to be shared (cheerfully, at that). I'm lucky to count him as a friend and colleague.

In that same category, Scott Hogg was equally encouraging and available, a true expert across every area of IPv6, and an abiding friend (with a surprisingly bent sense of humor). He's also living proof that the smartest, most capable experts are often the most humble and accessible.

Much appreciation and thanks to Cricket Liu, without whom it's exceedingly unlikely I'd have ever had the chance to write this book. I'll be forever grateful for the opportunity he afforded me to work at Infoblox and for all the subsequent opportunities for professional growth that have arisen since. His tireless enthusiasm, accessibility, and dear friendship made relocation and transition to the new job as painless as such challenges can be.

To these kind people and the many others in the Internet engineering community and IT industry I have had the privilege to learn from, and be inspired by, over the years, whatever might be valuable in this book is a reflection of their knowledge, experience, and patience. Whatever I've gotten correct and that proves to be helpful to the reader is entirely thanks to them, while any errors or omissions belong exclusively to me.

Finally, to my beautiful and talented partner, Eva Valencia, goes my deepest gratitude and love. Your patience, encouragement, friendship and love have sustained me not only through this project but through all of my previous professional and creative endeavors—truly, through my life of the last 18 years. I'm looking forward to many more years together. I love you, Eva!

## CHAPTER 1

Where We've Been, Where We're Going

Introduction

> I see it, but I don't believe it.
>
> — Georg Cantor

The standard LAN interface assignment in IPv6 is a /64. Or, to be more explicit, a subnet with 64 bits set aside for network identification and 64 bits reserved for host addresses. (If this is unfamiliar to you, don't fret. We'll review the basic rules of IPv6 addressing in the second chapter.) As it happens, 64 bits of host addressing makes for a pretty large decimal value:

$2^{64} = 18,446,744,073,709,551,616$

It's cumbersome to represent such large values, so let's use scientific notation instead (and round the value down, too):

1.8×10^{19}

That's a pretty big number (around 18 quintillion) and in IPv6, if we're following the rules, we stick it on a single LAN interface. Here's what that might look like in common router configuration syntax (Cisco IOS, in this case):

```
!
interface FastEthernet0/0
 ipv6 address 2001:db8:a:1::1/64
```

Now if someone were to ask you to configure the same interface for IPv4, what is the first question you'd ask? Most likely some variation of the following:

"How many hosts are on the LAN segment I'm configuring the interface for?"

The reason we ask this question is that we don't want to use more IPv4 addresses than we need to. In most situations, the answer would help determine the size of the IPv4 subnet we would configure for the interface. Variable Length Subnet Masking (VLSM) in IPv4 provides the ability to tailor the subnet size accordingly.

This practice was adopted in the early days of the Internet to conserve public (or routable) IPv4 space. But chances are the LAN we're configuring is using private address space[1] and Network Address Translation (NAT). And while that doesn't give us anywhere close to the number of addresses we have at our disposal in IPv6, we still have three respectably large blocks from which to allocate interface assignments:

- 10.0.0.0/8
- 172.16.0.0/12
- 192.168.0.0/16

Since we can't have overlapping IP space in the same site (at least not without VRFs or some beastly NAT configurations), we'd need to carve up one or more of those private IPv4 blocks further to provide subnets for all the interfaces in our network and, more specifically, host addresses.

But in IPv6, the question of "How many hosts are on the network segment I'm configuring the interface for?", which is so commonplace in IPv4 address planning, has no relevance.

To see why, let's assume x is equal to the answer. Then we'll define n as the ratio of the addresses used to the total available addresses:

$$n = \frac{x}{1.8 \times 10^{19}}$$

Now we can quantify how much of the available IPv6 address space we'll consume. But the value for x can't ever be larger than the maximum number of hosts we can have on an interface. What is that maximum?

Recall that a router or switch has to keep track of the mappings between layer 2 and layer 3 addresses. This is done through Address Resolution Protocol (ARP) in IPv4 and Neighbor Discovery (ND) in IPv6.[2] Keeping track of these mappings requires router memory and processor cycles, which are necessarily limited. Thus, the maximum of x is typically in the range of a few thousand.

---

1. RFC 1918, *Address Allocation for Private Internets* (*http://bit.ly/rfc-1918*).

2. RFC 4861, *Neighbor Discovery for IP version 6 (IPv6)* (*http://bit.ly/rfc-4861*). Keep in mind that RFCs are often updated (or even obsoleted) by new ones. When referring to them, check the *updated by* and *obsoletes* cross-references at the top of the RFC to make sure you have the most up-to-date information you might need.

This upper limit of *x* ensures that *n* will only ever be microscopically small. For example, let's assume a router or switch could support a whopping 10,000 hosts on a single LAN segment:

$$n = \frac{x}{1.8 \times 10^{19}} = \frac{1.0 \times 10^4}{1.8 \times 10^{19}} = 0.0000000000000005421011$$

So unlike IPv4, it doesn't matter whether we have 2, 200, or 2,000,000 hosts on a single LAN segment. How could it when the total number of addresses available in the subnet of a standard interface assignment is more than 4.3 billion IPv4 Internets?

In other words, the concepts of scarcity, waste, and conservation as we understand them in relation to IPv4 host addressing have no equivalent in IPv6.

 In IPv6 addressing, the primary concern isn't how many hosts are in a subnet, but rather how many subnets are needed to build a logical and scalable address plan (and more efficiently operate our network).

IPv4 only ever offered a theoretical maximum of around 4.3 billion host addresses.[3] By comparison, IPv6 provides *3.4x10³⁸* (or 340 trillion trillion trillion). Because the scale of numerical values we're used to dealing with is relatively small, the second number is so large its significance can be elusive. As a result, those working with IPv6 have developed many comparisons over the years to help illustrate its difference in size from IPv4.

All the Stars in the Universe…

Astronomers estimate that there are around 400 billion stars in the Milky Way. Galaxies, of course, come in different sizes, and ours is perhaps on the smallish side (given that their are elliptical galaxies with an estimated 100 trillion stars). But let's assume for the sake of discussion that 400 billion stars per galaxy is a good average. With 170 trillion galaxies estimated in the known universe, that results in a total of *6.8x10²⁵* stars.

Yet that's still 5 trillion times fewer than the number of available IPv6 addresses! It's essentially impossible to visualize a quantity that large, and rational people have difficulty believing what they can't see.

---

3. After reserved addresses (such as experimental, multicast, etc.) are deducted, IPv4 offers closer to 3.7 billion globally unique addresses.

Cognitive dissonance is a term from psychology that means, roughly, the emotionally unpleasant impact of holding in one's mind two or more ideas that are entirely inconsistent with each other. For rational people (like *some* network architects!), it's generally an unpleasant state to be in. To eliminate or lessen cognitive dissonance, we will usually favor one idea over the other, sometimes quite unconsciously. Often, the favored idea is the one we're the most familiar with. Here are the two contradictory ideas relevant to our discussion:

- Idea 1: We must conserve IP addresses.

- Idea 2: We have a virtually limitless supply of IP addresses.

- Result: Contradiction and cognitive dissonance, favoring the first, (and in this case) more familiar idea.

IPv4 Thinking

Idea 1 is the essence of *IPv4 Thinking*, a disability affecting network architects new to IPv6 and something that we'll often observe, and illustrate the potential impact of, as we make our way through the book.

We'll encounter a couple more of these comparisons as we proceed. I think they're fun —they can tickle the imagination a bit. But perhaps more importantly, they help chip away at our ingrained prejudice favoring Idea 1.

From my own experience, the sooner we shed this obsolete idea, the sooner we'll make the best use of the new principles guiding our IPv6 address planning efforts.

Figure 1-1 offers a comparison of scale based on values for powers of 2 (binary) and 10 (decimal).

2^x	10^x	Decimal	IP Quantity	Short Scale	SI Prefix	Equivalent Quantities
2^8	$\approx 10^2$	256	Single IPv4 interface (/24)			
$\approx 2^{10}$	10^3	1,000			kilo	
2^{16}	$\approx 10^5$	65,536	IPv4 Class B (/16)			
$\approx 2^{17}$	10^5	100,000				
$\approx 2^{20}$	10^6	1,000,000		million	mega	
2^{24}	$\approx 10^7$	16,777,216	IPv4 Class A (/8)			
$\approx 2^{30}$	10^9	1,000,000,000		billion	giga	Base pairs in the human genome (3x10^9).
2^{32}	$\approx 10^9$	4,294,967,296	Entire IPv4 space			
$\approx 2^{40}$	10^{12}	1,000,000,000,000		trillion	tera	Bacteria on you.
$\approx 2^{50}$	10^{15}	1,000,000,000,000,000		quadrillion	peta	Ants on earth.
$\approx 2^{60}$	10^{18}	1,000,000,000,000,000,000		quintillion	exa	Meters light travels in 100 years.
2^{64}	$\approx 10^{19}$	18,446,744,073,709,551,616	Single IPv6 interface (/64)			
$\approx 2^{70}$	10^{21}	1,000,000,000,000,000,000,000		sextillion	zetta	Grains of sand on earth's beaches.
$\approx 2^{80}$	10^{24}	1,000,000,000,000,000,000,000,000		septillion	yotta	Stars in the universe.
2^{80}	$\approx 10^{24}$	1,208,925,819,614,629,174,706,176	IPv6 Site (/48)			
$\approx 2^{90}$	10^{27}	1,000,000,000,000,000,000,000,000,000		octillion		Atoms in you (7x10^{27}).
2^{96}	$\approx 10^{28}$	79,228,162,514,264,337,593,543,950,336	IPv6 ISP/Large enterprise (/32)			
$\approx 2^{100}$	10^{30}	1,000,000,000,000,000,000,000,000,000,000		nonillion		Bacterial cells on earth (5x10^{30}).
$\approx 2^{110}$	10^{33}	1,000,000,000,000,000,000,000,000,000,000,000		decillion		Mass of the Sun in grams (2x10^{33}).
2^{116}	$\approx 10^{34}$	83,076,749,736,557,242,056,487,941,267,521,536	IPv6, RIR (/12)			
$\approx 2^{120}$	10^{36}	1,000,000,000,000,000,000,000,000,000,000,000,000		undecillion		Ratio of force of electromagnetism to gravity.
2^{125}	10^{37}	42,535,295,865,117,307,932,921,825,928,971,026,432	IPv6 GUA (2000::/3)			
2^{128}	$\approx 10^{38}$	340,282,366,920,938,463,463,374,607,431,768,211,456	Entire IPv6 space			
$\approx 2^{130}$	10^{39}	1,000,000,000,000,000,000,000,000,000,000,000,000,000		duodecillion		Molecules of H$_2$O in Great Lakes (53x10^{39}).

Recall that the character ≈ means *approximately equal to.*

Figure 1-1. Powers of 2 comparison

4,294,967,296 Versus 50,000,000,000

Let's look at a basic comparison between two rather large numbers.

Which is larger: 4,294,967,296 or 50,000,000,000?

If we re-express these values in scientific notation (rounding the first one up a bit), it's easier to more quickly determine which is larger:

4.3×10^9

5.0×10^{10}

You're probably suspecting that I didn't just happen to pick on two random numbers to remind you that scientific notation is useful in comparing larger integers. You may have recognized the first number as the decimal expansion of 2^{32}, or the total number of addresses defined in IPv4.

But what about the second number?

That tidy 50 billion is the number of Internet-connected devices by the year 2020 as predicted by Cisco.[4] Since 50,000,000,000 is greater than 4,294,967,296 by more than an entire order of magnitude, the IPv4-only Internet would appear to have a bit of an address supply problem.

---

4. Trends such as mobile device proliferation and the Internet of Things (or Everything) have produced wildly divergent estimates for Internet-connected devices by 2020. They range from 20 billion on the low end all the way up to 200 billion.

Of course, this isn't exactly news. As we'll read, early Internet engineers started musing about this supply problem at least as early as 1988. Even as the IPv4 Internet was taking off in the early 1990s, the Internet engineering community was already busy developing IPv4's eventual replacement. This would eventually lead to the development of IPv6, a new network address with 96 more bits than IPv4, or 2^{128} theoretical addresses.

The decimal expansion of 2^{128} is 340,282,366,920,938,463,463,374,607,431,768,211,456 (or as we've already seen it, rounded down to one decimal place and expressed in scientific notation, $3.4x10^{38}$). This is what math geeks might call a *nontrivially* larger value than either 4,294,967,296 or 50,000,000,000. In fact, it's significantly larger than 4,294,967,296 times 50,000,000,000—around a trillion trillion times larger![5]

In the Beginning

And finally, because nobody could make up their minds and I'm sitting there in the Defense Department trying to get this program to move ahead, we haven't built anything, I said, it's 32 bits. That's it. Let's go do something. Here we are. My fault.

— Dr. Vinton G. Cerf

Back in 1977, when he chose 32 bits to use for Internet Protocol addressing, Vint Cerf might have had trouble believing that in a few decades, a global network with billions of hosts (and still using the protocol he co-invented with Bob Kahn) would have already permanently revolutionized human communication. After all, at that time, host count on the military-funded, academic research network ARPANET was just north of 100.

By January 1, 1983, host counts were still modest enough by today's standards that the entire ARPANET could switch over from the legacy routed Network Control Protocol to TCP/IP in *one day* (though the transition took many years to plan). By 1990, the ARPANET had been decommissioned at the ripe old age of 20. Its host count at the time took up slightly more than half of one /19, approximately 300,000 IPv4 addresses (or about 0.007% of the overall IPv4 address space).

5. And in case it isn't obvious, the entire 50 billion devices would fit quite neatly into one /64 (360 million times, actually).

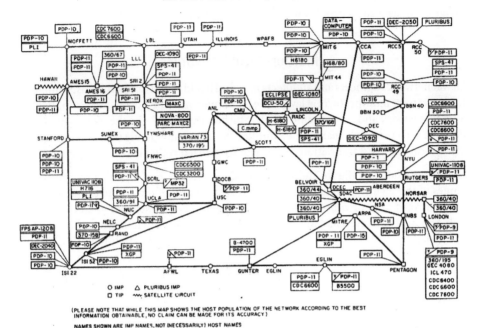

(PLEASE NOTE THAT WHILE THIS MAP SHOWS THE HOST POPULATION OF THE NETWORK ACCORDING TO THE BEST INFORMATION OBTAINABLE, NO CLAIM CAN BE MADE FOR ITS ACCURACY)

NAMES SHOWN ARE IMP NAMES, NOT (NECESSARILY) HOST NAMES

Yet, by then, the question was already at least a couple of years old: how long until 32-bit IP addresses run out?

A Dilemma of Scale

Concern about IP address exhaustion had been rising, due to the combination of the protocol's remarkable success, along with a legacy allocation method based on classful addressing that was proving tremendously wasteful and inefficient.[6] It was not uncommon in the early days of the ARPANET for any large requesting organization to receive a Class A network,[7] or 16,777,214 addresses. With only 256 total Class A networks in the entire IP space, a smaller allocation was obviously more appropriate to avoid quickly exhausting all remaining IP address blocks. With 65,536 addresses, a Class B network[8] met the host count needs of most organizations. Each Class B also provided 256 Class C subnetworks[9] (each with 256 addresses), which could be used by the organiza-

---

6. The success of IPv4 was (and is) at least partly a function of its remarkable simplicity. The formal protocol specification contained in RFC 791 (*http://bit.ly/rfc-791*) is less than 50 pages long and notorious for its modest scope: providing for addressing and fragmentation.

7. A /8 in Classless Inter-Domain Routing (CIDR) notation.

8. A /16 in CIDR notation.

9. A /24 in CIDR notation.

tion to establish or preserve network hierarchy. (This allowed for more efficient network management, as well as processor and router memory utilization.)

Multiprotocol Networks

Newer network engineers and architects may find it odd that at one point most computer networks were multiprotocol at layer 3 (i.e., multiple routed protocols co-existing within a single network and on the same wire). "Ships in the night" was the phrase coined to describe such protocols sharing the same link but never interacting (at least not without some form of layer 3 translation courtesy of specialized router code or appliances).

Even if you didn't configure and work with them directly, you probably recognize the names of these vintage routed protocols from the spines of old computer networking books at yard sales or from war stories your veteran colleagues told you down at the pub. You may have even had the unexpected challenge of troubleshooting these protocols in legacy networks where they probably ran alongside IP. AppleTalk, IPX, DLSw, DECnet, and NetBEUI are all examples of routed protocols that have been driven to virtual extinction by the ubiquity of IP. (And perhaps much like that of Homo sapiens, the enduring adaptability of IP has proven the key to its success over other contenders for evolutionary primacy.)

It is at least partly for these reasons that network admins who've been around a while are perhaps less perturbed by the requirement to adopt a new protocol that will run alongside IPv4. (Though I've encountered a few such folks, close to retirement, who've confided that they hope to be out the door before having to deploy IPv6. What *fun* they'll be missing out on!)

But allocating Class B networks in place of Class A ones was merely slicing the same undersized pie in thinner slices. The problem of eventual IP exhaustion remained.[10] In 1992, the IETF published RFC 1338 (*http://bit.ly/rfc-1338*) titled "Supernetting: an Address Assignment and Aggregation Strategy." It identified three problems:

- Exhaustion of Class B address space
- Growth of the routing tables beyond manageability
- Exhaustion of all IP address space

The first problem was predicted to occur within one to three years. What was needed to slow its arrival were "right-sized" allocations that provided sufficient, but not an excessive number of, host addresses. With only 254 usable addresses, Class C networks

---

10. From the remaining allocatable IP space to be carved up for Class B networks, you had to subtract the Class A networks already allocated.

---

were not large enough to provide host addresses for most organizations. By the same token, the 65,534 addresses available in a Class B were often overkill.

The second problem followed from the suggested solution for the first. If IP allocations became ever more granular to conserve remaining IP space, the routing table could grow too quickly, overwhelming hardware resources (this during a period when memory and processing power were more prohibitively expensive) and leading to global routing instability.

The subsequent recommendation and adoption of Classless Inter-Domain Routing (CIDR) helped balance these requirements. Subnetting beyond the bit boundaries of the classful networks provided right-sized allocations.[11] It also allowed for the aggregation of Class C (and other) subnets, permitting a much more controlled growth of the global routing table. The adoption of CIDR helped provide sufficient host addressing and slow the growth of the global routing table, at least in the short-term.

But the third problem would require nothing less than the development of a new protocol; ideally, one with enough addresses to eliminate the problem of exhaustion indefinitely. But that left the enormous challenge of how to transition to the new protocol from 32-bit IP. At the time, one of the protocols being considered appeared to recognize the need to keep existing production IP networks up and running with a minimum of disruption. It recommended:[12]

- An ability to upgrade routers and hosts to the new protocol and add them to the network independently of each other
- The persistence of existing IPv4 addressing
- Keeping deployment costs manageable

What We Mean by IPv6 Adoption

It's important to describe early what we mean (and don't mean) by IPv6 adoption. For most enterprises, it will mean configuring IPv6 on at least some portion of the existing network. We'll get into the details of how we logically carve up the network for the purposes of making IPv6 adoption easier in Chapter 5.

A second assumption is that any IPv6 configuration will occur on devices that already support IPv4 and that will continue to support IPv4 (likely for years to come). In other words, IPv4 and IPv6 will coexist in production on the same network interfaces pro-

---

11. This method of "right-sizing" subnets for host counts using CIDR would become an entrenched architectural method that, as we'll learn, can be a serious impediment to properly designing your IPv6 addressing plan.

12. And as you'll discover in Chapter 3, these IPv6 adoption requirements are still very relevant.

viding transport to applications for the foreseeable future.[13] This *dual-stack* configuration (as contrasted with IPv4 translation to and from IPv6) is currently considered the best practice for most networks.

You'll notice that over a long enough timeline, we are in fact migrating or transitioning to IPv6. But in the short-to-medium term, we're just adding IPv6 to our existing IPv4 network. That's why we prefer to say *IPv6 adoption* or *IPv6 deployment* rather than IPv6 migration or transition. It may seem like mere semantics, but it does serve a purpose: it helps dispel some of the FUD (fear, uncertainty, doubt) around IPv6 for those who are just getting started with it.

When my boss asked me to deploy IPv6, I knew he wasn't suggesting that we turn IPv4 off after IPv6 was up and running. Rather, it was essential to keep the existing IPv4 production network live and providing the services and applications the company relied on. IPv6 was then added to the network in tightly controlled phases. For nearly all organizations, such an approach will be more manageable, less disruptive, and cheaper than a premature attempt to transition entirely to IPv6 all at once.[14]

As part of our exploration of IPv6 address planning, we'll also learn strategies and methods for adopting IPv6 that have been reliably successful.

The one protocol meeting these requirements was known as SIPP-16 (or Simple IP Plus) and was most noteworthy for offering a 128-bit address. It was also known for being version 6 of the candidates for the next-generation Internet Protocol.[15]

IPv4 Exhaustion and NAT

While work proceeded on IPv4's eventual replacement, other projects examined ways to slow IPv4 exhaustion.

In the early 1990s, there were various predictions for when IPv4 exhaustion would occur. The Address Lifetime Expectations (ALE)[16] working group, formed in 1993, estimated that depletion would occur sometime between 2005 and 2011. As it happened, IANA

---

13. Enabling the forward march of human progress, as well as the reliable delivery of cat videos.

14. It's worth noting that some organizations running a dual-stack architecture today are taking steps to make their networks IPv6-only. For example, Facebook is planning on removing IPv4 completely from its internal network within the next year. Reasons for such a move may vary among organizations, but the biggest motivator for running a single stack is likely the aniticipated reductions to the complexity and cost of network operations (e.g., less time to troubleshoot network issues, perform maintenance and configuration, etc.).

15. The also-rans were ST2 and ST2+, aka IPv5 and IPv7, which offered a 64-bit address. Other next-generation candidate replacements for IP included TUBA (or TCP/UDP Over CLNP-Addressed Networks) and CATNIP (or Common Architecture for the Internet).

16. Based on the acronym, and their affinity for hotel bars as the best setting for getting things done at meetings, I shouldn't need to explicitly mention that this was an IETF effort.

(the Internet Assigned Numbers Authority) handed out the last five routable /8s to the various RIRs (Regional Internet Registries) in February 2011.[17] In all likelihood, IPv4 exhaustion would have occurred much sooner without the adoption of NAT.

The original NAT proposal suggested that stub networks (as most corporate or enterprise networks were at the time) could share and reuse the same address range provided that these potentially duplicate host addresses were translated to unique, globally routable addresses at the organization's edge. Initially, only one reusable, or *private*, Class A network was defined, but that was later expanded to the three listed at the beginning of the chapter.

The NAT proposal was attractive for many reasons. The obvious general appeal was that it would help slow the overall rate of IPv4 exhaustion. Early enterprise and corporate networks would have liked the benefit of a centralized, locally-administered solution that would be relatively easy to own and operate. From an address planning standpoint, they would also get additional architectural flexibility. Where a stub network might only qualify for a small range of routable space from an ISP, with NAT an entire /8 could be used. This would make it possible to group internal subnets according to location or function in a way that maximized operational efficiency (and as we'll see in Chapters 4 and 5, something IPv6 universally allows for). Privately addressed networks could also maintain their addressing schemes without having to renumber if they switched providers.

But NAT also had major drawbacks, many of which persist to this day. The biggest liability was (and is) that it broke the end-to-end model of the Internet. The translation of addresses anywhere in the session path meant that hosts were no longer communicating directly. This had negative implications for both security and performance. Applications that had been written based on the assumption that hosts would communicate directly with each other could break. For instance, a NAT-enabled router would have to exchange local for global addresses in application flows that included IPv4 address literals (like FTP). Even rudimentary TCP/IP functions like packet checksums had to be manipulated (in fact, the original RFC contained sample C code to suggest how to accomplish this).[18]

Whatever NAT's ultimate shortcomings, there's no question that it has been enormously successful in terms of its adoption. And to be fair, it has helped extend the life of IPv4 and provide for a more manageable deployment of IPv6 following its formal arrival in 1998.

---

17. More information on the RIRs, their function and policies, is provided in Chapter 6.

18. RFC 1631, *The IP Network Address Translator (NAT)* (*http://bit.ly/rfc-1631*).

Some Fundamental Design Principles

Before we proceed with the specifics of IPv6 address planning, it's probably worthwhile to articulate and examine some fundamental design principles where networks in general (and IP addressing plans in particular) are concerned. These principles are not unique to specific addressing protocols: they suggest the essence of what a network is and does. A different way of arriving at the same requirements might be to ask *"What problem(s) are we trying to solve?"*

It turns out that these basic requirements and first principles are really quite simple to articulate, if rather more difficult to instantiate thoroughly and maintain over time. They include:

Unique addressability
Every host or node on a network must be uniquely addressed or somehow distinguishable from other hosts.[19] IP is currently the dominant logical addressing method, while hardware addresses (typically MAC) identify individual physical interfaces. A viable network design requires a logical addressing method that will provide sufficient unique addresses (such as IPv6).

Manageability
Networks must be manageable, meaning that the methodology and tasks required to build and maintain the network must be well understood, relatively easy to replicate, and generally based on well-known protocols.

Scale
For a network to meet the needs of the business or organization, new users, applications, and services must be relatively easy to add and support. Any network design will need to plan for manageable (and cost-effective) growth.

Cost-effectiveness
As much as we might prefer otherwise, all network design must bow to economic realities. As the old engineering proverb states: "Fast, reliable, cheap: choose any two." But more often than not, we're obligated time and again to pick *cheap* first and hope for at least a modicum of *fast* and/or *reliable*. This can greatly challenge our ability to accomplish our other design principles.

Flexibility
As much as engineers might like to joke that the network would be great without all those pesky users, a network should ideally be configurable to support any existing or emerging business or organizational requirements. The difficulty in achieving such flexibility with traditional networking protocols has been one of the most persistent challenges in network engineering and has led to the development of technologies like software-defined networking (SDN).

---

19. In IPv6, we extend this requirement to the interface.

Resilience

All networks require some measure of fault tolerance and resilience. In cases where the mission of the network is merely to enhance general business productivity, such resilience may be adequately provided by the underlying protocols and good basic network design. However, the consequence of a network outage for some organizations could be loss of revenue (or even life), and the network design must accommodate this fact.

Simplicity

Network design reflects an aesthetic that extends from the disciplines of math, science, and technology. This aesthetic often prizes the elegance of the simplest solution for any complex problem. In network design, this kind of simplicity often correlates to efficiency and the realization of our other design principles, which in turn makes any network easier to build and run.[20]

You might notice that none of these articulated first principles demand a particular set of specific protocols, whether old or new, established or emerging. The importance of this is difficult to overstate at this particular moment in the history of the Internet. The above first principles are likely to be realized through whatever combination of technologies create the path of least technological and financial resistance in turning on the next generation of Internet and network services. Hyper-scale data centers, public and private cloud services, virtualization, the Internet of Things, and emerging SDN and NFV (network function virtualization) solutions challenge traditional protocols and entrenched architectural and operational paradigms in profound ways.

IPv6 Arrives

The first formal specification for IPv6 was published late in 1998, nearly 25 years after the first network tests using IPv4.[21]

Adoption of IPv6 outside of government and academia was slow going in the early years.

In the United States, the federal government has used mandates (with moderate success) to drive IPv6 adoption among government agencies. A 2005 mandate included requirements that all IT gear should support IPv6 to the "maximum extent practicable"

---

20. As we'll explore in Chapter 3 when we discuss what we mean by *IPv6 adoption*, the path to realizing this principle isn't necessarily a direct one.

21. RFC 2460, *Internet Protocol, Version 6 (IPv6) Specification* (*http://bit.ly/rfc-2460*). Also, *formal* in this case refers to the IETF *draft standard* stage as described in RFC 2026, *The Internet Standards Process—Revision 3* (*http://bit.ly/rfc-2026*). It's perhaps important to keep in mind that earlier IPv6 RFCs (especially *proposed standard* RFC 1883 (*http://bit.ly/rfc-1883*) from December of 1995) provided specifications critical to facilitating the development of the "rough consensus and running code" (that famous founding tenet of the IETF) for IPv6.

and that agency backbones must be using IPv6 by 2008.[22] These requirements almost certainly helped accelerate the maturation of IPv6 features and support across many vendors' network infrastructure products. IPv6 feature parity[23] with IPv4 was also greatly enhanced by the work of the IETF during this period: nearly 200 IPv6 RFCs were published (as well as hundreds of IETF drafts).

IPv6 adoption among enterprise networks was negligible during this same time period. With so few hosts on the Internet IPv6-enabled, it made little sense to make one's website and online resources available over it. Meanwhile, IPv4 private addressing in combination with NAT at the edge of the IT network reduced or eliminated any need to deploy IPv6 internally.

Why Not a "Flag Day" for IPv6?

Why not just set a day and switch all hosts and networks over from IPv4 to IPv6? After all, it worked for the transition from NCP to IP back in 1982. It should be obvious that even by 1998, the Internet had grown to such an extent that a "flag day" was no longer technically feasible. Even in relatively closed environments, flag days are difficult to pull off successfully—see Figure 1-2 for proof.

Much of the discussion around IPv6 adoption in this period focused on the possible appearance of a "killer app," one that would take advantage of some technical aspect of IPv6 not available in IPv4.[24] Such an application would incentivize broad IPv6 adoption and create an incontrovertible business case for those parties waiting on the sidelines. But without widespread deployment of IPv6, there was little hope that such an application would emerge. Thus, a classic *Catch-22* situation.[25]

---

22. See the official Transition Planning for Internet Protocol Version 6 (IPv6) (*http://bit.ly/ipv6-memo*) memorandum.

23. Feature parity, as you've probably inferred, refers to the equivalent support and performance for a given feature in both IPv4 and IPv6. We'll discuss this in more detail in Chapter 3.

24. As we have come to recognize, the "killer app" turned out to be the Internet itself. Without IPv6, the Internet cannot continue to grow in the economical and manageable way required for its potential scale.

25. "There was only one catch and that was Catch-22, which specified that a concern for one's own safety in the face of dangers that were real and immediate was the process of a rational mind...Orr would be crazy to fly more missions and sane if he didn't, but if he was sane he had to fly them. If he flew them he was crazy and didn't have to; but if he didn't want to he was sane and had to. Yossarian was moved very deeply by the absolute simplicity of this clause of Catch-22 and let out a respectful whistle. 'That's some catch, that Catch-22,' he observed. 'It's the best there is,' Doc Daneeka agreed." -Joseph Heller, *Catch-22*.

Figure 1-2. Stockholm, Sweden in 1967 on the day they switched from left-side to right-side driving.

To try to interrupt this vicious cycle, the Internet Society in 2008 began an effort to encourage large content providers to make their popular websites available over IPv6. This effort culminated in a plan for a June 8, 2011 "World IPv6 Day" during which Google, Yahoo, Facebook, and any others that wished to participate would make their primary domains (e.g., www.google.com) and related content available over IPv6 for 24 hours. This would give the Internet a day to kick the tires of IPv6 and take it out for a test drive, and in the process, gain operational wisdom from a day-long surge of IPv6 traffic.

The event was successful enough to double IPv6 traffic on the Internet (from 0.75% to 1.5%!) and inspired the World IPv6 Launch event the following year, which encouraged anyone with publicly available content to make it available over IPv6 permanently.

More recently, large broadband subscriber and mobile companies like Comcast and Verizon are reporting that a third to more than half of their traffic now runs over IPv6, and global IPv6 penetration as measured by Google has jumped from 2% to 4% in the last nine months (Figure 1-3).[26]

---

26. Google IPv6 Statistics (*http://bit.ly/google-ipv6-stats*). In the US, this figure is approaching 10%—or around 22.3 million users. IPv6 expert and O'Reilly author Silvia Hagen recently calculated that global user adoption of IPv6 will reach 50% by 2017.

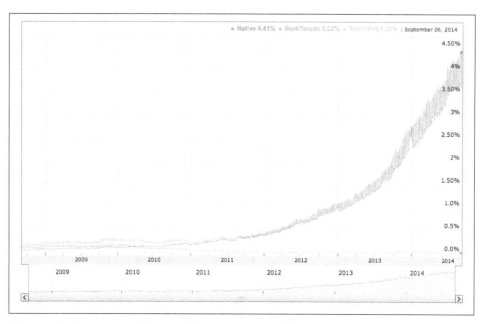

Figure 1-3. Percentage of IPv6 traffic accessing Google services

Conclusion

As mentioned previously, IANA had already allocated the last of the routable IPv4 address blocks in 2011. By April of that year, APNIC, the Asian-Pacific RIR (not to be confused with the Union-Pacific RR), had exhausted its supply of IPv4 (technically defined as running down to their last /8 of IPv4 addresses). And in September of 2012, RIPE, in Europe, had reached the same status. ARIN announced that it was entering the IPv4 exhaustion phase in April 2014, and Latin America's LACNIC followed in June, just two months later (Figure 1-4). Africa is good for now with AFRINIC having enough IPv4 to ostensibly last through 2019.)

RIR	Exhaustion Date	Remaining IPv4 /8s
APNIC	April 19, 2011	0.84
RIPE	September 14, 2012	0.98
ARIN	April 23, 2014	0.81
LACNIC	June 10, 2014	0.22
AFRINIC	June 19, 2019	3.05

Figure 1-4. IPv4 exhaustion by region

To put it bluntly, by the time you're reading this book, IPv4 will most likely be exhausted everywhere but in Africa. And as we've learned, IPv6 adoption is accelerating, by some metrics, exponentially. To stay connected to the whole Internet, you're going to need IPv6 addresses and an address plan to guide their deployment.

The Unequal Distribution of IPv4

Another critical factor that is impacting the rate of IPv6 adoption is the unequal distribution of IPv4 addresses globally.

The Internet originated and saw its early growth concentrated in the US. Early allocations of IPv4 addresses, especially of the class A type, eventually led to a disproportionate global distribution of IPv4, one that favored the US (Figure 1-5).[27]

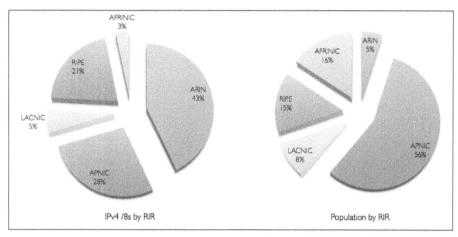

Figure 1-5. Percentage of IPv4 /8s compared to human population by RIR

Over time, as other regions began to expand their Internet penetration, this uneven distribution of addresses, combined with the explosive growth of mobile Internet, very likely led to earlier exhaustion of IPv4 in population-dense Asia and Europe.

A further consequence of this rapid growth and suboptimal distribution of addresses has been the proliferation of entries in the global IPv4 routing table, which has recently exceeded 512K entries. Because many older routers in the core of the Internet have memory or configuration limits on total IPv4 prefixes set at 512K, this has caused outages due to routes above and beyond the 512K limit being dropped.

We'll discuss this issue in relation to IPv6 routing in Chapter 10.

---

27. Source: *Internet World Stats* (*http://www.internetworldstats.com/stats.htm*).

## PART I

Preparation

The next three chapters seek to establish some critical context for the IPv6 address planning principles in the chapters that follow. You're welcome to think of it as kind of a crash course in IPv6: just the right depth of the right kind of IPv6 knowledge to create a better foundation for our main topic and task at hand. If the essentials of IPv6 addressing and adoption are already old hat to you, please feel free to skip ahead to Part II to get right to the design principles and practices.

## CHAPTER 2

What You Need to Know About IPv6 Addressing

We'll need to be familiar with the basics of IPv6 addressing as we learn and apply IPv6 address planning concepts and methods. If you already know this topic well, feel free to skip ahead to the next chapter.

Representation

Let's review the basic representation of the IPv6 address. The IPv6 address is 128 bits long:

```
00100000 00000001 00001101 10111000 00000000 00010000 10101010 00100000
00000000 00000000 00000000 00000000 00000000 00000000 00000000 00000001
```

Easy to write, easy to remember—that is, if you're a computer[1] or a savant.

For everyone else, it's easier to manage in its usual form, presented as 8 hextets[2] (each with up to 4 hexadecimal values) of 16 bits, separated by colons:

```
2001:0db8:0010:aa20:0000:0000:0000:0001
```

---

1. The binary representation is how a computer stores the address in memory and how it appears on the wire.

2. The technically precise (and fortunately seldom-used) term is *hexadectet*.

You'll notice that we're consistently using lowercase letters in our examples. IPv6 standards recommend lowercase letters when presenting addresses. But that's just for human consumption: when formatting IPv6 addresses for internal storage in a database or application, uppercase, lowercase, or any combination of the two can be used. Also, various OSes and types of networking equipment may present (or allow for configuration of) an IPv6 address in either uppercase or lowercase with no impact on functionality. However, keep in mind that consistent address representation becomes important to find addresses in databases and spreadsheets more easily (especially if you don't have, or can't soon deploy, an IPAM solution). A good choice for such representation might be the full (i.e., 32-character) address with lowercase letters like the example shown previously.

Even better, we can simplify the presentation of the address by following two easy rules to shorten it:

1. Leading zeros in any hextet can be dropped:

    ```
    2001:db8:10:aa20:0:0:0:1
    ```

2. One set of contiguous hextets of zeros can be replaced with a double-colon:

    ```
    2001:db8:10:aa20::1
    ```

 Note that the second rule can only be used once per address. If you did it twice in an address, you'd have no way of unambiguously determining how many hextets had been replaced with each double-colon. And since you may have more than one group of contiguous zero hextets, it's generally advised that you shorten the longest one.[3]

You may have noticed that after we apply the two rules to shorten our example, it has only two more significant characters than the longest possible IPv4 address. With a little planning, IPv6 addresses can often be just as easy to read and remember as IPv4. (But as we'll see, most host addresses end up being much longer and require DNS to track and manage them more easily).

---

3. An alternative recommendation suggests that you should compress the left-most zeros in an effort to keep the network part of the prefix as short and readable as possible.

Midnight at the Dead Beef Cafe

If you've ever played Boggle™ (or any of its variants), you may have found it amusing to see how many words you can come up with, given a limited number of letters.[4] Because IPv6 addresses use hexadecimal representation, the letters *a* through *f* (along with numbers substituting for letters) are available to rearrange into recognizable words. Since IPv6 has been around for more than a decade, examples of this kind of word play are now common:

```
2001:db8:dead:beef::1
2001:db8:cafe:babe::A90
```

And so on.

The most famous practical example of this comes courtesy of a well-known social networking site:

```
2a03:2880:2050:3f07:face:b00c::1
```

Cute, but should any such addresses generally be used in production? As with any design decision, there are trade-offs to keep in mind.

It's possible that it will be that much easier for operations personnel to keep track of network locations or functions by encoding recognizable and memorable words into IPv6 addresses or prefixes. (We'll see a more general example of this technique later.)

But it's also possible that malicious scans of IPv6 address space could be made easier with dictionaries of well-known words constructed using hexadecimal characters and common substitutions.

Security concerns aside, while possibly entertaining and memorable, such addresses aren't generally flexible or scalable enough for a production network, but may be perfectly suitable when configuring IPv6 prefixes and addresses for lab environments and testing purposes (as well as making packet captures more readable for training or demonstration).[5]

Structure

So now that we've looked at how the 128 bits of the IPv6 address can be more manageably represented, let's look at how those bits are structured.

---

4. After all, cabs anger faun man…er, anagrams can be fun!

5. One notable exception to this recommendation might include production DNS name server addresses. Such addresses, when memorable, can make any configuration or troubleshooting operations easier to perform.

Returning to the early days of Ye Olde IPv4e, recall that classful addresses, more specifically class A and class B networks, were the standard allocation sizes for most organizations. Early networks, though, were unlikely to need anywhere close to the 16.7 million class A (or even 65.5K class B) IP addresses for host addressing. From the standpoint of host addressing requirements, such extravagance is somewhat like asking for a new pair of pajamas for your birthday and instead getting a circus tent to wear to bed. It seems a bit short-sighted in hindsight given all the tweaking of subnets using VLSM and CIDR we've had to do in the intervening years. But as we've also already mentioned, the tremendous success and explosive growth of the Internet was still many years in the future.

In the meantime, sufficient host addressing was only one of the requirements of IP addressing anyway. The other requirement was met quite handily by all those class A and B allocations: namely, a hierarchy of consistently sized networks that made for simple prefix aggregation and efficient routing. This, in turn, kept the size of the global routing table manageable, improving routing stability, as well as conserving router memory and CPU cycles.

The idea was the right one; it's just that the address space was not sufficiently large to support it once the Internet really took off. The 128 bits of IPv6 addressing, on the other hand, enables both network hierarchy and prefix aggregation, as well as sufficient host addressing, all without running out of bits.

The most basic structure of the IPv6 address is the division of the address into some number of network bits for the *subnet prefix* and some number of host bits for *interface identification*. While theoretically the interface ID could use as many bits as are left over *after* subtracting the network bits from the 128 bits available in the overall address, in practice, interface IDs are always 64 bits (with subnet prefixes necessarily having no more than 64 bits).[6]

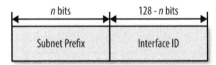

We'll be focusing mainly on the network (or subnet prefix) portion of the address, as we'll have a subset of those bits to work with in creating and maintaining our IPv6 address plan.

Keep in mind that IPv6 was designed to fully utilize 64 bits of host addressing. Thus, further subnetting the 64 host bits (i.e., the right half) of the IPv6 address is generally not recommended.

---

6. Perhaps this even division of bits suggests the equal importance of global routing efficiency and sufficient host addressing.

For one thing, address autoconfiguration mechanisms rely on a 64-bit host portion and can break if one tries to configure any subnets longer than 64 bits.

For another, when network architects new to IPv6 begin to think about what to do with all of the IPv6 space they've been allocated, a common reaction is the understandable desire to further divide the 64 host bits in order to reflexively conserve host addresses; just like the subnets they're used to in IPv4 (i.e., "right-sized" using CIDR and VLSM for network segment host counts).

There are, however, a few special use cases with associated subnets where such further subnetting of the 64 host bits is appropriate. We'll look at those later in the chapter.

Types

The original specification for IPv6 addressing defined three general types of addresses: *unicast*, *multicast*, and *anycast*.[7] The general description of each of these address types should be familiar from IPv4.

We'll introduce slightly more formal definitions for each IPv6 address type, but perhaps the easiest way to think of them is by the communication between nodes they're designed to enable, as shown in Table 2-1.

Table 2-1. Node communication by address type

Address type	Node to node(s) communication
Unicast	1:1
Multicast	1:Many
Anycast	1:Any

Unicast Addresses

Strictly speaking, a *unicast address* goes on an interface and allows packets to be sent specifically to that interface. It's convenient, and therefore habitual, to think of hosts as being configured with an address (or addresses). It's equally common to think of unicast communication as taking place between two hosts rather than two interfaces. That's perfectly appropriate for most situations. But if we want to get technical, in IPv6 a host is referred to as a *node*. Nodes can have any number of interfaces, but each is uniquely identified by at least one unicast address.

---

7. RFC 4291, *IP Version 6 Addressing Architecture* (*http://bit.ly/rfc-4291*). By the way, are you wondering from the table above where the *broadcast address* type went? If you're old enough and lucky enough to remember unintentional broadcast storms bringing all LAN traffic to a screeching halt, you'll be happy to learn that broadcast addresses don't exist in IPv6. They've been replaced entirely with multicast addresses and the much more efficient routing and switching logic they provide.

IPv6 unicast addresses contain several additional subtypes:

Loopback address
   `::1/128`

First is the loopback address, already familiar to us from IPv4 (e.g., 127.0.0.1). It serves the same function in IPv6, allowing the node to send packets to itself.[8]

Link-Local unicast addresses
   `fe80::/10`

Link-Local unicast addresses are defined by the first 10 bits of the address and are reserved for use on a single link. They play a critical role in Neighbor Discovery and auto-address configuration. They also provide for improved (i.e., largely automated) default gateway configuration and management (as compared with IPv4). A Link-Local address is automatically configured on an interface once the IPv6 stack is activated.[9]

Unique-Local unicast addresses
   `fc00::/7`

Unique-Local unicast addresses (ULA) reserve the first 7 bits of the address and are sometimes described as being the equivalent of RFC 1918 (i.e., private) addresses in IPv4. In general, they are redundant where an organization has received a Global Unicast Allocation, or *GUA* (see the next entry).

Global unicast addresses
   `2000::/3`

Next, the address range that we'll be spending the most time with is global unicast addresses (GUA).[10]

---

8. The loopback address has been helpfully described in the standards as "a Link-Local unicast address of a virtual interface to an imaginary link that goes nowhere."

9. The only instance where this should not occur is if a duplicate Link-Local address is detected on the same segment.

10. While technically the GUA space is everything left once we take out the other address ranges and addresses, only 125 bits (!) of that remaining address space has been allocated for immediate use.

To ULA or Not to ULA

Unique-Local addresses (ULA) merit a special discussion.[11] We need to understand their benefits and limitations and recognize when it's appropriate to utilize them.

ULA are most often compared to RFC 1918 addresses in IPv4. This is a useful comparison as far as it goes, but IPv6 ULA offer some advantages over IPv4 private addresses.

The most obvious of these is more address space per site. The standard site allocation for ULA is the same as it is for GUA: a /48. Compared to the largest IPv4 private address allocation of 10.0.0.0/8, a /48 offers 7.2×10^{16} times the number of addresses!

The global ID defining a ULA site prefix is designed to be allocated in a pseudo-random fashion.[12] This means that unlike IPv4 private addresses, the probability of any two ULA prefixes overlapping is extremely low.

Since it's very unlikely that ULA prefixes would be identical and contain overlapping space, consolidating networks after a merger or acquisition would be less problematic than in IPv4. Most organizations use the 10.0.0.0/8 space (often more than once in the same large network) and must rely on NAT or VRFs to overcome conflicting address space.

And just like all IPv6 site allocations, ULA prefixes can offer a well-defined /48 boundary that makes it easier to include in ACLs, either for routing policy prefix filtering and security policy firewall rules—as well as for IPv6-to-IPv6 Network Prefix Translation (NPTv6) use, something we'll look at a little more closely in Chapter 9.

The similarities of Unique Local addresses with RFC 1918 space make them intuitively appealing for most enterprise network architects and engineers new to IPv6. Using RFC 1918 addresses along with NAT in IPv4 at the enterprise network edge is the de facto standard for most enterprises (and has been for well over a decade). As a result, it's generally very well understood by network operations staff and well supported by vendors. Whatever its drawbacks (and there are keen ones), the practice of supporting IPv4 NAT and private addressing is quite mature.

Keep in mind, however, that IPv6 was designed to support multiple addresses (and address types) per interface. As a result, some organizations may wish to configure both ULA and GUA on the same host: The former for access to internal resources with the latter for Internet access.

---

11. RFC 4193, *Unique Local IPv6 Unicast Addresses* (*http://bit.ly/rfc-4193*).

12. The algorithm for this is described in RFC 4941, *Privacy Extensions for Stateless Address Autoconfiguration in IPv6* (*http://bit.ly/rfc-4941*).

This is the globally routable allocation that our organization will be assigned a block from by an RIR or an ISP. GUA allocations are of two types: provider independent (PI) and provider assigned (PA).[13] PI allocations are *portable*, meaning they can be announced and routed via any ISP. They are assigned by the RIR directly to an organization. PA allocations are assigned by the ISP and must be returned if switching to a new ISP, which requires network renumbering. PI and PA allocations are covered in more detail in Chapter 6.

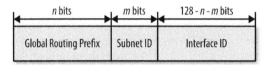

Multicast Addresses

In contrast, a *multicast address* is assigned to and identifies a group of interfaces.[14]

Multicast addresses
```
ff00::/8
```

The multicast address range begins with all ones in the first eight high-order bits. (The next four bits set various flags used to help characterize the address.)

The four bits that follow create various multicast *scopes*, i.e., the scope of the network the addressed packet is destined for. Multicast scopes are shown in Table 2-2.[15]

Table 2-2. Multicast scopes

Scope	Name
0	Reserved
1	Interface-local scope
2	Link-local scope
3	Realm-local scope
4	Admin-local scope
5	Site-local scope
6-7	Unassigned
8	Organization-local scope
9-d	Unassigned
f	Reserved

13. PA is sometimes also referred to as *Provider Aggregatable* space.

14. While these interfaces are usually on different nodes, there's no rule that says they have to be.

15. RFC 7346, *IPv6 Multicast Address Scopes* (*http://bit.ly/rfc-7346*).

Scope	Name
e	Global scope
f	Reserved

For operational purposes, the multicast addresses (and scopes) we're likely to interact with most frequently are displayed in Table 2-3.

Table 2-3. Common multicast addresses

Address	Scope/Destination
ff01::1	Interface-local, all nodes
ff02::1	Link-local, all nodes
ff01::2	Interface-local, all routers
ff02::2	Link-local, all routers
ff05::2	Site-local, all routers

With the first 16 bits of the multicast address spoken for, 112 bits remain for multicast group IDs (that's 5.2×10^{33} available groups per multicast prefix!).

Anycast Addresses

An *anycast address* is also assigned to multiple, different interfaces, but packets are delivered to the interface closest to the sender, as determined by routing metrics. Thus, an anycast address can actually be any unicast address.

Both IPv6 and IPv4 anycast addresses are used by large network operators in their WAN (or even global) DNS designs. Name servers maintained by these operators are configured with anycast addresses, and end-user DNS queries are then routed to the closest name server. This generally succeeds in improving overall session performance.[16]

Finally, not technically included in any of the above three types is the *unspecified address*.

The Unspecified Address

Unspecified address
   ::/128

This is an all 0s address. It signifies that the node doesn't yet have an address and, as such, is used as the source address in any IPv6 packets sent by a node before it has learned its own address.

Figure 2-1 compares the different IPv6 address types.

---

16. For example, Google's public DNS service uses the IPv6 anycast addresses 2001:4860:4860::8888 and 2001:4860:4860::8844 for its name servers.

IPv6 Address Range	IPv6 Address or Prefix	IPv4 Equivalent	Fraction of 2^{128}	Percentage of 2^{128}
Unspecified Address	::/128	0.0.0.0	n/a	0%
Loopback Address	::1/128	127.0.0.1	$1/3.4 \times 10^{38}$	≈0%
Unique Local Addresses	fc00::/7	10.0.0.0/8 172.16.0.0/12 192.168.0.0/16	1/128	0.78%
Link-local Addresses	fe80::/10	169.254.0.0/16	1/1024	0.098%
Global Unicast Addresses	2000::/3	n/a	1/8	12.5%
Multicast Addresses	ff00::/8	224.0.0.0/8	1/256	0.39%
Unassigned	n/a	n/a	≈6/7	85.74%

Figure 2-1. IPv6 address ranges

IPv4-Mapped Addresses in IPv6

In the early days of IPv6, a fair amount of effort was expended in finding ways to translate IPv4 addresses into IPv6 ones. Some of these methods were merely representational, while others were coded into actual transition mechanisms. In general, such methods have either not been widely adopted or have fallen out of favor, as they most often end up being more operationally taxing and much less manageable than a green-field dual-stack deployment.

Still, it's important to be aware of the methods that exist for representing or translating IPv4 into IPv6. We often end up responsible for networks we didn't design or build. Such networks may include one or more of these approaches, and we may need to manage them and develop a plan for their eventual replacement.

There are two IPv6 address types that have embedded IPv4 addresses. Either may be in use in an existing IPv6 network and may show up in an existing address plan (or IPAM system):

- IPv4-compatible addresses

- IPv4-mapped addresses

IPv4-compatible addresses

An IPv4-compatible address looks like this:

```
0:0:0:0:0:0:192.0.2.234
```

Because of the six repeated, leading 0 hextets, sometimes these addresses will be represented in this potentially confusing format:

```
::192.0.2.234
```

All of these addresses are to be found in the range ::/96

In any case, as we can observe, the left-most 96 high-order bits are set to 0 with following 32 low-order bits set to the IPv4 address.[17]

The original idea with these addresses was to create a dynamic transition mechanism where IPv6 packets would be tunneled over IPv4 networks. But IPv4-compatible addresses have been *deprecated*, which is the IETF's rather fanciful way of saying they're no longer to be supported by vendors or deployed in the wild. If they're in use in a network you administer, be aware that they won't be supported in any new hardware or software. You'll most likely want to decommission them as soon as reasonably possible.

IPv4-mapped addresses

An IPv4-mapped address looks like this:

```
0:0:0:0:0:ffff:192.0.2.234 (or, ::ffff:192.0.2.234)
```

These addresses are assigned from the range ::ffff:/96

The left-most 80 high-order bits in an IPv4-mapped address are set to 0, while the next 16 bits are set to 1 (ffff). The following 32 low-order bits are set to the IPv4 address.

While not formally deprecated, IPv4-mapped addresses are not commonly used.

Protocol Improvements

Recall that there were two primary reasons for developing IPv6. First, and most obvious, was the need to overcome address scarcity, given the limited 32-bit address space of IPv4. The second reason was to provide more consistent hierarchy and thus more efficient routing on the Internet. But the early decision to forgo backward compatibility with IPv4 meant that the designers of IPv6 also had leeway to make some additional improvements to the new protocol. These improvements include:

---

17. For the example, I've used an IPv4 address from the reserved documentation range, but in practice this address must be a globally unique IPv4 unicast address.

Simplified packet headers

IPv4's variable-length header has been replaced in IPv6 with a fixed 40-byte header. As a result, IPv6 packets are processed more quickly by routers and switches.

Improved header option and extension support

IP options have been relocated to appended header extensions, greatly increasing the flexibility, manageable length, and forwarding efficiency of IPv6 packets.

Flow labels

The ability to label packets as part of traffic flows that get special QoS processing by routers and switches has been integrated into IPv6.

Support for encryption and authentication

Authentication and Encapsulating Security Payload headers have been included as part of the general protocol specification.

Neighbor Discovery

ARP in IPv4 has been replaced with Neighbor Discovery in IPv6, which leverages Internet Control Message Protocol version 6 (ICMPv6) to provide a more efficient mechanism (multicast instead of broadcast) for mapping layer 3 to layer 2 addresses.

Other changes include built-in support for automatic host address configuration via stateless address autoconfiguration (SLAAC).[18]

As uptake of IPv6 has increased in production enterprise environments, and on the Internet, some of these changes have proven durable, while others appear to have an uncertain future. For instance, the fixed 40-byte header length in IPv6 (as compared to the variable-length header in IPv4) has greatly improved forwarding efficiency.

Meanwhile, flow labeling, while promising, has yet to be widely deployed and is mostly unused. Similarly, rarely used features like Mobile IP (which permit devices to maintain permanent IP addresses even while moving among different networks) have much better support in IPv6. Finally, protocol attacks on extension headers have led to proposals that some of them be deprecated.

Though it's definitely recommended that you explore these improved features thoroughly as part of your overall IPv6 training, we'll go ahead and leave the gory details to other texts (except where they may directly impact IPv6 address planning).

Subnetting Host Bits

We mentioned earlier that there are situations where it's appropriate to subnet the 64 bits of the host portion of the IPv6 address. Typically, there are two such cases:

---

18. Keep in mind that you'd still need a DHCPv6 server when using SLAAC to provide any DNS server and domain info to the host. See "DHCPv6 Basics" on page 182 for more information.

---

1. Loopback addresses

2. Point-to-point link subnets

Let's take a look at each of these.

Loopback Addresses

Just as in IPv4, in IPv6 the loopback address is not only used to permit a host to communicate with itself, it's also uniquely suitable as a way to address and identify network devices for various purposes. These include:

- Device access and management
- Interior gateway protocol (IGP) router ID

Loopback addresses can be configured from prefixes outside of the ones reserved for production addressing and interfaces. This makes it easier to create a security policy that isolates and better protects the internal management network.

Both interior and exterior gateway protocols (IGP and EGP) for routing rely on loopback addressing for sending and receiving routing updates, which are then used to calculate routing paths and provide network convergence.[19]

In IPv4, a prefix appropriately sized for the given routing domain (often a /24) may be reserved and individual /32 loopback addresses allocated from it may be assigned to routers. If more than one routing domain is part of the topology, an additional prefix for each is set aside from which to assign loopback addresses for that domain.[20]

In IPv6, the same concept applies, but rather than worrying about appropriately sizing the prefix, we simply allocate a /64 per routing domain and assign our /128 loopback addresses from it.

Point-to-Point Link Subnets

One of the seemingly endless religious debates in the IPv6 community is what size subnet to configure on a point-to-point link.

The original recommendation was simply to use a /64. As we discussed in our opening chapter, it makes little difference whether we use 10 or a billion of the addresses available

---

19. IGP and EGP routing protocols are covered in more detail in Chapter 10.

20. A routing domain can be loosely defined as a collection of routers under one administration and running the same routing protocol instance (e.g., a BGP AS, OSPF process, VRF, etc.). These loopback addresses often correspond to the router IDs used by the routing protocol as part of its route calculation.

to us with a 64-bit subnet. But nothing quite riles the anxiety inherent in *IPv4 thinking* like the idea of using only two addresses of the roughly 1.8×10^{19} available to us in a /64!

As it happens, there have been other, more legitimate, reasons for not using a /64 on a point-to-point link. At least two potential security vulnerabilities were identified in early IPv6 production environments: *Neighbor Discovery cache exhaustion* and the misleadingly fun-sounding *ping-pong attack*. Both of these vulnerabilities could result in a disabled point-to-point link (or evan a disabled router).

As a result of these vulnerabilities, an RFC was issued recommending the use of a /127 subnet (providing two addresses on a point-to-point link).[21] Alternately, some engineers chose a /126, perhaps out of misdirected nostalgia for the four addresses available in a 4-bit /30 subnet in IPv4. In another possible fit of nostalgia, /127s or /126s configured for point-to-point links could be taken from a single, parent /64 (just as /30s were often assigned from a /24).

Meanwhile, the major router vendors have largely eliminated (or created workaround configurations for) these vulnerabilities and made configuring a /127 optional.[22] The result of all of this is that you're likely to encounter one or more of these subnet sizes in different production networks.

The current recommendation is that you verify that your router vendor has eliminated the ND cache exhaustion and ping-pong attack vulnerabilities, and then use a /64 per point-to-point link. If they haven't and you must configure a /127, set aside an *entire /64 per point-to-point link*. Assigning a /64 per link (regardless of the actual interface configuration) helps keep your addressing plan consistent.

Host Address Assignment

Three primary methods for host address assignment exist in IPv6. Two of these methods (static addressing and DHCP) should be familiar from IPv4, while one, SLAAC, is unique to IPv6.

As with IPv4, static addressing is typically utilized for servers, routers, switches, firewalls, and network management interfaces for any appliances (or any instance where address assignments are unlikely to change over time).

SLAAC is available on router interfaces that support IPv6 and will allow hosts on such a segment to self-assign a unique address. (Default router information is provided via ICMPv6 Router Advertisements.) Because SLAAC does not provide any authentication mechanism and allows a host to connect to the network and communicate with other

---

21. RFC 6164, *Using 127-Bit IPv6 Prefixes on Inter-Router Links* (*http://bit.ly/rfc-6164*).

22. For example, Cisco recently introduced a feature called *Destination Guard* that explicitly protects an interface from Neighbor Discovery cache exhaustion attacks.

nodes, this addressing method is not recommended where security is required or preferred. Lab environments or totally isolated networks where tight host control isn't a requirement are good candidates for the exclusive use of SLAAC.

Another issue with the use of SLAAC may arise where privacy extensions are enabled on the host.[23] Privacy extensions allow the interface ID portion of a SLAAC-assigned address to be randomized in an effort to increase privacy for traffic originating from the host. (Otherwise, the SLAAC-assigned host address will always contain the traceable hardware address of the host's network interface.) Privacy extensions are enabled by default in the major host operating systems and may need to be disabled on the host if strict tracking and control of hosts is desired.

By contrast, Stateful DHCPv6 provides dynamic host address assignment, but also includes the ability to pass additional options to the client. These options include information such as DNS recursive name servers and the default domain name.

Stateless DHCPv6 is yet another configuration option. With Stateless DHCPv6, SLAAC is used to provide host address assignment and default router information while DHCPv6 provides a list of DNS recursive name servers or the default domain name.[24]

Host address assignment is covered in more detail in Chapter 8.

The Problem with NAT

As we discussed, NAT is a technology that we're all intimately familiar with. It's so much a part of everyday life in IPv4 network design, deployment, and operations that it's likely we often forget about or understate the problems it introduces. Let's review at least three of them.

NAT breaks the end-to-end model of the Internet

The Internet was originally conceived with an end-to-end model of host communication: any host on the Internet would be able to communicate directly with any other host. Of course, this model depends on unique host addresses.

As discussed, early Internet engineers faced a dilemma of scale. The simple aggregation and routing efficiency afforded by Class A and Class B network allocations came at the cost of many organizations having unused host addresses that couldn't easily be reclaimed or reallocated.

---

23. RFC 4941, *Privacy Extensions for Stateless Address Autoconfiguration in IPv6* (*http://bit.ly/rfc-4941*).

24. RFC 6106, *IPv6 Router Advertisement Options for DNS Configuration* (*http://bit.ly/rfc-6106*), proposes including DNS server and search list information in RAs to provide host configuration options for SLAAC currently provided by DHCPv6, but it isn't widely implemented among host operating systems.

So in addition to CIDR and VLSM methods to "right-size" allocations and help over-come this host address scarcity problem, it was also recognized that stub or leaf networks didn't necessarily need unique routable, or public, addresses. This was especially true of newly emerging enterprise networks being connected for commercial or business purposes. In the early days of the Internet, they simply wanted to be connected for a basic web presence, the use of the web as a tool for productivity and research, email, and perhaps for employees and customers to access company resources remotely. NAT provided a simple method to connect private addresses to the Internet. But the trade-off was that any hosts outside the enterprise network could no longer communicate directly with the hosts on the inside.

These early business adopters of the Internet didn't necessarily realize how the lack of end-to-end connectivity might limit application development, performance, and real security. Instead, many seized on the idea that having their network address topology obscured to the outside world provided an additional, "free" layer of security.

NAT reinforces the misperception of "security through obscurity"

Network security experts have long warned that this side-effect of NAT doesn't provide any true security. If anything, it reinforces an emphasis on the perimeter model of se-curity that in an age of booming malware threats and infected clients has long been insufficient.

Since firewalls often provide NAT functionality, it's also common to conflate NAT with stateful packet inspection, as if the two were one and the same. If internal enterprise network deployments use GUA prefixes and needn't rely on NAT, it can be somewhat easy to erroneously overlook the fact that stateful packet inspection is still in place (or certainly should be) at the edge of the network.

Shedding the belief that NAT is providing security (along with reestablishing the fact that NAT and SPI are not the same thing) can help properly deemphasize a perimeter model that is too-often insufficiently secure. This can result in an improved network security posture for many organziations.

NAT is operationally taxing

There's no polite way to put it: NAT breaks applications. It makes sense if you think about it. If you were designing a network application, would you want to start from the premise that one or more intermediate points in the network path would be changing the IP address of the destination host?

As a result, firewall and security appliance vendors have gotten pretty good over the years at fixing what NAT breaks. But these included fix-ups, or NAT helpers, then be-come largely invisible to network administrators.

Meanwhile, the application whose session flows are being NATed (and fixed-up) can behave erratically or suffer from performance issues that, while perhaps not breaking the application outright, can degrade user experience and cause headaches for IT staff.

Carrier-Grade NAT: NAT for ISPs

The economics of IPv4 exhaustion have created a major headache for service provider networks. While ISPs offering core routing infrastructure have arguably had an easier time deploying IPv6, broadband and mobile providers have a different challenge: namely, how to continue to add the users their business model depends on in an era of dwindling address resources.

One proposed and deployed solution is carrier-grade NAT (CGN, also referred to as large-scale NAT, or LSN). With CGN, new mobile and broadband subscribers are still connected via their cable or DSL modems using RFC 1918 IPv4 networks. But because the CGN architecture also uses private addressing for the provider's access layer, this results in two internal layers of NAT before any translation to a public address occurs (aka, NAT444; see Figure 2-2). Compare this scenario to the relatively simple, "traditional" NAT configuration of one device (or one home network) mapped to one public address. Instead, CGN sessions from thousands of customer devices (or networks) with private addresses are NATed to private addresses in the provider's access network, and then NATed again to a single public address. Such a configuration makes it much more likely that one or more of the problems detailed below will occur.

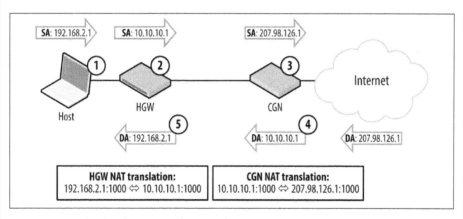

Figure 2-2. CGN (with NAT444) example

Figure 2-2 demonstrates the packet flow for a CGN architecture using NAT444.

The steps are as follows:

1. Host sends packet with private source address (SA).

2. Home Gateway (HGW) changes source address of packet.

3. Carrier-Grade NAT (CGN) maps private to public address.

4. CGN changes destination address (DA) and sends to HGW.

5. HGW changes destination address and sends to host.

The basic CGN/LSN cost-benefit analysis for service providers probes whether or not purchasing additional CGN/LSN hardware (or enhancing existing hardware with CGN/LSN functionality) and developing an operational practice to support CGN/LSN will be cheaper than either immediate or eventual IPv6 adoption.

It's also not simply a question of cost. Subscriber networks are adding hundreds to thousands of new users every day. To protect revenue, bringing these users online has to be done as quickly and economically as possible. The engineering practice to support such massive provisioning obviously has to be familiar enough to be rapidly scalable.

But you probably won't be surprised to learn that, like traditional NAT at the enterprise edge, CGN/LSN deployments introduce problems of their own. These issues include:

- Broken geolocation
- Difficulty with lawful intercept
- TCP port-exhaustion

Broken geolocation and reputation services

The maturity of IPv4 means that the IPv4 Internet becomes more like a village (and less like a jungle) with every passing year. Well-established policies and methods exist to track where, and to whom, IPv4 blocks are allocated. Network operators use this geolocation information to measure latency and help optimize traffic delivery. (Content providers and license-holders use the information to make sure that content isn't delivered to network locations where licensing agreeements haven't been secured.)

IPv4 reputation services have sprung up to provide the dirt on which networks are sourcing malware, spam, and hacker attacks. This information allows network administrators to block connections originating from IP addresses or ranges known to harbor malicious users.

Because CGN/LSN hides up to many thousands of private addresses behind one or a few public addresses, it can break both geolocation and reputation services.

Lawful intercept

Law enforcement agencies may need to issue requests to ISPs for information regarding Internet users' activities when those users are suspected of breaking laws. Since CGN/LSN hides user addresses, ISPs deploying it have the burden of tracking transaction data to the port level for thousands upon thousands of NATed sessions. The amount of data generated is voluminous yet must be stored for some period of time to make

available to law enforcement upon request, creating additional expense and administrative burden for the ISP.[25]

TCP port exhaustion

Many modern Internet-based applications use multiple TCP ports per session. A well-
known example of this is Google Maps, where every requested map is subdivided into
sections and each map section requires a new TCP port to be opened.

CGN/LSN appliances only have so much memory to track these ports and must share
that memory among individual addresses being NATed. Any given host behind a CGN/
LSN will thus have a limited number of TCP ports available to them for any particular
session. Once these ports are all in use, requests to open new ones must be dropped,
which can result in broken applications and degraded user experience (something the
content provider, and not the service provider deploying CGN in the first place, may
get unfairly blamed for).

Practical Example: Production Loopback Addresses

Managing a bunch of routers is much easier if each router is assigned a loopback address
from a single prefix. In IPv4, these addresses are usually /32s assigned from one /24 (or
larger prefix), while in IPv6, they are /128s assigned from one /64 (as covered in the
section on loopback addresses earlier in this chapter).

A logical numbering scheme can help make it easier for operational staff and processes
to track and manage routers. In networks with fewer routers, simple is perhaps best.
For example, if the prefix we've chosen to use is 2001:db8:aa:90::/64, we could use ::1 as
the first address (say for the HQ router) and then number up sequentially from there.

Sequential addresses are, of course, easier for hackers to scan, but we'll likely have a
security policy and set of ACLs in place that isolates our loopback network (while still
permitting legitimate device access).

But as we'll repeatedly demonstrate throughout the book, the abundance of bits available
in IPv6 provides the opportunity to encode operational significance into any given
address or prefix.

In this case, we have 64 bits to play with, which gives us 16 hexadecimal characters to
use for device identification.[26]

---

25. The regulations applying to lawful intercept requirements vary by jurisdiction, but in one example, ISPs must
keep these data for at least six months. Also, dynamic port assignment and changing port numbers amplify
an already staggering data management challenge.

26. Keep in mind that whatever name or function significance we encode into the address using the bits and
resulting characters available to us would be separate from whatever DNS entries we might (or might not)
create for it.

With 4 bits per character in the address, we could create groups and subgroups that are multiples of 2^{4n} (e.g., 16, 256, 4096, or 65536, etc). Note that any hierarchy we create will only be "on paper" and will not be reflected in the actual routing configuration as we're still just using an entire /64 per routing domain.

Routing domains will often be defined and configured according to geographical regions. This helps segment routing policy in a way that can make it easier to manage network traffic. Returning to our example, let's say we have a routing domain corresponding to our North American region. We allocate 2001:db8:aa:90::/64 to use for router and device loopback addressing in this region.

We can then examine our logical network topology to look for opportunities to reflect that topology in the loopback addressing.

Let's say our North American region is divided into three subregions: West, Central, and East. Each region has several core routers interconnecting the enterprise networks of various offices, including the company's headquarters. There are 30 routers in total. (The routers and switches at each of these locations are managed locally.) The routers are running OSPFv3 as the IPv6 IGP.

As mentioned, we could certainly just number from our /64 sequentially starting at ::1 and number through ::1e. Chances are our existing IPv4 loopback scheme does something similar. By keeping the values the same, we help retain some operational continuity with our IPv4 network.

 If you're planning on using whatever numbering scheme you're using in IPv4, remember that hexadecimal doesn't map directly to decimal. In general, we'll want to avoid IPv6 addressing schemes that restrict us to our existing IPv4 one. We'll discuss the reasons why in more detail in Chapter 5.

But by doing that we'd be missing the opportunity to encode the geography associated with our topology in our loopback addressing scheme. (This capability becomes especially valuable if we have lots of routers in our core network.)

To illustrate, let's break our /64 prefix into address groups. First, we'll look at the range of address values possible for the prefix:

    2001:db8:aa:90:0000:0000:0000:0000 - 2001:db8:aa:90:ffff:ffff:ffff:ffff

Next, to keep the addresses tidy, let's just focus on the last group:

    2001:db8:aa:90::[XXXX]/64

Since we already have more than 16 routers in one region, we'll need more than 4 bits per region. We'd likely want to use more than 4 bits anyway to leave room for the "growth" of our loopback ID scheme.[27]

By dividing the last group into 8 bits each, that gives us 256 levels of 256 addresses.

```
2001:db8:aa:90::[RR][DD]
```

(Where R represents the region and D represents the device.)

Which gives us:

```
2001:db8:aa:90::[00-ff][00-ff]/64
```

The simplest addressing scheme would only require three levels, one for each of our regions, and at least as many addresses as we had regional network devices. In our example, we have 30 total, with, say, 10 routers per region, so the previous address would provide more than enough room for expansion (all the way up to 256 regions with 256 devices per region).

Now we'll show some actual address-to-device mappings in Table 2-4:

Table 2-4. Address to device mappings

Looback address	Region	Description
2001:db8:aa:90::101/64	Central region	Chicago HQ core router
2001:db8:aa:90::102/64	Central region	Chicago HQ core router 2
2001:db8:aa:90::103/64	Central region	Minneapolis core router
2001:db8:aa:90::201/64	Western region	San Jose core router
2001:db8:aa:90::301/64	Eastern region	Boston core router

 We certainly could have added one or two bits to increase our available addresses in that group of addresses by 32 or 64 respectively. But recall that we want to stick to using groups of addresses that are always multiples of 2^{4n} so that each character in any given address is significant for the purposes of mapping that address to a particular location.

You might legitimately ask: Isn't this overkill? Don't I have DNS to handle the naming of devices? Chances are the great majority of your network management will rely on DNS entries for routers and other devices on the network. First-level operational staff with minimal training certainly will. Senior engineers responsible for building and

---

27. It's not that we'll ever run out of IPv6 addresses given that we have $1.8x10^{19}$ at our disposal, but it would be nice to keep our future loopback ID assignments contiguous with the previous per-region ones.

maintaining the routing configuration will rely on scripts or network management automation tools that use DNS names for devices.

But there are plenty of instances where DNS resolution might fail. Device identification via the IPv6 address protects an additional layer of operational transparency and thus effectiveness. The trade-off between this benefit and whatever additional complexity it entails is a specific instance of the general challenge of balancing the complexity of any operational practice with its general accessibility and extensibility; i.e., if an operational practice is so complex that only a few engineers can learn it and use it, its benefit to the organization may be constricted to only those individuals.

IPv6 as the Geologic Age of the Earth

Here's another size comparison between the IPv6 and IPv4 address spaces. According to geologists, the Earth is approximately 4.54 billion years old.

The first humans (the species *Homo habilis*) appeared on the scene over 2 million years ago. In the figure that follows, that slice of time is just before the very top of the circle.

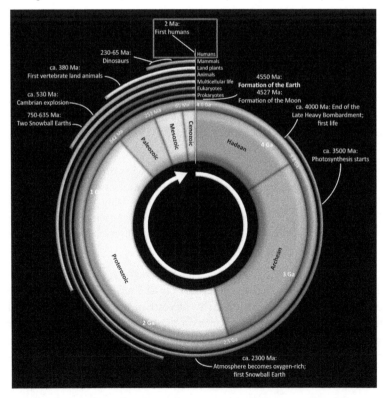

Just to get some sense of how much time that represents in the context of the age of the Earth, let's calculate the percentage of one arc degree (1°) that 2 million years represents:

$$\frac{2.00 \times 10^6 \, years}{4.54 \times 10^9 \, years} = (4.40 \times 10^{-4}) \times 360° = 0.1584°$$

So humans as a genus have been around for nearly 16% of one arc degree (where 360 arc degrees represent the 4.54 billion years the Earth has existed). Modern Homo sapiens are a bright-eyed and bushy-(non)tailed 50,000 years old, or approximately 0.4% of one arc degree in our circle.

For our comparison proper, let's make that 4.54 billion years equivalent to the total number of IPv6 addresses.

So, how much time would we need to represent all IPv4 addresses?

When I ask this question of audiences during IPv6 presentations, the estimates (by both IPv6 newbies and veterans) are typically in the range of seconds to months.

To find the actual answer, we first divide the number of IPv4 addresses by the number of IPv6 addresses to determine the ratio of IPv4 to IPv6:[28]

$$\frac{2^{32}}{2^{128}} = 1.3 \times 10^{-29}$$

Next, we'll multiply that ratio by 4.54 billion years (but first let's reexpress the years as seconds):

$$(4.54 \times 10^9 \, years) \times (3.15 \times 10^7 \, seconds \, / \, year) = 1.43 \times 10^{17} \, seconds$$

Finally:

$$(1.43 \times 10^{17} \, seconds) \times (1.30 \times 10^{-29}) = 1.86 \times 10^{-12} \, seconds$$

And we have our answer: Approximately 2 trillionths of a second (or roughly how long it would take light to traverse the period at the end of this sentence).

---

28. Keep this ratio of IPv4 to IPv6 handy if you *really* want to impress strangers at parties or your in-laws at the next holiday gathering.

## CHAPTER 3

Planning Your IPv6 Deployment

Introduction

Creating an IPv6 address plan is one of the most critical requirements for effectively adopting IPv6. But, of course, it's not the only one. So what else goes into a successful IPv6 deployment effort? Most organizations that succeed in adopting IPv6 take advantage of a relatively small number of reliable strategies and practices. In the following chapter, we'll explore these approaches and help you to align them with your own efforts. We'll discuss:

- The IPv6 business case you already have
- IPv6 as a cross-functional initiative
- A phased approach to IPv6 adoption

The IPv6 Business Case You Already Have

If you ask them, IT managers and executives will likely insist that they have been looking high and low—from the very beginning of time, even—for the elusive phantom known as The Business Case for IPv6 Adoption. This Business Case demonstrates the overwhelming and undeniable benefits of adopting IPv6: better network performance and security, lowered cost for IT operations, fresher breath, and World Peace™. But they haven't found it, so you should quit asking for a budget or additional personnel to deploy IPv6 (and please shut the door on your way out).

There are various reasons for the lack of an incontrovertible business case for IPv6 adoption. For one thing, although IT environments may utilize many common standards, hardware, software, and operational practices, it would still be difficult to prove a consistent and compelling bottom-line benefit for every company as business missions and organizational approaches are varied and not "one size fits all."

Part of the challenge is that, up till now, the overall rate of IPv6 adoption has been slow, especially among enterprises, and especially for their internal networks (i.e., corporate LANs and data centers). With fewer IPv6 deployments, the data that might reveal cost-savings or performance or operational benefits are harder to come by. And even once a large deployment base exists, it will still take time to assess the ways in which IPv6 is benefitting the business.

But that doesn't mean that there are no business cases at all for enterprise IPv6 adoption. It's just that for most organizations, the most compelling business case is based on managing the risks and costs that increase over time in the absence of an IPv6 adoption initiative.

We've already mentioned the exhaustion of IPv4 in North America, Asia, Europe, and Latin America. Examining Asia in particular, most companies see tremendous potential in reaching markets in China and India. Internet penetration in both countries is low when compared with those in Europe and North America, but it is increasing rapidly. The ongoing explosion in the number of new mobile devices connecting to the Internet in these countries proves that mobile networks are the most efficient way to get them online.

Recent data and predictions confirm that this is a global trend: according to Cisco, 2014 will be the year that the number of mobile-connected devices exceeds the human population of the earth (with 10 billion mobile devices by 2017).[1]

But as we've mentioned, in every global region (except Africa), IPv4 is exhausted. Meanwhile, hundreds of millions of potential users that remain unconnected are being aggressively marketed to by regional mobile providers. These providers have largely recognized the unprecedented operational nightmare they will face in attempting to use IPv4 private addressing and carrier-grade NAT (CGN) to scale their service to support these new users. Only IPv6 provides sufficient addressing that is also operationally scalable and manageable for the indefinite future.

This means that most new mobile users have devices configured with IPv6 addresses. These developments are changing the definition of what it means for a business to be connected to the Internet. The management of any organization is unlikely to quibble with the argument that Internet presence is a must-have in the new economy. Yet, out of necessity, millions of new subscribers are connecting to the Internet using only IPv6. What happens when they attempt to access an organization's IPv4-only website?

---

1. And as we mentioned at the end of Chapter 1, large mobile and broadband service providers in North America, like Comcast and Verizon, are not merely reacting to this trend. Instead, they're getting out in front of it with IPv6.

In the worst case, it's possible that they won't be able to access that organization's website at all. Since IPv4 and IPv6 are not directly interoperable, the session packets will have to be translated at least twice (both to and from the web server). If a company hasn't done any planning for IPv6 and has no IPv6 web presence, this mandatory translation of the user sessions from IPv6 to IPv4 will be entirely outside of its control. Even if users pass through one or more IPv6-to-IPv4 translation points to successfully connect to the website, how much might user experience be degraded given that each translation introduces the possibility of increased session latency?

Research shows that users seem preternaturally sensitive to delays in webpage loading times. A study by Google proved that a 250-millisecond delay—the time it takes to blink your eye—was enough to drive users to competitors' websites.

IPv6 Adoption as a Cross-Functional Initative

So let's say you've gotten executive buy-in for IPv6 adoption and are proceeding with management's approval. Or perhaps you've decided that you're not going to wait around for the corner-office types to pull their heads out of their ascots: you've launched a rear-guard action to deploy IPv6! Either way, IPv6 adoption in larger organizations can be painfully slow. But cross-functional initiatives are quite often susceptible to this kind of inertia, and the biggest reasons for this are easier to mitigate once identified.

Let's examine what an example of this challenge might look like in the Real World™.

Often, the IT network team gets the ball rolling with IPv6. Imagine then, that the network team at BellaLabs Corporation has successfully gotten through some initial testing of IPv6 deployed on lab gear. Now they'd like to try turning up IPv6 on a server in the DMZ to test some 6to4 tunnel connectivity using Hurricane Electric's tunnelbroker service. (They've already got a DMZ segment enabled and configured with public addressing to facilitate this type of testing.) So someone from the network team opens a ticket that gets forwarded to the security team: please open IP protocol 41 to IP address 192.0.2.35 to allow us to test IPv6 6to4 tunneling.

And they wait.

And wait.

Eventually, Ned from the network team follows up with the help desk and finally gets a call back:

"Hi Ned. It's Susan from security."

"Hi Susan. Thanks for getting back to me. Did you see my request?"

"I did Ned, and I was just trying to configure the firewall for your request, but I don't see anywhere to add or modify IPv6 entries."

"Well, it's really just an IPv4 rule that needs to be modified. We just need to get IP protocol 41 opened to the public IP of a server in the DMZ."

"Oh. OK. Let me look into it and call you back. What port and IP did you say?"

"IP protocol 41 and IP 192.0.2.35."

"Got it. I'll call you back in a bit."

A little later, Ned's desk phone rings again.

"Ned, this is Artesh from security."

"Hi Artesh. Is my request completed?"

"Sorry, no. I'm just trying to figure out if our security policy supports this. There's nothing in the existing policy docs about IPv6."

"Hmm. Well, it's IPv6 over IPv4, so at this point it's really only IPv4 on the firewall that we'd be modifying."

"But it's IPv6 on the server, right?"

"Yeah."

"OK. Well, let me check with my manager."

"OK. Thanks."

A day or two elapses, and Ned calls Artesh back.

"Hi Artesh, it's Ned. Did you get a response on our configuration request?"

"Yeah, Ned. I was just about to call you. The head of security said we can't support IPv6 at this time. I explained that it's really IPv4 on the firewall, but he said since IPv6 will be running on the DMZ server he can't approve it."

"He realizes that servers in the DMZ are using clustering that relies on IPv6 already, right?"

"Really? I didn't know that. I'll let him know, but for now we can't accommodate the request. Sorry."

Two obvious issues are at play here. The first is that security hasn't had any IPv6 training and doesn't have the requisite knowledge to handle what would otherwise be a simple request from the network team. The second is that the company's security policy hasn't been updated to include IPv6. (A related third issue is that lack of management buy-in may have made the first two issues much more likely.)

As a result, the IPv6 adoption effort is delayed. As with any cross-functional initiative, it's critical that any business unit or silo in the organization that might impact (or be impacted by) the effort receive at least minimal notification and training.

A Phased Approach to IPv6 Adoption

Many organizations have successfully deployed IPv6 by using a phased approach. Large IT projects are often broken into phases to better manage the associated risks and costs. Since IP addressing touches every part of the network, any changes to it can impact an organization's critical services, applications, and procedures. Unplanned network downtime is the bane of IT, and too much of it can lead to loss of productivity, lost revenue, negative brand impact, and employees throwing up their hands and heading for their cars at 2:30P.M. on a Tuesday. While a project manager with OCD could easily break up an enterprise's IPv6 adoption project into a bazillion phases, most organizations find that three phases will generally suffice.

1. Preparation
2. External adoption
3. Internal adoption

Phase 1: Preparation

For most enterprises, the first phase entails the least associated risk and cost while the last phase represents the most. (If your enterprise is different, feel free to shuffle the phases according to the principle at work, i.e., the phase with the lowest risk and cost should come first or next). The preparation phase usually consists of several individual steps, many of which can be accomplished in parallel. They include but are not limited to:

- Management buy-in
- IPv6 training
- Creating an IPv6 task force and selecting IPv6 stakeholders
- Verifying that your ISP supports IPv6
- Auditing your assets for IPv6 support
- Working with your vendors
- Obtaining an IPv6 address allocation

And finally the most exciting task of all:

- Creating an IPv6 address plan

Let's examine each of these first phase tasks individually. (*Creating an IPv6 Address Plan* is covered explicitly in later chapters.)

Management Buy-in

Management buy-in is, at the most basic level and for the purposes of our discussion, simply approval from management to move forward with some degree of IPv6 adoption. Ideally, such approval will lead to capital and operational budget allocations, specifically for an IPv6 deployment effort. Training, additional personnel or person-hours, hardware and software are all helpful in accelerating the completion of tasks in each phase of the initiative.

IT managers have been notoriously ambivalent about IPv6 for many years. And who can blame them? On the one hand, industry media frenzies about the imminent demise of all things IPv4 and the need to deploy IPv6 immediately have occurred frequently enough in the past few years to create a sense of panic fatigue (especially as IPv4 continues to work just fine). Yet in the face of such fear-mongering, business cases touting any authentic cost savings from adopting IPv6 have been virtually nonexistent. Small wonder then that most IT managers are continuing their "wait-and-see" approach to IPv6.

Of course, this can complicate management buy-in for IPv6 deployment. While it's often possible (or expected) to move forward with early-stage IPv6 adoption tasks, such steps are often taken with no formal project definition, additional personnel or funding, or explicit IT manager approval. In cases where it's simply expected that IT staff will absorb the additional effort around IPv6 into existing operational cycles and budget, efforts should still be made to define IPv6 adoption as a unique project, one that requires dedicated planning and resources.

Keep in mind that, depending on the size of the organization, a minimal level of management buy-in and participation may be necessary to allow IT and any other IPv6 adoption project stakeholders to work effectively across different business units, or silos, within the enterprise. Often, such buy-in may simply be an unfunded mandate to "go figure out what we need to do about IPv6." But even without any additional budget, management buy-in can help an IPv6 adoption initiative progress.

Remember also that the risks and costs of failing to adopt IPv6 don't vanish just because management chooses to ignore them. It's still possible to drive effective IPv6 deployment without management buy-in. Indeed, you or your team may be held accountable for failing to do so once management becomes aware that a lack of IPv6 adoption has compromised the company's *business agility, business continuity,* or *competitive advantage.*

We've already examined how an enterprise neglecting to make its website available over IPv6 may compromise its advantage over competitors who have already done so. (Remember that potentially costly 250ms delay in page load times?) Business continuity is potentially threatened by failure to effectively manage and secure the IPv6 that is already enabled on your network today. And the ongoing evolution of business agility is heavily dependent on the integration of cloud solutions, the architectures of which are ever-more reliant on IPv6 (due to its unlimited address supply, capacity for better address management and organization, more efficient layer 3 to layer 2 and multiple interface addresses management, and the multiple operational efficiencies that result).[2]

Training

Any unfamiliar technology has the potential to introduce fear, uncertainty, and doubt (FUD) into IT organizations. Because network addressing changes can impact every-thing, this FUD can be especially keen where IPv6 is concerned. Formal training is a great way to instill confidence in IPv6. Please visit *www.ipv6.works* for a current list of trainers.[3]

I probably don't have to convince you that independent study can go a long way toward dispelling IPv6 FUD. (You're reading this book, aren't you?) Sources of information include other books, RFCs, blogs, and white papers. Reading recommendations appear at the end of some chapters. And if it's in your budget, consider attending one of the many IPv6 conferences that are held around the world each year. Rubbing elbows with the folks who have adopted IPv6 early (and who have the operational scars to prove it) will boost your IPv6 knowledge and wisdom and instill confidence in your own IPv6 deployment effort.

Creating an IPv6 Task Force

Larger enterprises may have multiple IT or networking groups that will need to coor-dinate IPv6 deployment, especially if the cost and risk to existing operations are to be kept to a minimum. It's also possible that other business units outside of IT could be impacted by IPv6 adoption based on custom network, application, or service require-ments that are not well understood outside that silo (or even within) or effectively managed by IT.

As we discussed, some basic training on IPv6 across the organization should help iden-tify stakeholders and generate interest in IPv6 deployment project participation, but such training is unlikely to be budgeted in most organizations. It's much more likely that ad-hoc identification of IPv6 adoption stakeholders and allies in relevant business units will be necessary.

Ideally, an IPv6 task force would be created. It would include at least one member from every business unit or silo in the organization. Even just one meeting can be effective

---

2. The same will undoubtedly prove true of IoT networks as they increase in number and scale.

3. If formal training cannot be budgeted, check with your equipment vendors and partners to see if they offer any specialized training around IPv6, which can often be had for little or no cost (and can help you identify which of your vendors and partners are serious about their IPv6 support).

at establishing both basic awareness of the IPv6 adoption initiative and its backing by the executive team. This, in turn, can create accountability and an expectation of success that may help overcome what would otherwise be organizational inertia and lack of participation.

Auditing Hardware and Software for IPv6 Support

We mentioned that even though IT infrastructure among organizations is generally more similar than not, the ways in which organizations rely on the network, the resources they have at their disposal, their strategic visions, and their management philosophies can all vary widely. While this may make a one-size-fits-all project plan for IPv6 adoption less likely, there are tasks common to every deployment.

One of the first and potentially most daunting of these tasks is a complete inventory and audit of all IT assets to determine the degree to which (if any) they support IPv6. Any hardware or software that currently relies on the IPv4 network must be accounted for and then assessed (see Table 3-1 for a list).

Table 3-1. What to audit for IPv6 support

Routers/Switches	Remote-office CPEs
Servers	Operating systems
Desktops	Laptops
Critical desktop and laptop apps	Collaboration tools
Tablets/Smartphones	Transparent caching appliances
Optical gear	NMS software
IPv6 on network management interfaces	SNMP support
TFTP/RADIUS/SSH/NTP	Other authentication systems
IPS/IPS	Route server software/appliances
Geolocation database subscriptions	Kernel modules (e.g., TCP acceleration)
Wireless APs	WLAN controllers
TACACS/RADIUS software/appliances	Web and email content filters
NFS/CIFS	Stateful and stateless firewalls
Miscellaneous networking gear ACLs	CDP/FDP
VPN software/appliances	NATs
Security tokens	Middleware
Proxies, network and application level	Load balancers
Databases	Web server software/plug-ins
Mail transfer agents	Mail servers
Calendar/productivity servers	Source control/revision control systems
Accounting, payroll, financial systems	CRM systems

Embedded or specialty systems	PBX and SIP/VOIP
Manufacturing gear	Specialized systems with firmware-based OS/software
Card key systems	POS terminals
Printers and multifunction devices	Sensors/Sensor networks
Syslog/logging services	NetFlow/sFlow export

It's certainly a long list, and your organization may have additional elements not mentioned above.

A common lament heard when describing this task to IT personnel: gee, wouldn't it be swell if there was software that could automatically discover all your IT assets, determine their level of IPv6 support, and generate a nifty report/support matrix?

Why, yes, that would be swell. But that would really only be half—pardon, *one-third* of the battle. Those who are far along in their IPv6 adoption efforts may attest to the fact that there are (at least) three steps to fully validating whether or not a particular IT asset effectively supports IPv6. They are:

1. Determining vendor support
2. Verifying vendor support claims
3. Testing support under load

Of course, before you can tackle the first step, you'll need to have successfully completed the discovery of your IT assets. Once accounted for, this hardware and software will generally fall into one of three categories:

1. Determining vendor support
   a. IPv6: All systems go!
   b. Has known or possible upgrade path to IPv6 support
   c. Permanently unsupported (i.e., exiled forever from the New Eden of 128-bit addressing)

We'll talk about what to do with assets in the third category a bit later. Meanwhile, determining which of the first two categories a particular asset falls into will most likely require, at the least, checking with product documentation, but more ideally, verifying directly with the vendor and testing in a lab setting.

Independent IPv6 Equipment Validation

Many organizations, especially small- to medium-sized ones, may be limited to testing their equipment for basic IPv6 operational viability. While such testing can be vital to ensure the organization's smooth rollout of IPv6, it can't be expected to uncover and validate IPv6 protocol behavior beyond the somewhat narrow focus on the existing vendors and configurations. These are specific to the organization's current network, and as a result, future changes to them may expose protocol components that haven't been tested for reliable behavior and interoperability.

Fortunately, there are third-party testing laboratories that do rigourous IPv6 interoperability and standards conformance validation. For example, the University of New Hampshire InterOperability Laboratory (UNH-IOL)[4] offers "independent, vendor-neutral testing with a focus on quality assurance." Both the United States Government v6 (USGv6)[5] and the IPv6 Ready Logo[6] accreditation programs are facilitated through the UNH-IOL.

As part of the IPv6 support validation you do for your equipment, you may want to familiarize yourself with the UNH-IOL IPv6 test suites.[7] You may also want to investigate if any or all of it is USGv6 or IPv6 Ready Logo accredited (and if not, find out why not directly from the vendor).

Depending on your relationship with a given vendor, details regarding IPv6 support may be easy or hard to come by.

You'll likely discover that for any given asset, vendor claims of IPv6 support will be a mixed bag. Some critical features may already have support, while others may not.

4. *www.iol.unh.edu*

5. *http://bit.ly/nist-usgv6*

6. *www.ipv6ready.org*

7. *http://bit.ly/ipv6-testing*

Working with Vendors

You've probably noticed my use of the phrase *vendor claims* by now. This is not to suggest that vendors are inherently untrustworthy when it comes to assessing IPv6 support. Be aware that the path to effectively supporting IPv6 is often quite difficult for them. The IETF RFCs they rely on in whatever good-faith efforts they make to implement protocols in products or features can often be vague or operationally obtuse. Then there's the challenge of a potentially limited customer install base for IPv6 features. Even for their customers that *have* deployed IPv6, many of them are still in the early stages of IPv6 adoption. Their deployments may lack the kind of operational complexity or load that uncovers bugs, feature limitations, or general lack of performance.

As a result, try to get at least the following from your vendors:

- IPv6 RFC support
- Feature (and/or functional) parity list or matrix
- Known IPv6 bugs and issues
- Existing IPv6 customer deployments and references
- IPv6 feature roadmap

Obviously, there is always a fine line between working with your vendors to introduce and improve the features you need and letting them turn your production network into an extension of their test lab. The topic of technology vendor management itself is probably worthy of an entire book (though not likely a particularly exciting one). Just be aware that you'll need to work as closely as ever with your critical vendors as you tackle IPv6 adoption.

Regardless, once you have your list of critical features and the vendor insists that it supports IPv6, it's time to put on your skeptic's cap (or beret or fez or bonnet, if you prefer) and get to work testing, testing, testing (i.e., step 2). It's usually neither practical nor very wise to test new technology on the production network. Chances are you'll already have some methods, policies, and lab infrastructure in place for the controlled introduction of novel features.

Step three (testing support under load) may be difficult to accomplish before the levels of IPv6 production traffic on your network increase significantly (something that is unlikely to happen in the immediate term). Unless you have an established testing regime that includes specialized equipment like packet generators and protocol fuzzers, it's unlikely you'll be able to really put the performance of critical IPv6 features through their paces.

Even in the absence of any load testing, you should be able to deduce whether a particular vendor is ready for IPv6 primetime based on the quality and quantity of IPv6 feature support. Their timeliness in fixing bugs, improving performance, and adding features for IPv6 will let you know if you might need to find a vendor with a better IPv6 offering for a given asset. Further, any performance testing data they can provide should demonstrate that their gear performs adequately when configured the way you plan to deploy it.

Including IPv6 in Tech Refresh Cycles

As mentioned, vendor support for IPv6 has substantially improved in the last few years. As a result, organizations that have regularly performed tech refresh during this time period have also improved their IT infrastructure's IPv6 support (whether they intended to or not).

In fact, making general IPv6 support a *must-have* for any tech refresh cycle turns out to be an excellent way to accomplish one low-cost, low-risk goal of IPv6 adoption with little or no additional organizational effort.

Also, using regular tech refresh cycles to ensure that IPv6 is properly supported helps protect the enterprise's investment in internal infrastructure (which, in turn, helps make the business case for IPv6 adoption).

So if IPv6 support isn't already included in your tech refresh requirements, be sure to get it added as soon as possible.

Verifying That Your ISP Supports IPv6

The good news is that a great many ISPs currently offer IPv6 connectivity. The bad news is that they're all over the map in terms of the level of operational support for IPv6. Just because an ISP is effectively managing their IPv4-based network and products doesn't necessarily mean they are equally adept at providing good IPv6 services. Your first step is to verify that they support IPv6 at all. And if not today, then when? It's not hyperbole to say that an ISP without IPv6 on their roadmap has no future, no matter how affordable or reliable they currently might be. Dual-stack connectivity over your existing IPv4 connection(s) is ideal. ISPs that are relying on tunneling over IPv4 to deliver IPv6 Internet services may not be ready for IPv6 primetime.[8] If your ISP doesn't support IPv6 and has no plans to, it may be time to shop around for a new provider.

---

8. There are exceptions to this: certain IPv4/IPv6 transition technologies that rely on tunneling have historically been generally well-managed by providers like Hurricane Electric, Free Telecom (France), and Comcast.

Obtaining an IPv6 Address Allocation

If you've obtained IPv4 address space in the past, either from your ISP or from your RIR (regional Internet registry), the process is much the same in IPv6. Just like with IPv4, you'll need some information before submitting your request. In Chapter 6, we'll go into more detail regarding this necessary info, ISP and RIR policy, as well as what you can expect in navigating the process. For now, keep in mind that it is very common for enterprises to underestimate the amount of IPv6 space they need at the outset. If you're getting ready to request IPv6 address space and you already have a rough idea of how much you think you'll request, you may want to skip ahead to "RIR Allocation Request" on page 132 to read up on the criteria for how much address space you should be asking for.

Phase 2: External Adoption

The most basic definition of external adoption means that an organization makes its primary website available over the IPv6 Internet. Since there are a number of ways such a website can be traditionally served in IPv4, this task can be as simple as checking a box on a web-hosting (or content delivery network) services portal, or as complex as provisioning the IPv6 Internet to servers in data centers around the globe.

As we suggested earlier in the chapter, by making their websites available over IPv6, organizations ensure that requests for content from IPv6 hosts are not translated to and from IPv4. While this step is no guarantee that IPv6 user experience will be improved, it eliminates the possibility of a degraded experience for those users due to translation. The organization may enjoy a competitive advantage over those organizations that keep their websites exclusively in IPv4.

So let's examine what the most basic external IPv6 adoption configuration looks like (Figure 3-1). We'll assume that you're not using a CDN or web hosting service.

The diagram makes a logical distinction between the IPv4 and IPv6 Internet, given that the two protocols do not directly interoperate. Keep in mind, however, that most ISPs are relying on a dual-stack configuration in their core meaning that, although they are logically unique, the IPv4 and IPv6 networks share the same routers and switches.

The requesting hosts shown at the edge of these networks are configured accordingly: an IPv4-only host connected exclusively to the IPv4 Internet (our typical legacy configuration); an IPv6-only host connected to the IPv6 Internet; and a dual-stack host connected to both (via the same dual-stack CPE and ISP connection).

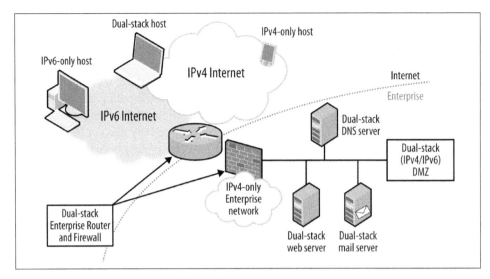

Figure 3-1. Enterprise external IPv6 adoption

An Internet border router that supports both IPv4 and IPv6 in a dual-stack configuration connects the enterprise network to both the IPv4 and IPv6 Internet. The dual-stack plumbing continues through a supporting firewall and onto a DMZ segment where a DNS and web server are connected (via dual-stack NICs). The OSes, DNS server, and web server applications support both IPv4 and IPv6.

Critically, the enterprise internal network remains IPv4-only, relying on NAT and private addressing to connect to the IPv4 Internet.[9]

With this configuration, requests from IPv6 hosts will be responded to natively over IPv6. IPv4 requests will be served over IPv4 as they always have been (though from a dual-stack server).

What about requests from a dual-stack host? To determine whether they'll be responded to over IPv4 or IPv6 (as well as how they'll decide which address family to use), we'll need to take a look at a little bit more IPv6 and Internet history.

Dual-Stack Eyeballs Are Happy Eyeballs

In the early days of IPv6, Internet engineers realized that, since no flag day was possible to transition all at once to IPv6, other more subtle mechanisms would have to be devised to help drive IPv6 adoption.

---

9. An IPv6 or dual-stack segment might be connected through to the DMZ in order to facilitate management and testing of the IPv6 resources located there.

One of these mechanisms is found in RFC 3484 (*http://bit.ly/rfc-3484*).[10] If a host has both IPv4 and IPv6 connectivity, it should prefer IPv6. It's a simple and effective method to encourage the use of IPv6 on dual-stack hosts. And it worked well enough where hosts were actually connected to the IPv6 Internet. But where they weren't, another mechanism, ostensibly designed to encourage IPv6 transition, broke things for these dual-stacked hosts: namely, that IPv6 AAAA (forward mapping) DNS records can be delivered to a host using IPv4.

For example, let's say a residential subscriber's cable modem is connected to the Internet using only IPv4. The ISP doesn't yet support IPv6 services but plans to offer IPv6 connectivity within the next six months. In the meantime, the subscriber connects his laptop to the home network. The laptop is running Windows 7 and gets a private IPv4 address from the DHCP server running on the cable modem. The cable modem has a public IPv4 address it is using to NAT[11] any internal private addresses it assigns.

But let's also imagine that someone else in the household hooked up an additional home router to the local network (not to use as a router but merely to test out the device's WLAN capabilities). The additional home router supports IPv6 out of the box and is sending out IPv6 ND RAs on the local network segment.

Someone then connects a laptop to the network. The laptop gets an IPv6 router advertisement from the second home router and proceeds to self-configure a Link-Local address. The laptop now believes it has both an IPv4 and IPv6 address.

When the laptop user opens a browser, a DNS query for the start page is sent. The query requests an A record for www.example.com and gets a response. Because it has an IPv6 address configured, the querier then requests and receives a AAAA record as well (see Example 3-1).

Example 3-1. Forward A and AAAA record for www.example.com

```
www    A      192.0.2.34            ; example.com's web server
       AAAA   2001:db8:667:776::34  ; same web server's dual-stack IPv6 address
```

Both responses are delivered over the existing IPv4 connection. Now, to get to the www.example.com website, the subscriber's laptop has an IPv4 address and an IPv6 address to choose from. Which one will it choose?

Up until a few years ago, the default address selection policy found in RFC 3484 was the one commonly used in dual-stack implementations. This policy gave IPv6 preference over IPv4. In that instance, the laptop, having a valid IPv6 address, would make the assumption it's connected to the IPv6 Internet. It would first attempt to connect to

---

10. RFC 3484 has since become obsolete by RFC 6724 (*http://bit.ly/rfc-6724*), which includes updates to the address preferences and selection algorithm.

11. Technically, PAT (or port address resolution).

2001:db8:667:776::34. But because the laptop is not actually connected to the IPv6 Internet, it wouldn't be able to connect. After some period of time set by the OS (as long as several minutes in some cases), the attempted connection to IPv6 would time out and another connection would then be attempted over IPv4 (which, in our example, would succeed).

This was the situation prior to World IPv6 Day in June of 2011 and the reason that no major content providers had yet enabled AAAA records for their primary websites (i.e., www.google.com, www.yahoo.com, etc.). Knowing that some nontrivial number of Internet subscribers (much less than 1% of all Internet users but still likely numbering in the tens if not hundreds of thousands) had the same configuration as our hypothetical subscriber's laptop from our previous example meant that configuring these AAAA records would result in impatient users believing that www.google.com was down (then maybe switching over to www.yahoo.com, which, not having a AAAA record configured, would come up immediately). Result: possible brand damage to content providers daring to significantly adopt IPv6 early.

World IPv6 Day was organized to test the extent of this *IPv6 brokenness* while avoiding exposing individual content providers to any exclusive brand damage it might do. If *all* the major content providers enabled AAAA records for 24 hours, users with broken configurations would have trouble getting to any of their sites (not just to those providers brave or foolhardy enough to have unilaterally configured AAAAs prior to World IPv6 Day).

At this point, you're probably wondering why couldn't the OS or browser just test the connection to IPv4 and IPv6 simultaneously and pick the one that works (and perhaps even performs better)? Well that's precisely what most OSes and browsers do now, thanks to *Happy Eyeballs*.[12] Following the success of World IPv6 Day, another event was planned for June of 2012. World IPv6 Launch aimed, among other goals, to have major content providers, as well as anyone else who wanted to participate, configure AAAA records for their main websites and leave them permanently enabled. Though the content providers decided that the actual levels of IPv6 brokenness were acceptably low, the rapid and significant adoption of the Happy Eyeballs approach to address selection in browsers and OSes made the issue even less of a potential concern for them.

And that's the reason why organizations today should feel confident in configuring AAAA records, leaving them enabled, and making their primary websites permanently available over IPv6.

---

12. RFC 3484 (along with its replacement, RFC 6724) technically allows for alternate address selection policy and methods, such as Happy Eyeballs (*http://bit.ly/rfc-6555*) and Windows Network Connection Status Indicator (NCSI).

IPv6 CDNs and Web Hosting

Many major web hosting companies and content delivery networks (CDNs) offer IPv6 support for at least some of their services. For organizations already using CDNs or hosting services, this can be the easiest way to accomplish external IPv6 adoption.

Some forward-thinking providers are even moving to an IPv6 *on-by-default* or *opt-out* posture where any newly provisioned service offers IPv6 by default unless the customer explicitly chooses not to enable it.

Regardless, as is true with these services in IPv4, the potential advantages are many and include:

- More rapid provision of IPv6 accessibility for websites and online content
- Dynamic scale of services over time to support increasing levels of IPv6 traffic
- Geographical diversity to shorten distance to content (and improve performance and user experience) for requestors
- Dual-stack or IPv4-only interfaces to make website and content management and upload easier

If you're already using a web hosting or CDN service, you'll need to check with them to see what level of IPv6 support they offer. You may want to find out the following:

Do you offer IPv6 everywhere you offer IPv4?

As we mentioned, a key advantage of using a web hosting service or content delivery network is geographical ubiquity and diversity of services and the improved performance that may offer. But for this performance advantage to be uniformly realized in IPv6, the provider in question would need to have IPv6 provisioned anywhere IPv4 currently is. As with provisioning these services in-house, it might be initially acceptable to have less ubiquity and diversity, especially if you are in a proof-of-concept phase for deploying IPv6. Regardless, you'll want to know what the provider's roadmap to full IPv6 parity is in this area.

Are your management and IPv6-content upload interfaces available in IPv4 (or IPv4-only)?

A possible advantage for companies leveraging a web hosting or CDN in order to make their websites and content available over IPv6 is that little or no in-house IPv6 infrastructure may be needed right away. You'll want to check with the provider to make sure that you'll be able to manage and upload content from your IPv4-only or dual-stack hosts and servers (depending on where your organization is at with overall IPv6 adoption). You'll also want to make sure that the provider either currently offers, or has a plan for offering, content management and upload via IPv6.

Do you offer IPv6 reporting and visibility equal to what's currently available in IPv4?

Another critical benefit of using a web hosting or content provider is the visibility into, and detailed reporting for, the services they offer. The data from these features can often be used not just to ensure performance but also to generate metrics that can improve the reach of the company into better target markets. Of course, all of this reporting and visibility needs to work for IPv6 traffic as well as IPv4, and you'll want to make sure that the provider supports, or plans to support, all such features equally well in IPv6.

Phase 3: Internal Adoption

For most organizations, the final phase of IPv6 adoption is the deployment of IPv6 on internal networks. Traditionally, most enterprises have been slow in tackling this phase, likely due to a number of unique factors, including:

- Reliance on NAT and private address space architecture and practice for internal networks
- Business models and revenue streams not reliant on continually scaling network services (and the IP address supply such services require)
- Little or no need to be seen as early adopters of transformative technologies
- Little or no operational best practice to leverage from other enterprises due to slow overall adoption
- Discouraging assumptions that internal adoption is more complex or expensive than other phases

Let's examine a few of these factors individually before discussing the potential risks and costs of delaying internal IPv6 adoption. We'll then look at steps that organizations can take to make internal IPv6 adoption more manageable.

Reliance on NAT

We've already discussed the pros and cons of NAT for enterprise networks.

On the plus side, NAT reduced the rate of consumption of limited public IPv4 addresses by networks and hosts that didn't need to be directly accessible from the Internet. This delayed the inevitable arrival of IPv4 exhaustion. NAT also allowed enterprises to take advantage of the relatively larger space available with private IPv4 in planning their address architectures. It has also given enterprises much more flexibility to schedule (and frankly, delay) their internal adoption of IPv6.

Meanwhile, this flexibility has too often led to an insufficient recognition of the potential risks and costs of failing to adopt IPv6 internally.

But setting aside IPv6 altogether, IPv4 NAT's deficiencies are often ignored or overlooked. We mentioned in Chapter 2 both the misperceptions of improved security through obscurity, as well as the operationally taxing impact of NAT on application features and performance.

IPv6 Business Case Redux

A more general business case for IPv6 adoption is perhaps easier to make for the first two phases of IPv6 adoption. Given the growth of IPv6 adoption across the Internet, it's impossible at this point to argue that any enterprise IT organization can avoid IPv6 altogether. It would almost certainly be a form of career suicide for individual network or system administrators or engineers to studiously ignore IPv6 simply because their current company has mistakenly decided to do so. Thus, while the scope of what you'll need to know and plan for in IPv6 might vary from organization to organization, there should be little doubt that some knowledge and planning are absolutely essential.

Since IPv6 deployment by mobile and broadband subscriber service providers is already happening at accelerating rates due to the lack of routable IPv4 (and the additional expense and operational complexity of CGN/LSN solutions), making websites and content available through external IPv6 adoption is the only way for organizations to directly reach these new subscribers.

The business case for internal enterprise IPv6 adoption is usually more general, focusing on how even modest uptake of IPv6 among internal enterprise networks will, over time, result in evolution of operational practices (and, as elaborated on below, premium costs for continued IPv4 support provided by vendors and SPs).

IPv6 (In)Security

Considering that all modern OSes now have IPv6 enabled by default, IPv6 is already running on any network where you haven't explicitly disabled it (not an option for reasons we'll see next). This means that IPv6 is running essentially unmanaged. As a result, the requirements of the existing network security policy where IPv4 is concerned (as well as the security tools providing visibility and mature operational practice that go with it) are not being met for IPv6.

This lack of operational awareness and practice results in a weakened state of network and host security that threatens business continuity, whether by error or misconduct. And without the security tools and operational practice in place to effectively monitor IPv6 traffic, the security policy is either being directly and actively violated or is out-of-date with no reference to IPv6. This noncompliance will become more costly over time.

Considering that it is only a matter of time before new services will need to be enabled in an IPv6 environment, an ongoing lack of training, proper tools, and operational experience will continue to erode business continuity.

The Latent Costs of IPv4

There's an effort at large among the hardcore IPv6 adoption community that skeptics could be perhaps excused for deriding as mere semantics: IPv6 should now simply be called *IP* while IPv4 should now and forever be referred to as the *legacy* protocol.

Before you scoff, though, keep in mind that a common effort among some organizations (both service providers *and* enterprises) that have widely adopted IPv6 using the preferred dual-stack approach is now trying to figure out how to decommission IPv4 sooner rather than later.

There are a few reasons for this.

It's absolutely the case that dual-stack is a necessary intermediate step to facilitate the introduction of IPv6 into the network while simultaneously protecting the existing IPv4 production network (not to mention controlling the risks and costs associated with failing to adopt IPv6 in time). But it should be uncontroversial to point out that managing two address protocols over time (however necessary initially until IPv6 operational and architectural practice has matured) is more complex (and potentially costly) than managing one.

Service providers have seen their historical revenue sources (mere bandwidth and connectivity) commoditized out of profitability. The razor-thin margins that remain have left these providers scrabbling for any opportunities to recognize new revenue streams. As a result, they're really looking forward to charging you an added premium for any aspect of their legacy IPv4 service, from connectivity to services to addresses. If you're not running IPv6 and have no upgrade path, you'll have to pay what they're asking (or go with a bargain IPv4 provider: how retro!).

At some point in the near future, vendors will be making similar assessments as they allocate product and feature strategy resources. While continued IPv4 feature support may not directly cost more, customers may discover that vendor support and engineering are slower to resolve issues with the *legacy* protocol. This could result in additional operational expense (not to mention much aggravation!).

Internal Adoption and Operational Wisdom

While IPv6 deployment on the internal networks of large, multinational companies has accelerated, these organizations are generally not inclined to publicly share too many of the details of their IPv6 initiatives. This makes it difficult to derive business cases from their IPv6 adoption efforts, and it reduces any *bandwagon* effect among other enterprises we might otherwise see. It also reduces the operational wisdom and guidance available to enterprises.

A lack of operational guidance can cause enterprises to make unforced errors at the early stages of their internal adoption efforts.

For instance, members of the enterprise security team may learn that IPv6 is on by default and perhaps recognize that it is generating unmonitored traffic on the network. The network security monitoring tools in use may not offer IPv6 support, or unfortunately more likely, the team may lack IPv6 expertise, as well as the time and resource commitment needed to obtain it. Rather than addressing these causes, and with the best intentions for proper security, they'll insist that IPv6 be disabled on servers and hosts.

A side effect of this step may be to weaken or break OS features like Failover Clustering in Microsoft Windows Server, which currently prefers IPv6 both in production and in vendor test environments. Other features like Microsoft Direct Access rely on IPv6 to provide end-to-end addressing (something not really possible to do with IPv4). And like many other Microsoft services, Exchange Server 2013 is considered out-of-scope for technical support when IPv6 is disabled.

Another possible error is for enterprise IT to assume that the existing architecture leveraging NAT and private addressing in IPv4 should be replicated in IPv6. This can lead to ULA being deployed internally with either NAT66 or NPTv6 at the edge. While there certainly could be network and business requirements that make this configuration desirable, the recommended architecture for nearly all enterprise networks uses global unicast addresses everywhere.

## PART II

Design

When I am working on a problem, I never think about beauty but when I have finished,
if the solution is not beautiful, I know it is wrong.

— R. Buckminster Fuller

Luck is the residue of design.

— Branch Rickey

The next four chapters will cover the topics essential to designing an IPv6 addressing plan. In Chapter 4, we'll take a deeper look at IPv6 subnetting while Chapter 5 discusses the core concepts and principles behind IPv6 address planning. In Chapter 6, we'll review the methods of obtaining IPv6 address allocations (as well as the key policies that impact how we get and use them). Chapter 7 puts it all together to walk you through the creation of an IPv6 address plan.

## CHAPTER 4

IPv6 Subnetting

As I was going to St. Ives,

I met a man with seven wives,

Each wife had seven sacks,

Each sack had seven cats,

Each cat had seven kits:

Kits, cats, sacks, and wives,

How many were there going to St. Ives?

— Traditional Nursery Rhyme

Introduction

We've discussed how early efforts to successfully slow the depletion of IPv4 included techniques like VLSM, CIDR, and NAT. In particular, the granular subnetting provided by VLSM became a common (and engrained) practice in IPv4 network architecture and address planning. But the enormous scale of IPv6 and the resulting bounty of additional bits in a given address require new subnetting methods. These methods provide opportunities to improve both the ease and effectiveness of IPv6 address planning. In this chapter, we'll cover these IPv6 subnetting techniques and the legacy IPv4 subnetting methods they differ from (and improve upon).

Subnetting IPv4: A Brief Review

Before we dig into IPv6 subnetting methods, let's briefly review their counterparts in IPv4.

As we've already discussed, subnetting in IPv4 optimistically started out as *class-based*; i.e., using only two classes of subnets to facilitate aggregation and reduce the demand placed on router memory and CPU resources (as well as create some hierarchical consistency within the Internet).

The first two classes of subnets in IPv4 were as follows:

Class A
    8 bits to identify the network, 24 bits for host addressing

Class B
    16 bits to identify the network, 16 bits for host addressing

But as the Internet began to grow, most organizations discovered that they had an abundance of unused address space. In general, this situation was beneficial to them individually: they had plenty of addresses for current use and future growth, plus they could aggregate their networks efficiently and maintain improved router performance.

The situation was not so beneficial for the addressing needs of a rapidly expanding Internet. So class C networks were proposed as a way to allow for much more granular allocation to smaller organizations with more modest addressing requirements.

Class C
    24 bits to identify the network, 8 bits for host addressing

The 254 host addresses available in a class C network[1] made them ideal for assigning to organizations that had more modest host requirements, especially leaf or stub networks.

But many more organizations (especially small- and medium-sized ISPs) would need multiple class Cs for their host addressing, though perhaps not as much as an entire class B. Allocating more than 1 class C but fewer than 256 of them meant that there would potentially be many more routing table entries. In addition, for some network architectures and topologies, even a class C could end up being wasteful if assigned to one segment or interface.

Either way, even with class Cs, the classful addressing approach was simply not sophisticated enough to support sufficient host addressing *and* efficient routing. Some other mechanism would be needed to allow the aggregation of any number of smaller subnets into larger ones.

VLSM and CIDR provided this mechanism. It allowed for any number of the 32 bits of the IPv4 address to be used for the network ID while those bits that remained would define the host addressing. As an example, say we had a class C network that we wanted to use to number hosts on various segments:

    192.0.2.0

---

1. Recall that the first and last addresses of any subnet (in this case .0 and .255) are reserved for the *network* and *broadcast* addresses respectively.

Because it's a *class C*, I know that I have 254 usable host addresses.

```
192.0.2.1 to 192.0.2.254
```

As with any IPv4 address, the subnet mask must accompany it so that it's clear what bits are reserved for the network (with the remaining bits set aside for the hosts). The subnet mask for a class C looks like this:

```
255.255.255.0
```

The mask works by a bitwise logical AND operation:

```
192.0.2.55          =     11000000 00000000 00000010 00110111
255.255.255.0       =     11111111 11111111 11111111 00000000
                          _____

          Logical AND:    11000000 00000000 00000010 00000000
```

You'll notice that the host bits are "zeroed out" by the operation, while the network bits "pass through" the mask. Converting from binary back to decimal gives us:

```
192.0.2.0
```

In my hypothetical network, let's stipulate that I have two segments that each have 50 servers and that I expect to grow by 25% a year for the next three years:[2]

```
50 + 3(50 x 0.25) = server count on segment after 3 years
```

After three years, neither segment will have more than 90 servers. I need enough bits to support a subnet with a host count of at least 90. According to binary math, the smallest subnet to support 90 servers is provided by 7 bits (though recall that I lose 2 addresses to the network and broadcast addresses):

$$(2^n) - 2 = (2^7) - 2 = 128 - 2 = 126$$

90 servers using 126 available addresses equates to just a little above 70% utilization, so I've still got a little room for growth before I'll potentially need to renumber.

Since we'll need 7 bits for host addressing for each segment, that leaves 25 bits for the network, giving us the following subnet mask:

```
255.255.255.128
```

or

```
11111111 11111111 11111111 10000000
```

Recall that our original class C network had a mask of 255.255.255.0 and 24 bits.

The two possible values of the 25th bit give us two networks:

```
192.0.2.0           =     11000000 00000000 00000010 00000000
255.255.255.128     =     11111111 11111111 11111111 10000000
```

---

2. Sorry, no compound interest.

```
                    Logical AND:   11000000 00000000 00000010 00000000 = 192.0.2.0

192.0.2.128             =          11000000 00000000 00000010 10000000
255.255.255.128         =          11111111 11111111 11111111 10000000

                    Logical AND:   11000000 00000000 00000010 10000000 = 192.0.2.128
```

The 7 bits remaining provide 128 addresses, giving our two new networks 128 total addresses each:

```
192.0.2.0 to 192.0.2.127
```

and

```
192.0.2.128 to 192.0.2.255
```

Computers rely on binary operations that require the inclusion of a subnet mask whenever an IPv4 address is represented. It's more convenient for humans to represent the subnet mask as either a dotted quad of octets (e.g., 255.255.255.0) or using CIDR notation; i.e., "/nn" notation where the network bits (represented by "nn") of an address are appended to the end of the address after a "/" (e.g., *192.0.2.0/24*). IPv6 uses CIDR notation exclusively.

The CIDR and VLSM methods led to a chain of significant design and operational consequences. Since it allowed for aggregation of networks beyond the 8-bit boundaries of the classful networks, the need for efficient aggregation and routing could be balanced against the need for sufficient host addressing.

This, in turn, led to the practice of defining and assigning to a link the smallest practical subnet to support immediate and anticipated host counts. Proper aggregation and efficient routing, while still possible, were more often a secondary concern (or a lucky accident). Thus, the definition of what makes a particular address plan efficient changed over time. It went from one that emphasized the importance of fewer routes in the routing table and consequent router resource conservation to one that emphasized the preservation of host addresses. As mentioned earlier, this is the essential element of *IPv4 thinking*.

A Note on Efficiency

The original challenge with IPv4 subnetting was defining and assigning subnets that provided sufficient host addresses per segment while at the same time not having too many unused addresses left over. We might have heard an address plan exclusively referred to as "efficient" merely because it provided sufficient IP addressing for the network.

But this form of efficiency is impossible to maintain and improve, given an ever-dwindling supply of addresses. Because it's often not feasible to reliably predict how quickly any given network might grow, administrators could face either running out of available addresses on a segment and having to renumber in order to increase subnet size (or having underutilized subnet assignments tying up subnet bits that could be assigned elsewhere to support growth).[3]

In the first chapter, we reviewed the dilemma of scale and the difficulty of balancing the requirements of sufficient host addressing with *efficient routing* (e.g., conservation of router memory and CPU by aggregation of prefixes) in IPv4. IPv6 was designed in a way to eliminate the tension between these two requirements. It does this by first providing a standard interface subnet with 64 bits of host addressing. With 1.8×10^{19} addresses, overutilization of addresses on a single network interface simply isn't possible. This, in turn, allows network engineers designing a site to aggregate interface subnets for, among other potential benefits, routing efficiency.

But what the heck do we need routing efficiency for anyway? To answer that is to get at why we need routing at all.

We often talk about networks being flat or hierarchical, where, in the simplest terms, the former suggests a switched network while the latter usually implies a routed one. Each type of network has pros and cons. Flat networks are simple. The flattest network is a collection of hosts sharing a transmission medium and communicating with each other directly. As long as I've got enough unique network addresses, switch ports, and bandwidth, I can keep adding hosts. That is, up to a point.

Eventually, however, the network becomes overloaded. The protocols allowing communication between the hosts have overhead that consumes bandwidth. The switch ports have to keep track of hardware addresses and have limited memory with which to do so. And we need some way of keeping those switches from forming loops and causing address table corruption and broadcast storms. The physical limitations of the transmission medium itself begin to interfere with reliable network state information once too great a distance separates hosts and latency increases.

It turns out that all networks require state information: Where are the hosts? What paths are available to connect them? Is a particular host still connected?

Network segmentation is a way of limiting the amount of state information that must be managed for a given collection of hosts. Routing was invented to help accomplish this by providing a way to aggregate host addresses and reduce the amount of state information any single router or switch had to manage and maintain. But beyond just overcoming the limitations of the networking equipment and physics, the hierarchy that results from segmentation and routing creates a logical framework that makes it much easier for humans to effectively manage and maintain networks.

---

3. Notice that this approach leaves aggregation to facilitate routing and security policy as an afterthought.

Summarization creates logical boundaries that can be correlated to the administrative entities for which we created the networks in the first place. These boundaries are essential for making distinctions about what constitutes the inside and outside of the network (and which side a given host or set of networks should be on). From these distinctions, administrative responsibilities and lines of demarcation are established. Security policies are designed and instantiated. And so it goes.

Summarization

We've mentioned *summarization* as well as its synonym *aggregation* (both sometimes referred to as *supernetting*) at different times in the previous chapters. It's a subject that should already be familiar to us from designing, building, and running IPv4 networks. But it's probably a good idea to review it in the context of our current IPv6 subnetting discussion.

Simply stated, summarization is the combining of smaller networks into larger ones. Recall that only contiguous networks of the same size (i.e., bit length) can be summarized:

```
/64 + /64 = /63
/63 + /63 = /62
/62 + /62 = /61
etc.
```

Summarization provides multiple benefits:

It reduces the total number of routes (and routing table entries) that routers in the network must learn and keep state information on.

This is by far the most important benefit of network aggregation. By reducing the number of routes that routers must learn and keep track of, memory and CPU resources are preserved, potentially delaying costly router upgrades or replacement.[4]

A reduced number of routes can also lead to faster convergence and improved performance of the network as fewer network prefixes mean that updates between routers can be sent and processed faster.

It can reduce the administrative overhead associated with tracking address assignments.

Aggregation can reduce the number of entries in network management and IPAM systems, reducing the amount of overall data network operations personnel and process must track and potentially reducing operational expenditures.

---

4. Recall that data plane performance is enhanced by pushing routing information down to an individual port's FIB (forwarding information base). Each port has a limited amount of ternary content addressable memory (TCAM) to store its FIB. As a result, per-port costs are dependent on the amount of TCAM needed, which proper prefix aggregation can help reduce.

> **It can help create well-defined network and administrative boundaries that allow us to simplify security policy and improve operations performance.**
>
> Often, network aggregation correlates to well-defined administrative boundaries. This can greatly simplify the definition and configuration of security policy through ACLs and policy documentation. It can also improve network operations efficiency, leading to faster isolation and resolution of issues and problems on the network.

These logical boundaries facilitated by summarization are much easier to establish in IPv6. And because renumbering and resubnetting to support changes in interface host counts are no longer necessary, such logical boundaries are also much easier to maintain over time.

With IPv6, host address conservation (and whatever limited form of efficiency it provided) is effectively obsolete. We can now optimize our design choices for the superior efficiencies of network scale and operational ease.

Nibble Boundaries

A *nibble* is 4 bits. Since IPv6 addresses are expressed using hexadecimal characters, subnetting exclusively in multiples of four bits has several important benefits for address planning (and operations).

The first and most obvious of these is that our CIDR notation for any prefix will always be a multiple of four. For example, starting from a /64 (as that's the smallest typical subnet size):

/64, /60, /56, /52, /48, /44, etc.

From an operational standpoint, this makes any subnetting transcription errors in configuration or documentation immediately apparent. For example:

/53, /47, /39, etc.

The next benefit is that we have a smaller possible set of subnet groups to account for, as shown in Table 4-1:.

Table 4-1. Binary nibbles

n	2^{4n}
1	16
2	256
3	4096
4	65536
5	1048576
6	16777216

n	2^{4n}
7	268435456
8	4294967296

As we get into our address plan design based on our network topology, it's uncommon that we'll have any network entities (VLANs, buildings, business units, etc.) in groups larger than 65536.

Also, much of our address planning will be focused on either the 16 bits of the individual site subnet ID (from /48 to /64) or the 16 bits of the overall organizational assignment (typically from /32 to /48, though possibly larger for the largest enterprises). As a result, the first four values (i.e., 16, 256, 4096, and 65536) are the most often used and thus most usefully remembered.

The final benefit takes a bit more explaining.

Prefix Legibility

The final benefit of adhering to the nibble boundary when subnetting in IPv6 is improved prefix legibility (or, to put it another way, human-readability).

What do we mean by legibility? Let's demonstrate with an example. Say we've been assigned a /48 for the headquarters site of a large enterprise. (We'll explain in detail why we might get such an assignment in Chapter 5.)

The site has 20 buildings, and we've designed our plan to allocate one subnet per building. (We've been told to anticipate very little growth as the company is planning on moving the HQ sometime in the next two to five years.) We'll set aside an additional subnet for infrastructure between buildings for a total of 21 subnets.

The minimum number of bits we'd need to use to support 21 subnets would be 5, which gives us a total of 32 subnets. We've got 11 subnets to spare in case any need arises to assign additional ones. The *N*s represent these 5 bits below, while the *X*s are unspecified:

```
2001:db8:abcd:[NNNNNXXXXXXXXXXX]::/53
```

Note that while this provides sufficient subnets, the resulting prefixes aren't as immediately legible because the bit boundary doesn't align with the 4 bits used to define the hexadecimal character in the address:

```
2001:db8:abcd:0000::/53
2001:db8:abcd:0800::/53
2001:db8:abcd:1000::/53
2001:db8:abcd:1800::/53
...
```

Continuing with our example, the abundance of addresses available in IPv6 allows us to use 8 bits (instead of only 5), which makes the hexadecimal representation of the resulting subnets much tidier:

```
2001:db8:abcd:000::/56
2001:db8:abcd:100::/56
2001:db8:abcd:200::/56
2001:db8:abcd:300::/56
...
```

For each subnet group, only one value is possible for the hexadecimal character that corresponds to the 4-bit boundary in the IPv6 prefix (in this case, a /56). This makes the resulting prefix more immediately readable.

Obviously, the use of more bits gives us more subnets: 256 in this case, 21 of which we'll use immediately along with 235 for future use. But fewer host ID bits also reduces the number of available /64 subnets in each parent subnet. In our above example, we went from 2048 /64s available per /53 to 256 /64s available with a /56.

Visualizing Hierarchy

As mentioned in the last section, much of our address planning will be focused on either the 16 bits of the individual site subnet ID (from /48 to /64) or the 16 bits of the overall organizational assignment (typically from /32 to /48).

As it turns out, dividing either of these 16-bit groups along their nibble boundaries gives us a very simple way of visualizing the hierarchy available to us when defining our addressing plan. We'll pick the typical subnet ID range to demonstrate, i.e., /48 to /64 (Figure 4-1).

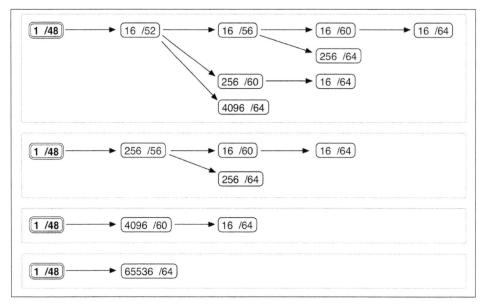

Figure 4-1. IPv6 site prefix visualization

To create an IPv6 subnetting hierarchy from a /48 using the above diagram, simply choose one of the four boxes and then a single path in that box from left to right.

The first box gives us four unique possibilities, as shown in Figure 4-2:

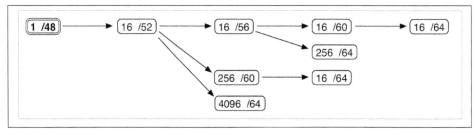

Figure 4-2. IPv6 site prefix visualization (detail 1)

Box two provides two possible paths (Figure 4-3):

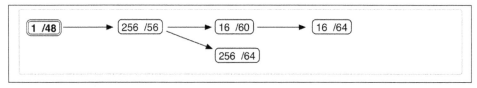

Figure 4-3. IPv6 site prefix visualization (detail 2)

One path each is provided by the third and fourth boxes (Figure 4-4):

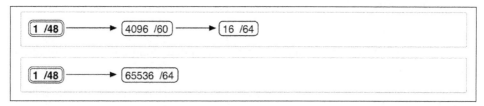

Figure 4-4. IPv6 site prefix visualization (detail 3)

Adding the possibilities up, we end up with only eight paths to choose from.

As it happens, this simple expression of subnetting hierarchy will often prove more than adequate to guide a basic topology for many organizations. It strikes a good balance between the minimum amount of complexity required to instantiate operational efficiency and the simplicity to make and keep the plan extensible and flexible.

Let's take a look at the same figure with actual subnets added for clarity (Figure 4-5):

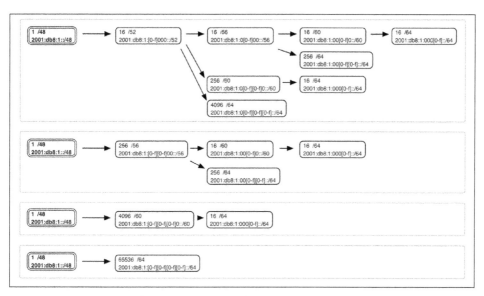

Figure 4-5. IPv6 site prefix visualization with subnets

In this figure, the range of possible values to enumerate the subnets available at that level of hierarchy is bracketed. For example, starting in the upper left-hand corner and moving to the right, we observe that the 16 /52s at that level will be enumerated by modifying the first character of the fourth hextet:

```
2001:db8:1::/52 (or, expanded for clarity, 2001:db8:1:0000::/52)
2001:db8:1:1000::/52
2001:db8:1:2000::/52
...
2001:db8:1:F000::/52
```

From there, each of our /52s could be further subnetted along one of three different paths.

The first path gives us 16 /56s enumerated by the second character (and next 4 bits) of the fourth hextet. Choosing the first /52 from the step above, we get the first group of 16 /56 subnets:

```
2001:db8:1::/56
2001:db8:1:0100::/56
2001:db8:1:0200::/56
...
2001:db8:1:0F00::/56
```

The second group of 16 /56 subnets would be:

```
2001:db8:1:1000::/56
2001:db8:1:1100::/56
2001:db8:1:1200::/56
...
2001:db8:1:1F00::/56
```

The second path gives us 256 /60s enumerated by the second and third character (and 8 middle bits) of the fourth hextet. Again choosing the first /52 subnet from our first example, we get the first group of 256 /60 subnets:

```
2001:db8:1::/60
2001:db8:1:0100::/60
2001:db8:1:0200::/60
...
2001:db8:1:0FF0::/60
```

The second group of 256 /60 subnets would be:

```
2001:db8:1:1000::/60
2001:db8:1:1100::/60
2001:db8:1:1200::/60
...
2001:db8:1:1FF0::/60
```

The final path gives us 4096 /64s enumerated by the second, third, and fourth characters (and right-most 12 bits) of the fourth hextet. Once more, starting with the first /52 subnet, we get the first group of 4096 /64 subnets:

```
2001:db8:1::/64
2001:db8:1:0100::/64
2001:db8:1:0200::/64
...
2001:db8:1:0FFF::/64
```

The second group of 4096 /64 subnets would be:

```
2001:db8:1:1000::/64
2001:db8:1:1100::/64
2001:db8:1:1200::/64
...
2001:db8:1:1FFF::/64
```

Hopefully, these images (and the method associated with them) give you a better sense of how to visualize and enumerate the subnets and hierarchy options available to you for a site. With a few uses, you'll quickly be able to mentally map out your options.[5]

Non-Nibble Subnetting

As we discussed, we'll want to use nibble boundary subnetting whenever possible. Recall that if we stick to the nibble boundary when subnetting a site prefix with 16 bits, we always get 16, 256, 4096, or 65536 prefixes. Also, enumeration is simple, as each hexadecimal character represents a nibble and prefixes will never "divide" a hex character.

However, there may be instances that arise where we'll need to use the non-nibble "in-between" bits to provide sufficient subnets for our site address plan.

Here's a method for IPv6 subnetting using any number of bits in the subnet ID. This will allow you to calculate and enumerate groups of prefixes other than the ones adhering to nibble boundaries, i.e., 16, 256, 4096, 65536, etc.[6]

Let's walk through this method with an example allocation. Say we've received 2001:db8:abba::/48 to number a campus LAN.

With a little planning, we've determined that we're going to need at least 16 subnets for each building. So this first group of prefixes will not require our method because we simply adhere to the 4 bits of the first nibble boundary.

This gives us 16 prefixes enumerated by the first character of our fourth hextet:

```
2001:db8:abba::/52
2001:db8:abba:1000::/52
2001:db8:abba:2000::/52
...
2001:db8:abba:f000::/52
```

Now, let's say for the sake of illustration that our typical campus building uses 20 VLANs. Since allocating 4 more bits to take us to the next nibble boundary only yields 16

---

5. As mentioned, this approach will work just as well for the 16 bits between a /32 and a /48 (thus, for any address planning necessary between sites).

6. This method is derived in part from the one presented in Joseph Davies' excellent book *Understanding IPv6: Your Essential Guide to IPv6 on Windows*.

additional prefixes, we'll need more than 4 bits. By standard IPv6 address planning principles, we should be entirely comfortable simply allocating an additional 4 bits for a total of 8 bits. This would give us 256 additional prefixes (with 4 bits remaining for 16 /64s per prefix). But to demonstrate our method, let's get more granular and only use as many bits as gives us sufficient prefixes for the number of elements in this level of our design (i.e., 20 VLANs). Since the least number of bits that produces an integer value greater than 20 is 5 ($2^5 = 32$), we'll use 5 bits to subnet our /52 prefix.

First, where p = *prefix length* of the parent subnet and a = *number of fixed bits in the subnet ID*:

$a = p - 48$

From our example:

$a = 52 - 48 = 4$

$a = 4$

So we have 4 bits that are fixed (which we already knew, but the value is used in later formulae).

Next, where s = *subnets created* and b = *bits used to subnet*

$s = 2^b$

$s = 2^5 = 32$

$s = 32$

As we outlined above, we'll create 32 subnets using 5 bits.

Next, where i = *the (decimal) increment value between the created subnets* (which we must convert back to hexadecimal):

$i = 2^{16-(a+b)}$

$i = 2^{16-(4+5)} = 2^{16-9} = 2^7 = 128$

$i = 128$

Converted to hexadecimal:

$i = 0x80$

Next, where p_1 = *the prefix length of the created subnets*:

$p_1 = 48 + a + b$

$p_1 = 48 + 4 + 5 = 57$

So now that we know the increment and prefix length value, we can enumerate the new subnets:

```
2001:db8:abba::/57
2001:db8:abba:80::/57
2001:db8:abba:100::/57
2001:db8:abba:180::/57
...
2001:db8:abba:f80::/57
```

Et voilà: Our 32 new subnets.

We could, of course, subnet each of these /57s further in order to provide additional hierarchy for other organizational or operational requirements.

But assuming we don't, how many /64 interface subnets would each of these /57s provide?

Finally, where n = *number of /64 subnets provided by each new subnet*:

$n = 2^{(64-p1)}$

$n = 2^{(64-57)} = 2^7 = 128$

So each /57 will provide us with 128 /64 interface subnets.

With a little practice, you'll be able to dispense with the formulae and do this in your head.

A Bit to the Left, a Bit to the Right

There are many bit-allocation methods to help take advantage of the tremendous subnetting flexibility in IPv6. It's a Good Thing™, too, because there are many sizes of networks with many different business requirements. And, of course, networks are constantly growing, shrinking, adding new applications and services, etc. As a result, it's sometimes difficult to know in advance what size allocations will be ideal for an existing or planned set of networks. (We'll review IPv6 address allocation methods in the next chapter.)

Let's look at three ways we could assign bits in an allocation to create subnets. We'll start with a sample allocation:

```
2001:db8:aa00::/40
```

The same allocation expressed in binary:

```
00100000 00000001 00001101 10111000 10101010 00000000
```

For illustration purposes, we'll focus on the next 8 bits available to us (from /41 to /48). Keep in mind that the maximum number of subnets with 8 bits is 256.

Subnets from the Right-Most Bits

The first method would be to begin with and increment the right-most available bits (Table 4-2):

Table 4-2. Subnets from Right-Most Bits

Name	Binary	Hex
Subnet1	00000000	2001:db8:aa00::/48
Subnet2	00000001	2001:db8:aa01::/48
Subnet3	00000010	2001:db8:aa02::/48
Subnet4	00000011	2001:db8:aa03::/48
…	…	…
Subnet256	11111111	2001:db8:aaff::/48

This method has some advantages. It's certainly the simplest of the allocation methods. A major disadvantage, however, is that if an allocation turns out to be too small to accommodate growth, there is no easy way to increase its size contiguously.[7]

Subnets from the Left-Most Bits

The second method starts from the left-most available bits and assigns them from left to right (Table 4-3).

Table 4-3. Subnets from Left-Most Bits

Name	Binary	Hex
Subnet1	00000000	2001:0db8:aa00::/48
Subnet2	10000000	2001:0db8:aa80::/48
Subnet3	01000000	2001:0db8:aa40::/48
Subnet4	11000000	2001:0db8:aac0::/48
Subnet5	00100000	2001:0db8:aa20::/48
…	…	…
Subnet256	11111111	2001:0db8:aaff::/48

It's hard to perfectly visualize, but it's pretty obvious that early in our list there is plenty of space between subnets. (Although as we assign bits from left to right, we would

---

7. You may notice, however, that when using this method, by simply skipping some fixed number of subnets in between allocations, you'll automatically leave subnets in reserve for future contiguous assignments. For example, start at 2001:db8:aa01::/48 and allocate every other prefix: 2001:db8:aa03::/48, 2001:db8:aa05::/48, etc. That would leave in reserve 2001:db8:aa00::/48, 2001:db8:aa02::/48, 2001:db8:aa04::/48, etc. The CLI tool *ipv6gen*, which is used for automatically generating IPv6 subnets, offers this capability. We'll examine this, as well as other features of *ipv6gen*, in more detail at the end of this chapter.

eventually account for every possible subnet and fill in the space between the prefixes at the start of our list.)

The disadvantage here is that since we've started with the left-most bits, we're right at the edge of our allocation. We can always create smaller subnets, but there's no way to create any larger subnets, contiguous or otherwise.

Can you guess where the third method begins? That's right! With the middle bits!

Subnets from the Middle Bits

The algorithm for assigning bits for this method is a little more complex.[8]

If we have an odd number of bits, we start with the middle one:

000000000

If we have an even number of bits (as we do in our example), we divide them in half and choose the left-most bit of the second half:

00000000

Next, we count up through the available bits in our set. Since we've only selected one bit so far, there are only two possibilities:

00000000 00001000

In our example, these would correspond to the following subnets:

```
2001:db8:aa00::/48
2001:db8:aa08::/48
```

We now say that we've completed the first *round* of bit selection and subnetting.

Each subsequent round will add an additional bit to the previous round's set of bits. If we're in an even-numbered round, we add the first available bit to the left of our previous set. If we're in an odd-numbered round, we add the first available bit to the right of the previous round's bit set. Then we count up through all the available bits in that set. Rinse. Repeat. (See Figure 4-6.)

---

8. RFC 3531, *A Flexible Method for Managing the Assignment of Bits of an IPv6 Address Block* (*http://bit.ly/ rfc-3531*).

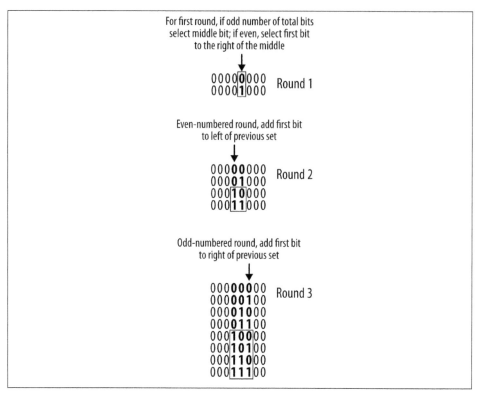

Figure 4-6. RFC 3531 middle bits method

The power of this method is two-fold.

By leaving unused bits to the left, we're effectively leaving space between subnets. By numbering into these bits, we can arbitrarily increase the size of a previous allocation.

By leaving unused bits to the right, we can create smaller subnets as needed.

Perhaps we could refer to this as *tentative allocation*. If all or part of our network is very dynamic, we might reasonably infer that we'll have to modify our allocation scheme to accommodate any change and growth. This method gives us a way to do it more easily.

Since this method is a bit more involved, there are multiple tools available to help manage it (including *ipv6gen*, detailed below).

Using Only Numeric Subnets

We've seen how subnetting from the left-most or middle bits can leave ample space between subnets for future use. Another way to preserve space in a group is to select those subnets containing only numbers (and no hexadecimal characters).

For example:

```
2001:db8:abba:0[0-9][0-9]0::/56
```

Enumerating the numbers-only subnets would give us blocks of /60s, according to the following pattern:

```
2001:db8:abba::/60
2001:db8:abba:0010:/60
2001:db8:abba:0020:/60
...
2001:db8:abba:0090:/60
```

Here are the subnets containing hexadecimal characters from the same range:

```
2001:db8:abba:00a0:/60
2001:db8:abba:00b0:/60
2001:db8:abba:00c0:/60
...
2001:db8:abba:00f0:/60
```

Out of the 256 total subnets available, 100 numeral-only subnets would be used. This method leaves 61% of any group of subnets in reserve for future use. (It's also helpful operationally because production subnets are immediately identifiable by the absence of hexadecimal characters in a given group.)

ipv6gen

ipv6gen (*http://bit.ly/ipv6gen*) is a very handy open-source, Perl-based tool for generating and enumerating subnets from a larger prefix.

You enter the prefix you want to subnet, as well as the size of the prefixes you want to generate (Figure 4-7).

It's especially useful for accurately enumerating prefixes when subnetting away from the nibble boundary (Figure 4-8).

With no argument, ipv6gen allocates from the right-most bits of the entered prefix. But the tool also lets you allocate from the left-most bits, which is a useful approach if you think you might need to create additional contiguous subnets in the future (Figure 4-9).

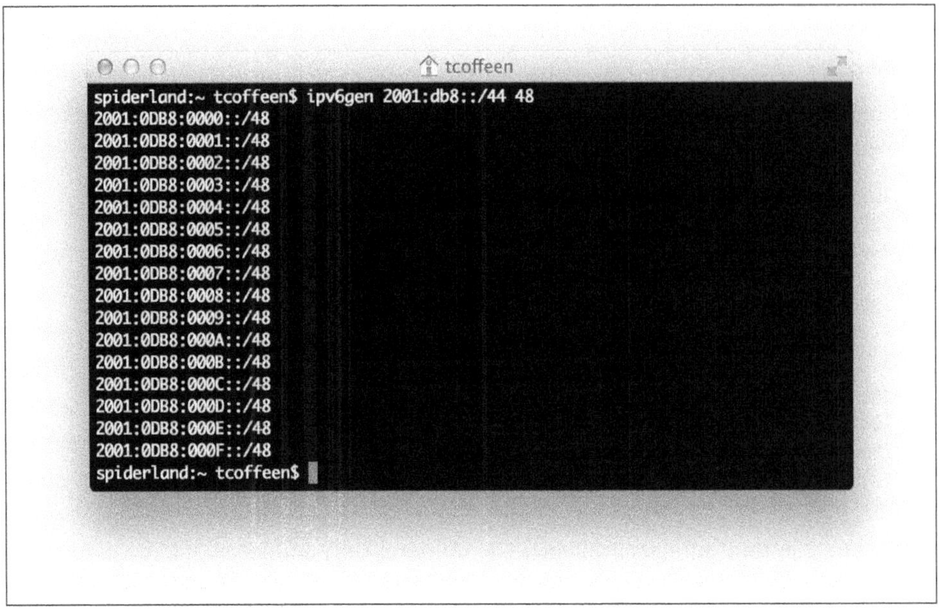

Figure 4-7. ipv6gen, example 1

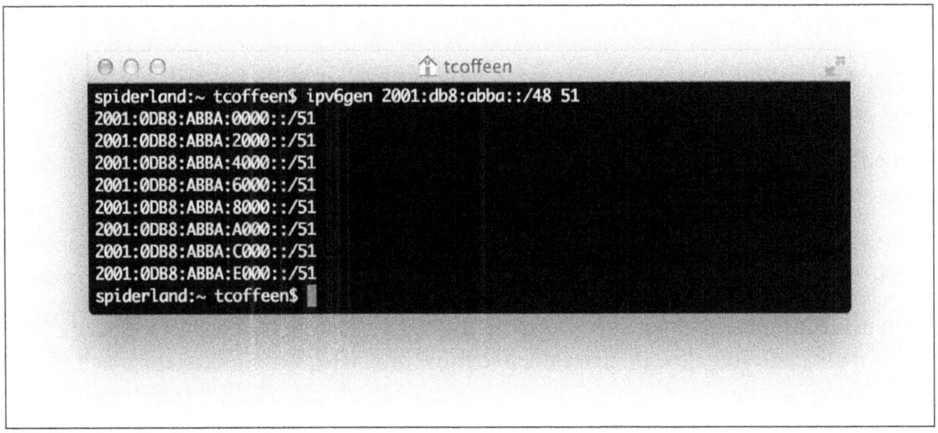

Figure 4-8. ipv6gen, example 2

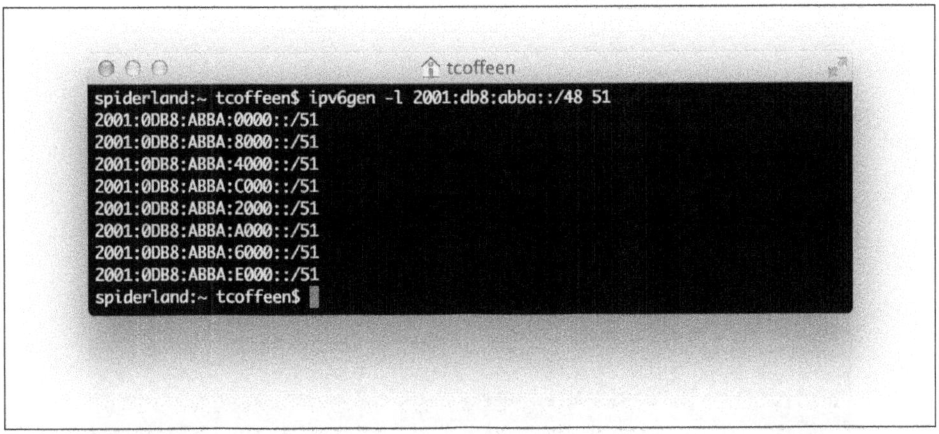

```
spiderland:~ tcoffeen$ ipv6gen -l 2001:db8:abba::/48 51
2001:0DB8:ABBA:0000::/51
2001:0DB8:ABBA:8000::/51
2001:0DB8:ABBA:4000::/51
2001:0DB8:ABBA:C000::/51
2001:0DB8:ABBA:2000::/51
2001:0DB8:ABBA:A000::/51
2001:0DB8:ABBA:6000::/51
2001:0DB8:ABBA:E000::/51
spiderland:~ tcoffeen$ 
```

Figure 4-9. ipv6gen, example 3

Finally, you can allocate from the middle bits, allowing contiguous subnetting for both larger and smaller prefixes (shown here with the debug flag set in Figure 4-10).

ipv6gen also has a sparse allocation function that skips the enumeration of intervening prefixes. Here's the example from Figure 4-7 using the "step between prefixes" argument set to 4 (Figure 4-11).

For each prefix, the three prefixes that would have followed are dropped. These prefixes could be held in reserve and allowed for future assignment and aggregation (in this example, to a /46).

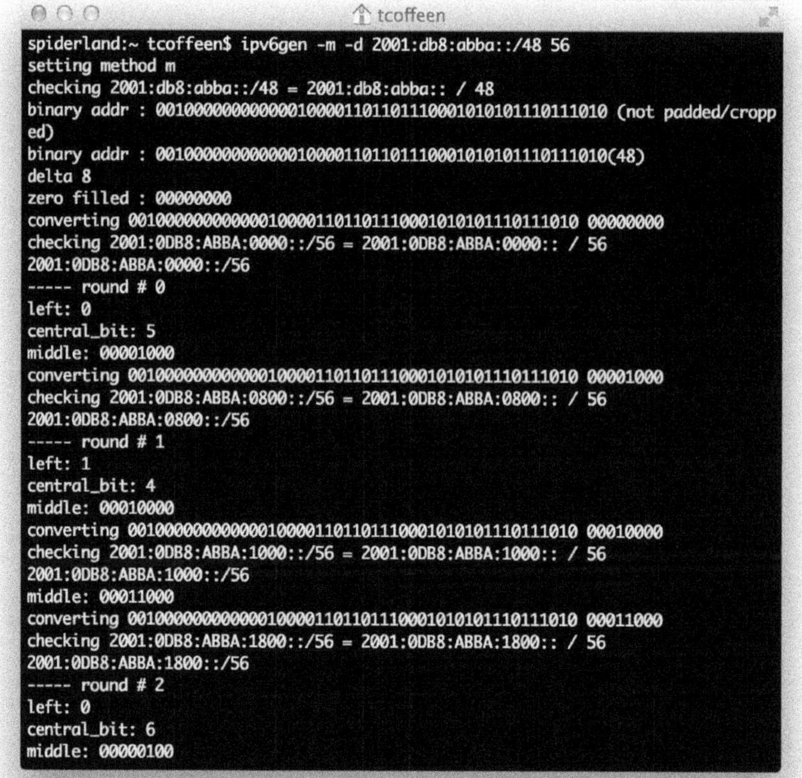

```
⊝ ○ ○                          ⬆ tcoffeen                              ⬈
spiderland:~ tcoffeen$ ipv6gen -m -d 2001:db8:abba::/48 56
setting method m
checking 2001:db8:abba::/48 = 2001:db8:abba:: / 48
binary addr : 00100000000000010000110110111000101010111010111010 (not padded/cropp
ed)
binary addr : 00100000000000010000110110111000101010111010111010(48)
delta 8
zero filled : 00000000
converting 00100000000000010000110110111000101010111010111010 00000000
checking 2001:0DB8:ABBA:0000::/56 = 2001:0DB8:ABBA:0000:: / 56
2001:0DB8:ABBA:0000::/56
----- round # 0
left: 0
central_bit: 5
middle: 00001000
converting 00100000000000010000110110111000101010111010111010 00001000
checking 2001:0DB8:ABBA:0800::/56 = 2001:0DB8:ABBA:0800:: / 56
2001:0DB8:ABBA:0800::/56
----- round # 1
left: 1
central_bit: 4
middle: 00010000
converting 00100000000000010000110110111000101010111010111010 00010000
checking 2001:0DB8:ABBA:1000::/56 = 2001:0DB8:ABBA:1000:: / 56
2001:0DB8:ABBA:1000::/56
middle: 00011000
converting 00100000000000010000110110111000101010111010111010 00011000
checking 2001:0DB8:ABBA:1800::/56 = 2001:0DB8:ABBA:1800:: / 56
2001:0DB8:ABBA:1800::/56
----- round # 2
left: 0
central_bit: 6
middle: 00000100
```

Figure 4-10. ipv6gen, example 4 (output truncated)

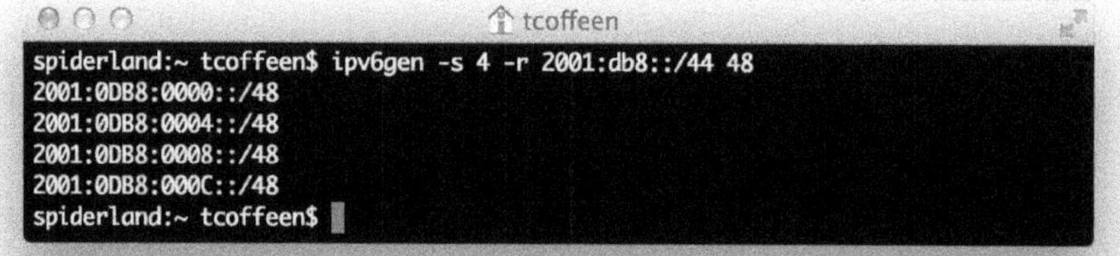

```
⊝ ○ ○                          ⬆ tcoffeen                              ⬈
spiderland:~ tcoffeen$ ipv6gen -s 4 -r 2001:db8::/44 48
2001:0DB8:0000::/48
2001:0DB8:0004::/48
2001:0DB8:0008::/48
2001:0DB8:000C::/48
spiderland:~ tcoffeen$ █
```

Figure 4-11. ipv6gen, example 5

## CHAPTER 5

IPv6 Address Planning Concepts

> Practice safe design: use a concept.
>
> — Petrula Vrontikis

Introduction

It's been said that design is where science and art break even. In this chapter, we'll focus primarily on the science part of IPv6 address planning and be as thorough as we can be with the design concepts and principles that you'll need to be familiar with to tackle your plan. As we proceed, however, we'll be sure to consider the art of address plan design as well, an art based on accumulated operational knowledge and practical experience and the best-practices that have evolved from it.

IPv6 Address Planning Principles

We've already mentioned earlier that IPv6 address planning should *not* be based on (e.g., sufficient host addressing).

But given that, what *should* it be based on (and why)? Let's examine the fundamental IPv6 address planning principles in brief before looking at each more closely. They are:

Properly sized initial allocations
> This is arguably the most critical of all the address planning principles we'll discuss. The reason is that all of the principles that follow are more or less dependent on getting a sufficiently large allocation at the start.

Sparse assignment of subnets
> With a sufficiently sized allocation, we'll be able to assign subnets sparsely, i.e., leave unused space between our assigned subnets adequate for future growth or network reconfiguration.

Hierarchical organization of subnets

A sufficiently sized allocation also allows for the organization of subnets into hierarchies or levels that follow one or more organizational attributes of the network or enterprise: geographical location, organizational role, security classification, etc.

Adherence to nibble boundaries

Where practical, assigning subnets based on 4-bit boundaries provides for the operational benefit of increased legibility (i.e., human-readability) for IPv6 subnets.

Uniform subnetting and summarization

Equal-sized subnets (or groups of subnets) help simplify the overall address plan. They're easier to assign, administer, and track. They're also easier to summarize, potentially providing for smaller routing tables and tidier ACLs.

Let's look at each of these principles in more detail.

Properly-Sized Initial IPv6 Allocations

It seems to be an all-too-common occurence for enterprises to end up with an IPv6 allocation that's too small. A typical example of this is an enterprise that has multiple networks in multiple locations but receives only a single /48. Such scenarios often occur because enterprise network or IT personnel have gotten conflicting, insufficient, or out-of-date information on how much IPv6 space they need, so they end up asking for too little. The absolute enormous scale of a /48 can trigger an analysis that is misinformed by IPv4 thinking: "We've got 1,208,925,819,614,629,174,706,176 IPv6 addresses to use. Let's see…(does calculation)…that's 281 trillion Internets! But…we don't want to eventually be in the same boat as we are with IPv4 exhaustion. Better play it safe and figure out how to best carve up our one /48. After all, it's more than enough host addresses."[1]

So now that we know we're going to need a *properly-sized initial IPv6 allocation*, what's the proper size? Naturally, organizations come in many sizes and have differing missions. Though there are some common allocation sizes by organization type (as depicted in Chapter 3), there typically isn't a one-size-fits-all allocation. So our more general definition of a proper-sized IPv6 allocation is *one that allows for the realization of all the other IPv6 address planning principles*. Such principles will help ensure more specific operational benefits like prefix legibility (or human-readability), better route aggregation, more manageable ACLs, and more accurate tracking of IPv6 prefix assignments. The goal is to futureproof the address plan and keep it operationally viable through the growth and change that inevitably occurs in any network.

---

1. While it's certainly theoretically possible to receive too much IPv6 space, any conclusion that too much space has been allocated needs to be scrutinized through a careful assessment of the proposed IPv6 address plan. Such an assessment should focus on the operational viability of the plan. In other words, does it make network operations over time easier rather than harder?

Of course, attempting to accurately determine how much IPv6 space will be needed *before* you've completed at least an initial version of an address plan means that you may need to make some educated inferences (aka, guesses). Meanwhile, creating an IPv6 address plan relies on knowing how much space you have to work with. As a result, it may be helpful to tackle this sizing conundrum in a couple of stages:

1. By making an initial, approximate estimate based on the relative size of the organization (generally, with regard to the number of *sites* as uniquely defined in IPv6 terms).

2. Reassessing the estimated allocation size after a detailed plan based on solid IPv6 address planning principles and best-practices has been constructed.

For the first stage, allocations range in size from a /48 at the smallest end (usually for a single site) all the way to a /16, depending on the size of the requesting organization. While there could always be exceptions, ISPs are more likely to receive larger allocations, between a /16 and /32, while enterprises are often allocated between a /48 and /32 of IPv6 space (Figure 5-1).

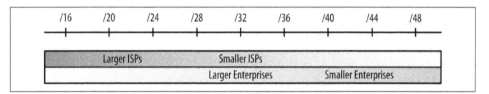

Figure 5-1. Allocation size according to type of organization

We'll cover RIR and ISP requirements for justifying IPv6 allocations in Chapter 6, but planning on assigning at least a /48 per site is a good rule of thumb for estimating the necessary size of your IPv6 allocation.[2]

Also, for those that have already received an allocation from a RIR or ISP: as you create or revise your first plan, you may come to realize or believe that your allocation is insufficient. We'll cover what to do in that scenario in the next chapter.

Sparse Assignment of Subnets

The next principle of IPv6 address planning is *sparse assignment of subnets*. We saw a few of the methods for creating subnets that allow for sparse allocation in the previous chapter, such as subnetting from either the left-most or middle bits, either of which leaves additional bits to create additional contiguous subnets in the future.

---

2. Recall that a *site* in IPv6 is a logical concept and can apply to any consistently defined network, location, function, etc.

Hierarchical Organization of Subnets

By grouping subnets into hierarchies (or more simply put, levels), the addressing plan can more closely track the organization of the network: e.g., its physical topology, its security policies, or any other attributes that might make sense to map into the address plan. Each level of the hierarchy should be easy to aggregate into the next level. It follows then that when creating a new level below an existing one, subnets should be equally sized to continue to allow for aggregation. This recommendation is our next principle.

Uniform Subnetting and Summarization

Anytime new subnets are defined for a hierarchy level within an addressing plan, every effort should be made to make sure that they are uniform in size. This requirement makes sense when considered in the context of the previous principle: hierarchy is easier to establish and maintain when using subnets of equal size. This principle also makes for more efficient network operations (and IP address management) when equal-sized subnets are assigned to particular locations or functions in the network. Finally, uniform subnet sizes can help simplify security policies and any resulting ACL entries (reducing the risk of configuration errors).[3]

Subnets in Reserve

Getting a big enough block of IPv6 addresses from an RIR or ISP at the outset (as well as using techniques like sparse allocation) should help automatically preserve blocks of subnets sufficient for future use. That said, the principle of holding subnets in reserve should be kept in mind as you develop and iterate your address plan. Having enough subnets in reserve at each layer of hierarchy will help ensure the future flexibility and scalability of the plan.

As the network grows or changes, the ability to maintain the above principles is evidence of a successful addressing plan.

Why Don't I Use My Existing IPv4 Plan in IPv6?

When getting started with IPv6 address planning, we might be tempted to use an existing IPv4 address plan as a guide or framework. The reasons for this impulse are perfectly understandable. For instance, without the foundation in IPv6 address planning concepts and methods this book seeks to provide, an architect can lack the proper organizing principles with which to build a proper address plan in IPv6. An existing IPv4 plan provides at least some structure (and the concepts and methods that gave rise to

---

3. Note that this principle has been reflected in the IPv6 standards suggesting /48 site prefixes and /64 interface prefixes.

it) and seems to offer a manageable entry point into a new planning effort. It's also already familiar to network administrators.

But there are multiple reasons why this is the wrong approach.

We've already discussed some of the common methods resulting from *IPv4 thinking*. Attempting to somehow correlate our new IPv6 plan with our existing IPv4 one may lead to improper subnetting and summarization.

For example, because IPv4 allocations are often necessarily limited in size, it's much more common to allocate adjacent subnets. But IPv6 allocations are obviously much larger, and as a result, allocating subnets along boundaries separated by a nibble is the technique preferred in IPv6 address planning. This sparse allocation method leaves intervening bits to number into later, a luxury not afforded to us by the limited bits available in IPv4.

Another reason too much thoughtless deference to our existing IPv4 address plan can be a bad idea is that, unless we're doing a lot of translation between IPv4 and IPv6, our preferred IPv6 deployment method will be dual-stack. Since the IPv4 and IPv6 networks are logically separate in such an environment, we have the freedom to develop a new and unique address plan for IPv6. The potential benefits of this green-field opportunity cannot be overstated (and are partly the reason this book exists).

A final trap that an existing plan can lay for us is the impulse to map IPv4 addresses into IPv6 addresses for an attempt at operational consistency (with the hopes that it will lead to increased operational efficiency). Some or all of the IPv4 octets could be encoded into the hexadecimal characters of the IPv6 address.

For instance, here's the IPv4 host address 192.0.2.234 mapped into the last eight nibbles of the IPv6 subnet 2001:db8:777:::

```
2001:db8:777::c000:02ea
```

You'll notice that we immediately sacrifice the more familiar decimal representation of the IPv4 address (along with whatever operational benefit it might have otherwise provided). An alternative would be not to convert the decimal characters to hexadecimal, but just represent them using the numbers characters of hexadecimal:

```
2001:db8:777::192:0:2:234
```

While this method forgoes any of the benefits of auto-addressing via SLAAC or DHCPv6 (and the tighter host control, DNS, and IPAM potentially available when using it), it might be useful in limited instances where static addressing is usually used, such as specific, well-known servers.[4]

---

4. Though I've used the IPv4 and IPv6 documentation prefixes for the example above, in an actual production configuration, the mapped address would be constructed from globally unique (i.e., *public*) addresses.

Finally, no matter what might be perceived as the immediate operational ease or benefit of mapping our IPv6 address plan into our existing IPv4 one, keep in mind that IPv4 is headed toward *legacy protocol* status: at some point, organizations will be removing IPv4 from the network. Whatever interim operational benefit was missed out on by commiting to IPv4 address plan logic at the outset, add to that the complexity and expense of revising or redoing the IPv6 address plan according to the established and new best practices.

Address Plan Structure

 At its most basic, the IPv6 addressing plan method is defining and assigning blocks of subnets based on the structure of the network or the organization.

We'll look at some general best-practice IPv6 address planning principles a little later in the chapter. But first, let's look at an example of the *basic address plan structure* (Figure 5-2).

In this example, the *level 0* represents an organization's primary IPv6 allocation from the ISP or RIR. *Level 1* represents blocks of subnets defined and assigned to some network or attribute within the organization. *Level 2* represents the smallest assignable subnet (in most cases a /64).

More specifically, the example above might correspond to a /48 being carved into 256 /56s, each yielding 256 /64s (or, alternatively, a /32 being carved into 256 /40s, each with 256 /48s). Figure 5-3 shows another example with an additional level added.

As before, *level 0* represents an organization's primary IPv6 allocation from the ISP or RIR. *Level 1* represents blocks of subnets defined and assigned to some network or attribute within the organization. *Level 2* would be the next block of assigned subnets within each *level 1* subnet. *Level 3* would likely be the smallest assignable subnet (again, with each instance of *level 3* fitting into each *level 2* subnet).

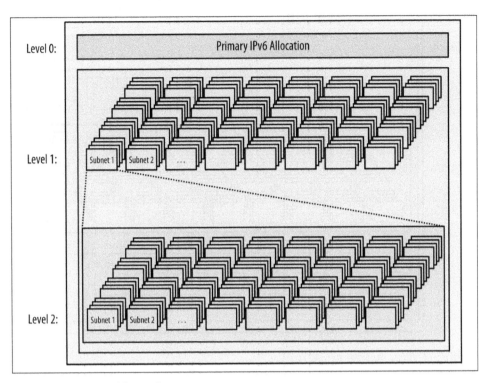

Figure 5-2. Basic address plan structure

As we'll see in the addressing plan example in Chapter 7, most organizations have fewer than 256 attributes requiring subnet blocks. They also typically have subattributes requiring additional levels. As a result, most address plans end up with many unused subnets in each block (Figure 5-4).[5]

When we talk about blocks of subnets defined and assigned to a level, each level typically corresponds to some well-defined network or organizational attribute, and the most significant of these (and typically the first to be defined) is the *site*.

---

5. Recall that this is an ideal outcome according to the general principle of "Subnets in Reserve" on page 94 we covered earlier in the chapter.

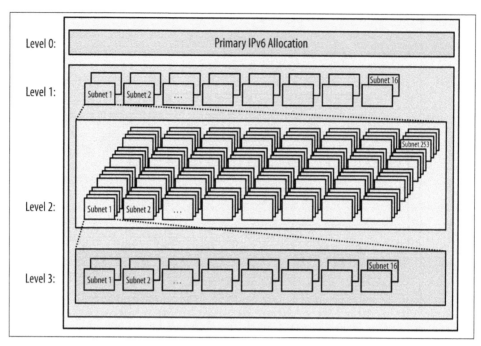

Figure 5-3. Basic address plan structure

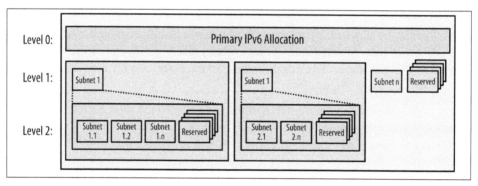

Figure 5-4. Address plan structure with reserved (unused) subnets

What Is a Site?

We should already have some concept of what constitutes a *site* when it comes to general network architecture and addressing. Since the network exists to provide services to the organization, a site is very often defined by its generic role: e.g., headquarters, remote office, research campus, home network, data center, point-of-presence, etc. Often, these designations are prepended with actual geograhical locations: e.g., Atlanta HQ, Fresno remote office, Frankfurt POP, etc.

We also might think of sites more abstractly: e.g., as discrete LANs behind routing aggregation points, IGP areas, security domains, etc.

 In the context of IPv6 address planning, it can be helpful to think of a site as *a fundamental network (or organizational) unit that receives a uniform network prefix*. Keep in mind that we shouldn't define a site in a way that prevents us from realizing our basic address planning principles (an outcome that is more likely if we have defined too few or too many levels of hierarchy).

Thus, our choice of how we define a site within our network or organization will have a critical impact on our IPv6 address plan; specifically, how much IPv6 address space we should request from an RIR or ISP (and can reasonably expect to receive).

A little bit of background on the subject should help provide some helpful context for this process.

In the early days of IPv6 adoption, members of the IETF wanted to create some useful guidelines for allocating IPv6. As a result, way back in 2001, the Internet advisory board (IAB) recommended that the allocation for "the boundary between the public and the private topology" be a /48, except "for very large subscribers."[6]

As we've covered, such an allocation left 16 bits available for additional subnetting before reaching the /64 host ID boundary and was seen as a good balance in size for small and large enterprises, as well as home networks.

A fixed /48 allocation size for all sites offered a number of operational and administrative benefits for both the allocating agency and the recipient.

For an RIR or ISP, a fixed allocation meant they didn't have to worry too much about whether requests were appropriately sized or know too many of the gory details of the recipient's network or plans for growth. A fixed allocation of sufficient size could prevent the recipient from having to come back for additional space any time soon after the initial allocation, a potential boon to both the end-user and the RIR or ISP.

For the recipient, benefits included things like the relative ease of renumbering (should it be required). With a fixed allocation size for sites, any new allocation would have the same number of bits in the network portion of the address, making renumbering much simpler. Another benefit would be being able to use and manage one reverse DNS zone per site. And perhaps most compelling of all (at least for our discussion) is that a

---

6. RFC 6177, *IPv6 Address Assignment to End Sites* (*http://bit.ly/rfc-6177*).

fixed /48 allocation size made address planning and management much simpler and more consistent.

At the time, the issue of conservation was considered. Would a /48 allocation for all sites create premature scarcity in IPv6 overall (i.e., shortages within the address protocol that was designed explicity to overcome a scarcity problem in the first place).

The answer was a resounding *no*. The 35 trillion available /48s in the existing global unicast allocation were deemed sufficient (and with approximately 87% of the total IPv6 address space remaining unallocated, any misjudgements or miscalculations on this question would be easily absorbed by a newly defined GUA, potentially one with tighter allocation policies).

In the Year 2100 CE

Perhaps it's time for another demonstration of the sheer magnitude of the IPv6 address space.[7]

The current global unicast allocation 2000::/3 is defined by the three highest-order bits of the 128-bit address being set to 001. A little arithmetic reveals that this allocation is 12.5% of the overall IPv6 address space:

$$\frac{2^{125}}{2^{128}} = \times\ 100 = 12.5\ \%$$

Next, we'll calculate the number of /48s in the GUA. This quantity can be easily determined by subtracting the number of bits defining the network portion of the GUA (indicated by the /3 of its CIDR notation) from the number of bits defining the network portion of the site allocation (indicated by the /48 of its CIDR): e.g., 48 - 3 = 45. Thus, there are 2^45 /48s in the GUA.

$2^{45} = 35,184,372,088,832$

The UN predicts that by 2100 the Earth could have a human population of as many as 16 billion people. Will posterity have enough IPv6?

$$\frac{35\,184\,372\,088\,832}{16\,000\,000\,000} = 2\,199$$

---

7. This one is courtesy of IPv6 solutions manager, Cisco Press and Network World author Jeff Doyle (CCIE #1919).

So even with a potential population of 16 billion, there are still enough /48s in the GUA to provide every person on Earth with almost 2,200 of them (and that's with approximately 86% of the IPv6 space still held in reserve).

Based on these numbers, the argument goes that over the next 80 years IP will, in all likelihood, be superseded by other communications protocols.

Since then, the recommendations have been updated to allow for subnets smaller than a /48 (e.g., /56) to be assigned to sites.[8] This was done less out of any concern for the potential to "waste" IPv6 space and more as a recognition that some operators would want the flexibility to use a smaller assignment to make their plan more operationally manageable. In particular, broadband service providers might want to assign more than a /64 to CPE devices inferring that future home networks will need additional subnets to support new services (without perhaps requiring the 65,536 /64s provided by an entire /48).

Of course, the individual sites in our plan could also require an IPv6 allocation larger than a /48. As we develop our plan according to the concepts and principles within this chapter, it's perfectly acceptable to conclude that a /48 per site would be insufficient to realize the benefits of an IPv6 address plan. RIR policies for IPv6 are still evolving, but a well-designed plan that maximizes operational benefit for the requestor and hastens the overall deployment of IPv6 should be favorably viewed and accommodated, even if said plan requires more than a /48 per site.

Intra-Site Versus Inter-Site Planning

Because of the suggested subnet size for sites (/48) and for interfaces (/64), there is a certain amount of structure already implied for any addressing plan.

In most IPv6 addressing plans, this structure is applied geographically, i.e., to network or organizational topology.

If we think about the 16 bits between a /48 and a /64 prefix as most generally being reserved for *intra-site* addressing (i.e., subnets within sites), and the 16 bits between a /48 and a /32 prefix as generally reserved for *inter-site* addressing (i.e., subnets between sites), we've identified a basic structure that can help organize our initial effort (Figure 5-5).[9]

---

8. RFC 6177.

9. If your IPv6 address plan is for a large service provider or enterprise, you may receive an allocation larger than a /32, but the principle is essentially the same.

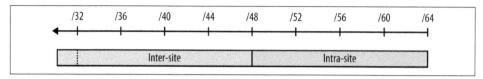

Figure 5-5. Inter-site and intra-site planning

Recall that the standards and RIR policies provide a very broad definition of what a *site* can be. As a result, an organization has tremendous latitude to assign site designations. Such flexibility is beneficial because there may be multiple site types, each with potentially differing topologies.

In the last chapter, we saw Figure 4-1, which demonstrated eight possible hierarchies (created by choosing different nibble-aligned combinations of the available 16 bits) that we could use for a site's IPv6 address plan. These hiearchies can be mixed and matched to create unique intra-site address plans for groups of sites that share the same organizational or network topology. An organization might need a small library of address plan templates for when new sites of any type are to be added.

While multiple types of sites could exist (with variations on the intra-site address plan for each type of site), it's more desirable to attempt to keep the address plan uniform for all sites. In any case, for most enterprises there is typically only one topology between sites.[10] As a result, only one inter-site address plan is usually needed. (Although as with the intra-site address plan, variations of the inter-site plan based on regional or architectural differences might be necessary or desirable.)

---

10. If the enterprise is large enough, it may have multiple routing domains in multiple regions, perhaps requiring different address plans depending on the topology (or topologies).

AS, Region, Site

A common way to structure the inter-site part of an address plan is based on a hierarchical network topology corresponding to an autonomous system (AS), regions, and sites (Figure 5-6).

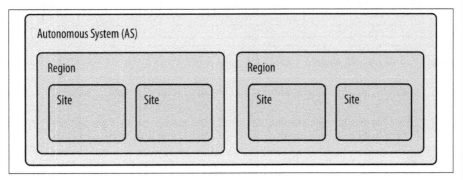

Figure 5-6. Inter-site structure using AS/Region/Site

Typically, the entire IPv6 allocation would be assigned to the *AS*. An AS is "a set of routers under a single technical administration"[11] and with one or more interior gateway protocols (IGPs) providing routing within the AS. An exterior gateway protocol (EGP)— usually Border Gateway Protocol (BGP)—provides routing to other external autonomous systems.[12]

The next level of the topology for the inter-site part of our address plan is generally based on *regions*. The initial allocation is carved up into prefixes of equal size, which are then assigned to specific geographical regions. Regions might be global, continental, national—any designation that works for the organization.

Finally, each of those assignments are themselves divided equally among the sites within the region.

Here's a more specific example of how a large US enterprise might apply this concept (Figure 5-7):

---

11. RFC 1930, *Guidelines for creation, selection, and registration of an Autonomous System (AS)* (*http://bit.ly/ rfc-1930*).

12. It's natural and appropriate to associate the idea of autonomous system with the autonomous system numbers (ASNs) used in BGP. But while some enterprises may not run BGP, they will almost certainly have an AS (according to the above definition) to administer and assign their IPv6 allocation to.

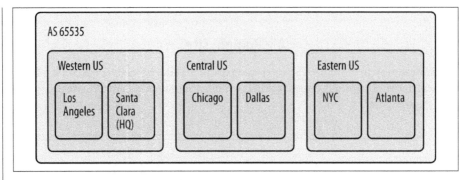

Figure 5-7. Inter-site structure large US enterprise

 For many organizations, especially those with very simple network topologies and operational requirements, this basic division is sufficient for coming up with a workable address plan.

But for everyone else, some additional structure will be required. Here's the general address plan process:

1. Obtain a primary IPv6 allocation.
2. Identify or define the organizing attributes and hierarchy of the network or the business (e.g., geographical location, organizational role, security classification, etc.).
3. Assign blocks of subnets within each attribute or hierarchical level to satisfy their immediate and future subnet requirements.

Another way of conceiving of this approach is that it is a *top-down*, compared to the *bottom-up*, approach in IPv4 relying on host counts.

As we covered in the last chapter, by adhering to the nibble boundary when allocating bits for subnets within a site or between sites, a limited structure or hierarchy can be achieved. Of course, we're not restricted to only using 4-bit boundaries.

In fact, we can represent in our addressing plan as many branches and sub-branches as we like to correlate to network function, location, names of US presidents, etc. But we need to keep in mind that the more levels we create, the more complex our plan becomes, and the less flexible and scalable it potentially gets. That's why we should learn and keep in mind some general, best-practice principles.

IPv6 Allocation Methods

When you're putting together your initial IPv6 addressing plan, you'll obviously need to allocate subnets to the various entities you've defined (e.g., regions, sites, buildings, applications, VLANs, etc.).

When we talk about IPv6 address allocation methods, we're really talking about the same basic technique that we use in IPv4, i.e., designating bits to define subnets for assignment. The minor technical difference, of course, is that rather than converting from binary to decimal as we did with IPv4, we're converting from binary to hexadecimal.

But we're still dealing with the basic process of bit math and subnet definition that we're already intimately familiar with from IPv4. As a result, the same allocation methods we use in IPv4 are available to us in IPv6.

Besides the minor technical difference mentioned above, there's a major conceptual difference in how we perform IPv6 address allocations. With IPv6, we're allocating from abundance rather than from the scarcity of IPv4.

Let's review the IPv6 allocation methods at our disposal:

- Best-fit
- Sparse
- N+1
- Random

Best-Fit Allocation

Best-fit allocation usually refers to the following method:

1. Find the smallest unassigned block in the overall address space that the request fits in.
2. If possible, successively halve that block until the smallest block that will meet the needs of the request is defined.
3. Allocate this block.

First, an example from IPv4: say a data center required 375 IPv4 addresses in the same subnet to assign to servers. The organization is using 10.0.0.0/8 as its overall allocation, and the subnet 10.10.0.0/16 has just been assigned to the region that the data center is in. Using the best-fit method, we don't have to think too hard about the first step because no space has been assigned from this allocation yet. Proceeding to the second step, we halve the original allocation and halve each resulting half until we reach the smallest block that will accommodate the request; in this case, a /23 for 512 total addresses, 375 of which are right around 75% utilization. A pie graph is helpful in visualizing this process (Figure 5-8).

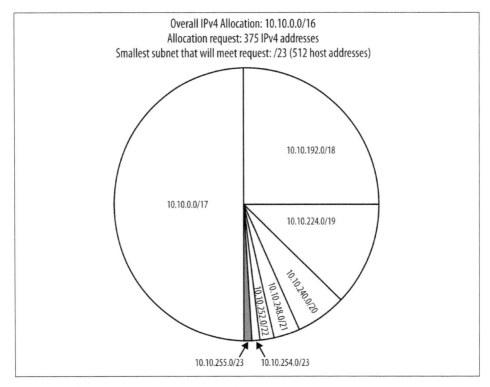

Figure 5-8. IPv4 best-fit allocation example

This result and the method behind it might typically be considered the "most efficient" in terms of IPv4 allocation. But keep in mind that such efficiency is defined as maximum utilization of the IPv4 host addresses available within the smallest assignable subnet, and therefore, is primarily about host address (and subnets for host address) conservation (i.e., IPv4 thinking).

If future allocation requests are of a similar size, it may be possible to consistently use adjacent subnets as you allocate. This, too, will result in more of the available space being "filled in" (i.e., a more thorough utilization of scarce IPv4).

More likely, allocation requests competing for the same overall address space will arrive at different times from different segments or functions in the network topology. The best-fit method pretty much ensures that the resulting discontiguous subnets will be very difficult to summarize for purposes of routing aggregation or access-list (ACL) manageability.

The basic method of best-fit allocation is the same in IPv6, but instead of host address requirements, the allocated block provides the number of subnets needed for a particular assignment.

For example, if the data center from our first example has 375 VLANs that it needs /64s for, the smallest block that will accommodate the request is a /55 (Figure 5-9):

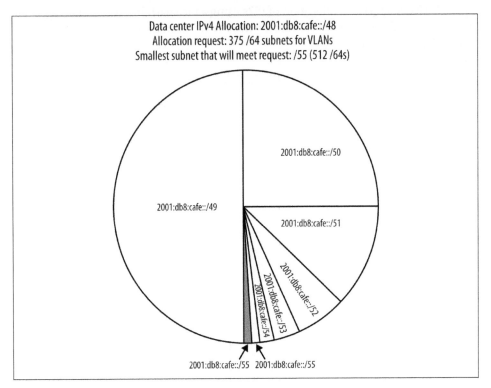

Figure 5-9. IPv6 best-fit example

Though in IPv6 we're defining and allocating a block to provide subnets instead of individual host addresses, the logic of the best-fit allocation method is still about "right-sizing" the block to use. Later, when our plan is operational and we're allocating blocks based on changing requests, the subnet size requirements will vary, depending on the number of elements the requestor needs subnets for.

As a result, best-fit allocation is typically a poor first choice when designing an initial address plan.

Sparse Allocation

As you might have guessed, sparse allocation is about leaving a lot of space in between allocations. Sparse allocation is sometimes referred to as *bisection*. And though it shares the *successive halving* process with the best-fit allocation method, the sparse approach allocates the block at the edge of each new half.

Figure 5-10 depicts sparse allocation of /52s using a pie chart. In this example, only the 1st, 5th, 9th, and 13th /52s are allocated, while the remaining space between allocations is held in reserve for future use.

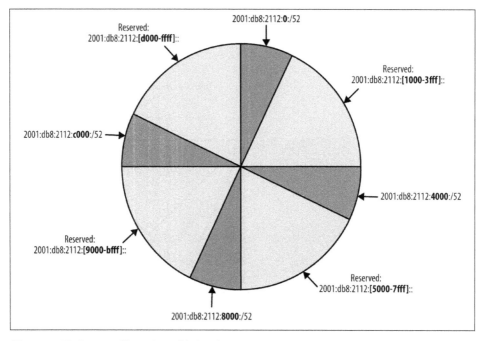

Figure 5-10. Sparse allocation of /52 subnets

Figure 5-11 depicts sparse allocation of /56s using a pie chart. In this example, only the 1st, 64th, 128th, and 192nd /56s are allocated, while the remaining space between allocations is held in reserve for future use.

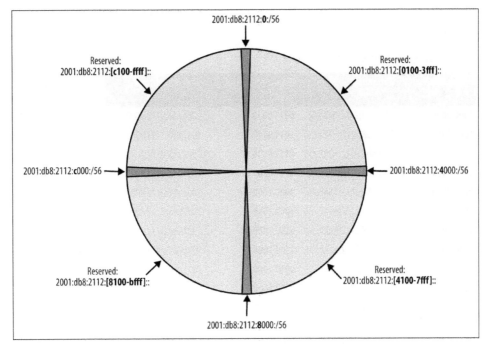

Figure 5-11. Sparse allocation of /56 subnets

Recall the subnetting method from Chapter 4 in which we created subnets by starting with and incrementing the left-most bits.

Let's use the same site allocation from the above best-fit example:

```
2001:db8:2112::/48
```

We can safely ignore the first three hextets of the network ID and focus on the bits of the fourth hextet:

```
0000 0000 0000 0000
```

Next we'll modify our best-fit example a little and say that we have 20 buildings at our site. The minimum number of bits we'd need to provide allocations for all 20 buildings would be 5 ($2^5 = 32$).

But recall also from the previous chapter the advanatage of adhering to the nibble boundary. Rounding to 8 bits give us:

$2^{4(n)}$ (where n=8) = 256 possible subnets

Since we're using 8 of the sixteen available bits for our fourth hextet, the resulting network length will be /56. As a result, we don't care about the right-most eight bits:

```
0000 0000 XXXX XXXX
```

The next step would be to begin with the remaining left-most bits and increment bitwise (Table 5-1):

Table 5-1. Sparse allocation example

Binary, 4th hextet	IPv6 subnet	Binary, 4th hextet (cont.)	IPv6 subnet (cont.)
0000 0000	2001:db8:2112:0000::/56	0011 0000	2001:db8:2112:3000::/56
1000 0000	2001:db8:2112:8000::/56	1011 0000	2001:db8:2112:b000::/56
0100 0000	2001:db8:2112:4000::/56	0111 0000	2001:db8:2112:7000::/56
1100 0000	2001:db8:2112:c000::/56	1111 0000	2001:db8:2112:f000::/56
0010 0000	2001:db8:2112:2000::/56	0000 1000	2001:db8:2112:0800::/56
1010 0000	2001:db8:2112:a000::/56	1000 1000	2001:db8:2112:8800::/56
0110 0000	2001:db8:2112:6000::/56	0100 1000	2001:db8:2112:4800::/56
1110 0000	2001:db8:2112:e000::/56	1100 1000	2001:db8:2112:c800::/56
0001 0000	2001:db8:2112:1000::/56	0010 1000	2001:db8:2112:2800::/56
1001 0000	2001:db8:2112:9000::/56	1010 1000	2001:db8:2112:a800::/56
0101 0000	2001:db8:2112:5000::/56	0110 1000	2001:db8:2112:6800::/56
1101 0000	2001:db8:2112:d000::/56	1110 1000	2001:db8:2112:e800::/56

Now we'll look at how these subnets increment graphically. But because we don't want our graphic to become too cluttered, we'll focus on the first 10 entries in the table to establish the sparse allocation pattern (Figure 5-12).

Between Figure 5-12 and Table 5-1, you may observe that the subnets increment in a way that corresponds to a new allocation at the edge of each new half of the available space.

One of the key advantages of creating an IPv6 address plan from scratch is that you can plan equal-sized address blocks for levels of hierarchy in the network. These equal-sized blocks can then be sparsely allocated, leaving room for growth between allocations and allowing for easier aggregation and ACL maintenance. As a result, the sparse allocation method is typically the most appropriate one to use when creating a new IPv6 addressing plan.

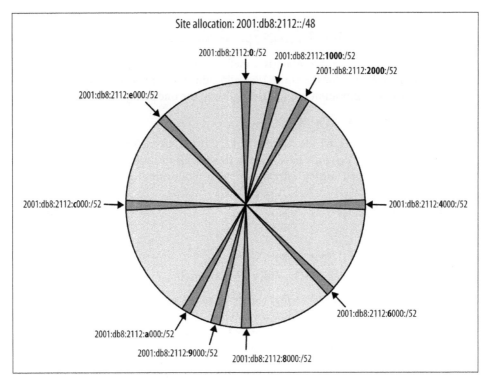

Figure 5-12. Sparse allocation of /56 subnets

 One variation of the sparse allocation method is referred to as *growth-based*. In this method, the unused space contiguous with the slowest growing allocation is selected next to be halved again to generate a new subnet allocation. This approach is arguably more useful in service provider environments where allocations may go to different customers and be under independent control. (It conserves the maximum amount of contiguous space for faster growing customers.)

N+1 Allocation

N+1 allocation (which could also be referred to as *sequential*, or *strict sequential* allocation) is pretty much what it sounds like: a larger allocation is divided evenly among smaller subnets that are assigned in numerical order. As a result, there is no space between subnets to accommodate future growth for any of the assignments. Any original assignment that required additional space (except the most recent assignment) would necessarily receive a noncontiguous new subnet.

N + 1 Versus Sparse Allocation

For this discussion, *N + 1 allocation* is a method for a strict sequential allocation of subnets within a site (or for the entire IPv6 allocation), where N is equal to the hexadecimal value of the allocation immediately prior to the one being allocated.

Let's look at an example of this approach.

Recall that a /48 gives us 65,536 /64 networks. Given that each of these subnets has 1.8×10^{19} addresses, we certainly have enough to allow us to simply begin to assign /64 networks in a sequential fashion without worrying about running out of addresses.

```
2001:db8:1100::/64          Subnet 1
2001:db8:1100:1::/64        Subnet 2
2001:db8:1100:2::/64        Subnet 3
...
2001:db8:1100:ffff::/64     Subnet 65536
```

There are some glaring deficiencies with such a method.

First, unless our network never changes after our initial address allocation, we're obviously going to need to assign additional subnets. If we're merely grabbing the next available subnet in our list, there's no guarantee that this subnet will be needed for the same physical or logical area of the network as the subnet before it or after it.

As a result, over time, subnets that should otherwise be grouped together for the same location or function in the network become sporadic and disconnected with less efficient ways to logically associate them with each other for management purposes. Also, if a particular network location or function requires a contiguous block of prefixes, it may be necessary to allocate a previously unused block.

In the typical hierarchical network topology, these discontiguous networks mean that our routing tables are larger than they have to be, with many /64 prefixes routed to disparate network locations that would otherwise be aggregated. Larger routing tables slow down convergence times and require more router memory. The potential results are a slower and more expensive network.

From a security standpoint, such discontiguous networks also require more effort to maintain secure access to using ACLs. Single prefixes can result in longer ACLs, which become more prone to configuration errors. Abandoned and out-of-date ACL entries can lead to costly security breaches. Security policies in hardware and software that assume logical groupings of network prefixes according to business roles and compliance rules can become unnecessarily complex or even unenforcable.

Limited or no correlation of business or administrative logic to summarized groups of network prefixes means that it becomes harder and more costly to operate the network. Any single prefix could potentially belong to any location or function and additional context may be required to isolate and effectively troubleshoot hosts or services addressed with it (or otherwise relying on it). Operational costs for troubleshooting are increased.

Sporadic and discontiguous assignment of subnets can increase the cost and difficulty of maintaining the address plan itself, especially in the absence of specialized IP address management (IPAM) systems that allow dynamic representation of the network prefixes and addresses.

By comparison, sparse allocation of network prefixes within an IPv6 address plan can prevent the above issues. It helps provide:

- Sufficient, contiguous IP space in reserve for future growth
- Well-defined and stable boundaries leading to more efficient routing and easier management of security policy and associated ACLs
- A better basis for correlating the topology of the network to the structure of the organization
- Easier network operation and troubleshooting
- Cleaner, tidier, and more error-free creation and administration of the plan itself

Finally, keep in mind that *within* sparsely allocated subnet groups themselves, N + 1 allocation is not necessarily problematic. In fact, allocating the next available subnet is often the preferred method of assigning /64s within a larger sparse allocation.

Random Allocation

Random allocation also divides a parent allocation evenly among smaller subnets, but as compared with N+1 allocation, assigns them not in order but rather in a random fashion. Such a method may be of use where assignments are more dynamic since it could be used to provide a minimal layer of security by obscuring assignment logic (as compared with any of the other allocation techniques). While this method increases the probability that a contiguous subnet would be available for growing a previous assignment, we'll go ahead and infer that any deployment utilizing this approach isn't too concerned with summarization or ACL manageability.

Assigning Subnets by Location or Function

Two of the most common organizational attributes used to define and assign subnets within a site are *location* and *function.*

Location, as the name implies, is usually physical in nature and corresponds to an actual geographical location within the organization that contains some part of the network: e.g., buildings, floors, IDFs (if you're into old-school telco jargon), etc.

Functions, meanwhile, can be any logical or administrative entity and are often associated with some specific set of users (e.g., students, guests), hosts (e.g., mobile devices), servers (e.g., development, finance), or roles (e.g., accounting, engineering).

Either function or location significance assigned within a site prefix can be generalized and kept consistent across multiple sites for maximum operational consistency and efficiency, even as the site prefix changes.

Let's look at assigning location signifcance to subnets created from a sample site prefix. Here's a generic site assignment:

```
2001:db8:2112::/48
```

As we reviewed in Chapter 4, we can create subnets and groups of subnets using any of the 16 bits available to us from /48 to /64. The *Xs* in the brackets of the fourth hextet represent binary bits:

```
2001:db8:2112:[XXXXXXXXXXXXXXXX]::
```

Recall also that adherence to the nibble boundary when defining subnets helps keep resulting address prefixes readable (also, consistently sized, easy to aggregate, and more operationally manageable, etc.):

```
2001:db8:2112:[XXXX XXXX XXXX XXXX]::
```

Choosing to adhere to the nibble boundary also reduces the number of available hierarchy levels, which can greatly simplify our address planning. The only requirement is that this simplifed hierarchy needs to fit the underlying network topology or organizational structure.

Let's give the first nibble location significance:

```
2001:db8:2112:[LLLL XXXX XXXX XXXX]::
```

This creates 16 /52 subnets. Expressed in hexadecimal (where *Us* represent unused hexadecimal characters):

```
2001:db8:2112:[0-f]UUU::/52
```

So, in this case, the first level of hierarchy for a site would be 16 /52 subnets that we've assigned location significance; e.g., say we're creating an address plan for a campus with fewer than 16 buildings (Figure 5-13).[13]

---

13. Or, if we'd like to leave room for growth, 12 buildings or fewer to stick to a ≤75% utilization factor.

Prefix: 2001:db8:2112::/48				

	Associated Location	Subnet (CIDR)	Address Prefix	Location
		/52	2001:db8:2112:0000::/52	*reserved*
		/52	2001:db8:2112:1000::/52	Building 1
		/52	2001:db8:2112:2000::/52	Building 2
		/52	2001:db8:2112:3000::/52	Building 3
		/52	2001:db8:2112:4000::/52	Building 4
		/52	2001:db8:2112:5000::/52	Building 5
		/52	2001:db8:2112:6000::/52	Building 6
/48	Site 1	/52	2001:db8:2112:7000::/52	*future use*
		/52	2001:db8:2112:8000::/52	*future use*
		/52	2001:db8:2112:9000::/52	*future use*
		/52	2001:db8:2112:a000::/52	*future use*
		/52	2001:db8:2112:b000::/52	*future use*
		/52	2001:db8:2112:c000::/52	*future use*
		/52	2001:db8:2112:d000::/52	*future use*
		/52	2001:db8:2112:e000::/52	*infrastructure*
		/52	2001:db8:2112:f000::/52	*future use*

Figure 5-13. 16 /52s, Location significance in first nibble

12 bits remain to assign to additional locations (or 3 nibbles to keep the example consistent).

Recall that groups of subnets assigned a location are often defined to correspond to a point of aggregation within the network. And, of course, we're not limited to location in assigning any of the next nibbles. Functional assignments for groups of subnets often correspond to security policy and ACL entries.

With that in mind, we'll give the next nibble functional significance:

```
2001:db8:2112:[LLLL FFFF XXXX XXXX]::
```

This creates 16 /56 subnets:

```
2001:db8:2112:L[0-f]UU::/56
```

L represents the location subnets, while *Us* still represents unused hexadecimal characters.

So now we have 16 /52 subnets for each network location, each with 16 /56 subnets that can be assigned to network function (Figure 5-14).

	Associated Location	Subnet (CIDR)	Address Prefix	Function
		/56	2001:db8:2112:**1000**::/56	*reserved*
		/56	2001:db8:2112:**1100**::/56	Accounting
		/56	2001:db8:2112:**1200**::/56	IT
		/56	2001:db8:2112:**1300**::/56	Lab 1
		/56	2001:db8:2112:**1400**::/56	Lab 2
		/56	2001:db8:2112:**1500**::/56	*future use*
		/56	2001:db8:2112:**1600**::/56	*future use*
/52	Building 1	/56	2001:db8:2112:**1700**::/56	*future use*
		/56	2001:db8:2112:**1800**::/56	*future use*
		/56	2001:db8:2112:**1900**::/56	*future use*
		/56	2001:db8:2112:**1a00**::/56	*future use*
		/56	2001:db8:2112:**1b00**::/56	*future use*
		/56	2001:db8:2112:**1c00**::/56	*future use*
		/56	2001:db8:2112:**1d00**::/56	*future use*
		/56	2001:db8:2112:**1e00**::/56	*future use*
		/56	2001:db8:2112:**1f00**::/56	*reserved*

Figure 5-14. 16 /56s, Function significance in second nibble

In the example above, we've selected four functions (Accounting, IT, Lab 1, and Lab 2) that correspond to groups of hosts sharing a particular security policy. Administration of their associated ACL entries is greatly simplified by each function's well-defined (and human-readable) prefix.

At this point, we could use the 256 /64s in each /56 for individual router or switch segment interface assignments.

```
2001:db8:2112:LF[0-f][0-f]::/64
```

You may recall that this progressive allocation of bits along the nibble boundary corresponds to one of the paths in the IPv6 site visualization example from Chapter 4 (Figure 4-2).

Note also that we've held the first subnet (2001:db8:2112:1000::/56) and last subnet (2001:db8:2112:1f00::/56) in reserve. There are two reasons for this.

The first reason applies only to the first subnet (and its equivalent in other subnet groups). It's explained in greater detail in "*Zero* Subnets Have a Problem" on page 153, but to briefly summarize: any subnet uniquely identified by a zero can cause confusion for operational personnel. It's common sense to want to identify the first subnet in any group with the number *1* (as opposed to *0*).

The second is that, whatever other subnets we might hold in reserve for future use, we have at least two "last-resort" subnets reserved at this level of hierarchy.

VLAN-Mapped IPv6 Addresses

While it's generally not recommended to tie the IPv6 addressing plan to the existing IPv4 one, some network administrators have historically found it beneficial to map VLAN numbers into IPv4 addresses.

This practice is even easier to accommodate in IPv6, given the much larger standard prefix assignment sizes and the additional bits available to represent and encode information like VLAN numbers.

The easiest method to accomplish this is to simply use decimal values in the address to represent the VLAN. For example, say a site receives the standard /48 assignment:

```
2001:db8:b0b0::/48
```

Our example site has a few dozen VLANs defined and configured. Because of changes to the network over time, these VLANs are not contiguous and are not consistently numbered but range in value from VLAN 2 up to VLAN 3030. Here's a small sample of the VLANs in use:

```
VLAN 2
VLAN 5
VLAN 10
VLAN 12
VLAN 200
VLAN 210
VLAN 1501
VLAN 3030
```

Using the four characters of the fourth hextet allows us to easily map these VLANs into our site assignment prefix:

```
2001:db8:b0b0:2::/64
2001:db8:b0b0:5::/64
2001:db8:b0b0:10::/64
2001:db8:b0b0:12::/64
2001:db8:b0b0:200::/64
2001:db8:b0b0:210::/64
2001:db8:b0b0:1501::/64
2001:db8:b0b0:3030::/64
```

This simple method makes it easy to track and troubleshoot VLANs and their associated address ranges. But you may observe that since these are actually hexadecimal values being interpreted as decimal, the associated subnets are distributed piecemeal throughout the overall assignment. Look at the distribution of bits within the fourth hextet (Table 5-2):

Table 5-2. VLAN hex-as-decimal values into binary

Hexadecimal interpreted as decimal	Binary
0x0002	00000000 00000010
0x0005	00000000 00000101
0x0010	00000000 00010000
0x0012	00000000 00010010
0x0200	00000010 00000000
0x0210	00000010 00010000
0x1501	00010101 00000001
0x3030	00110000 00110000

This distribution of bits prevents easy summarization or subnetting of the remaining address space. If the site is relatively small and topologically flat (and likely to remain that way indefinitely), the simplicity and operational benefit of this method may offset any resulting liability.

But most sites will have at least some network hierarchy or other logical structure that makes it beneficial to preserve some bits to use for consistent summarization or subnetting.

This can be accomplished by converting VLAN decimal values to hexadecimal (Table 5-3):

Table 5-3. VLAN decimal values into hexadecimal

VLAN number	Hexadecimal
2	0x0002
5	0x0005
10	0x000a
12	0x000c
200	0x00c8
210	0x00d2
1501	0x05dd
3030	0x0bd6

Since the maximum number of VLANs is 4,096, all possible VLAN values can be represented with 12 bits. Here's how the original addresses would be expressed hexadecimally:

```
2001:db8:b0b0:2::/64
2001:db8:b0b0:5::/64
2001:db8:b0b0:a::/64
2001:db8:b0b0:c::/64
2001:db8:b0b0:c8::/64
```

```
2001:db8:b0b0:d2::/64
2001:db8:b0b0:5dd::/64
2001:db8:b0b0:bd6::/64
```

With this configuration, 4 bits remain for a total of 15 additional subnets (each with up to 4,096 VLANs):

```
2001:db8:b0b0:[1-f]XXX::/52
```

Using this method, some of the immediate operational benefit is arguably lessened: operations personnel would now need to first convert hexadecimal into decimal before correlating a given subnet with its associated VLAN. However, the architectural benefit of reserving at least some subnets for additional assignments will make the trade-off worthwhile for most planners.

Summary

When the proper concepts are understood and the right principles are applied, IPv6 offers the opportunity to create an address plan that is scalable, flexible, extensible, manageable, and durable far beyond what is possible with IPv4 networks. Moreover, the operational benefits of a proper plan extend beyond the simple, effective management of the IPv6 prefixes themselves. The ability to encode network location and function in prefixes provides another layer of useful data for effective identification, isolation, and troubleshooting of network issues.

The basic method in IPv6 address planning of defining and assigning blocks of subnets based on the structure of the network or the organization moves us away from the *IPv4 thinking* that obliged us to consider scarcity and waste and to allocate addresses and prefixes primarily on the basis of host conservation. There are certainly risks of too much deference to our existing IPv4 address plan and allocation, especially considering that IPv4 will soon become the legacy protocol.

A broad and flexible definition of what constitutes a site along with inter-site and intra-site planning concepts provides a simple but powerful framework to apply to our own address plans and the networks they serve. These also allow for the attainment of the address planning principles that will ensure that our plan endures through the inevitable growth and change of our respective organizations and networks. These principles include properly sized initial allocations, sparse assignment of subnets, hierarchical organization of subnets, adherence to nibble boundaries where practical, and uniform subnetting and summarization.

## CHAPTER 6

Getting IPv6 Addresses

Introduction

Creating our first IPv6 address plan presents another minor catch-22 scenario: it's a little more complicated to construct an address plan without knowing up front how much IPv6 address space we'll need. On the other hand, it's also difficult to know how much IPv6 address space to request until we've worked through enough of our plan to be confident that we're asking for the right amount.

So we'll actually have to do a bit of address planning design before we request an IPv6 allocation. While we've established that the enormous size of the typical allocation makes sufficient host addressing concerns generally irrelevant, we still need enough groups of subnets to make sure our address plan provides operational efficiency and manageable growth.

Keep in mind that since we're constructing an address plan geared toward operational efficiency, one where conservation of address space is in nearly all cases a negligible concern, it should be possible to use the ideas and methods in this book to develop a plan based on the assumption that we'll be granted the address space we need from the allocating agency. While a rough estimate of the right amount of address space may be useful to help us get started with developing our plan, we should be perfectly comfortable with coming to realize as we work through the planning process that we need more (or less) address space than we initially assumed.

 Your plan should drive your ultimate allocation size. Avoid constraining your plan within a smaller allocation if you could make your plan more operationally efficient with additional address space.

The IP Address Supply Chain

It's probably a good idea to review the global allocation structure of IP addressing (Figure 6-1).

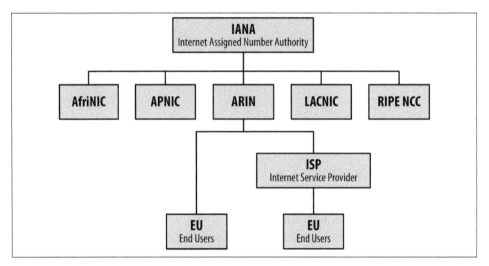

Figure 6-1. Global IP address allocation structure

The Internet Assigned Numbers Authority (IANA) is the centralized global authority that allocates all IP addresses (and AS numbers) to the Regional Internet Registries.[1]

There are five RIRs, correlating roughly to five of the seven continents:

- American Registry for Internet Numbers (ARIN) for North America
- Réseaux IP Européens Network Coordination Centre (RIPE NCC) for Europe (as well as the Middle East and parts of Central Asia)
- Asia-Pacific Network Information Centre (APNIC) for Asia and Oceania
- Latin American and Carribean Network Information Centre (LACNIC)
- African Network Information Center (AFRINIC)

Each RIR in turn allocates IP address blocks to downstream ISPs—aka Local Internet Registries (or LIRs). RIRs may also allocate addresses directly to large end-user organizations. These have traditionally been large corporate and government enterprises that typically have more than one ISP providing conncetivity to the Internet. But smaller

---

1. They're also responsible for coordinating a number of other foundational Internet technologies, including the DNS Root, .int and .arpa domains, and protocol number assignments.

enterprises and organizations desiring better network resiliency, routing performance optimization, and always-on access to cloud services can multihome their networks as well. As a result some enterprise networks are requesting portable provider independent IPv6 address space (i.e., routable via any ISP, at least within one region) directly from their RIR.

So Where Will Your IPv6 Addresses Come From?

Well, that depends.

At its most basic, the process for getting IPv6 address space is pretty much the same as the process for getting IPv4 addresses. But you'll need to request them from the right organization. Though it's probably reasonable to assume you'll be getting your IPv6 from whence came your IPv4, it's also possible your requirements for IPv6 may differ enough from IPv4 that your best source for IPv6 address space may differ as well.

In any case, there are generally three types of organizations that will provide you with IPv6 addresses:

- A RIR (or RIRs)
- An ISP (or, in the lingo of the RIRs, a Local Internet Registry, i.e., LIR)
- A department within your organization

Which of these you get your IPv6 addresses from typically depends on a few criteria, including your network and routing topology, as well as the specific addressing requirements of your organization (or department).

How Many ISPs Do You Connect To?

Asking the number of ISPs you connect to is another way of asking are you *single-homed* or *multihomed*? In other words, does your organization connect to a single ISP or more than one? The reason this is important is that organizations with multiple ISPs for redundancy must have *portable* IP allocations. Portable allocations are assigned by RIRs directly to the organization. As we covered in Chapter 2, these allocations are formally referred to as *provider independent* (PI) and should be able to be routed, or *announced*, through any ISP.

An organization that is single-homed typically receives a nonportable, *provider assigned* (PA) assignment from an ISP. The ISP has administrative authority for the addresses they use for PA assignments. If the organization changes ISPs, they'll have to renumber out of their old ISP's PA assignment (and into a PA assignment from their new provider). Meanwhile, portable allocations allow an organization to keep the same addresses and internal numbering scheme, regardless of which ISP (or ISPs) they connect to.

Another advantage of PI space is that it allows an organization to maintain a highly available network via multiple providers without any manual routing changes or other special configurations. Consistent routing policy can be developed over time to influence and optimize inbound traffic in a scalable way that may be difficult or impossible where an organization is single-homed and relying on a PA allocation.

How Large Is Your Organization?

Other criteria for determining where your IPv6 address space request should go include the amount of IPv6 address space your organization may need and the amount of network growth or change you anticipate.

As we covered in the last chapter, if you're a large enterprise, you may need as much as a /32 of address space (or more). Depending on the ISP, that could be all the space they've been allocated! And, of course, large enterprises are more likely to rely on multiple ISPs, making PI space a requirement.

Larger organizations are also more likely to have areas of the network that require renumbering (either through growth or change or from merger and acquisition activity), making PA space problematic.

So Why Doesn't Everyone Just Get a PI Allocation?

From our network operator perspective, a provider independent address allocation appears more desirable than a provider assigned allocation in how it can add and insure some operational ease in the network (e.g., more flexible routing policy, reduced likelihood of having to renumber, etc). And while RIRs like ARIN have gone to great lengths to create policies that favor easier network growth and operation, giving PI space to everyone is problematic.

Remember the *dilemma of scale* from Chapter 1? While IPv6 creates a better balance between an individual organization's addressing needs and keeping the global routing table small, it doesn't eliminate the tension between these two conflicting goals entirely.

Every additional PI allocation for an organization creates at least one more entry in the ISP's and global routing table—an entry that would otherwise be subsumed in an ISP allocation that the same organization's PA space would be assigned from (Figure 6-2).

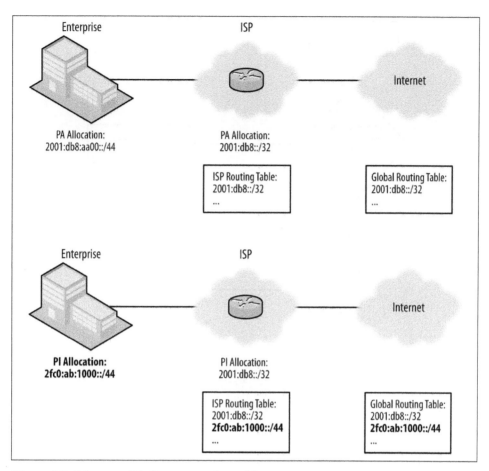

Figure 6-2. PA versus PI effect on routing tables

So with all that in mind, here's a simple flowchart for determining what kind of IPv6 allocation your organization is likely to need and from whom to request it (Figure 6-3).

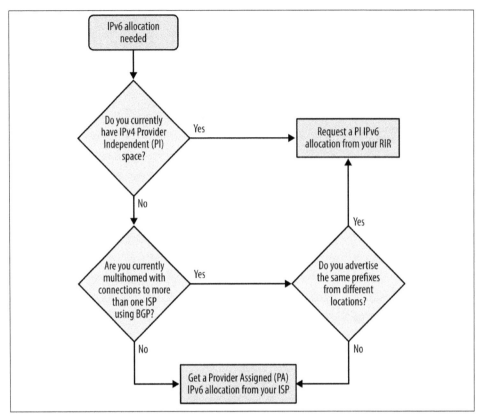

Figure 6-3. Determining best type and source for a new IPv6 allocation

ARIN PI Requirements

Keep in mind that the requirements for PI IPv6 address space allocations directly to end-users (as opposed to ISPs) vary among RIRs.[2] For example, here are ARIN's initial assignment requirements:

Organizations may justify an initial assignment for addressing devices directly attached to their own network infrastructure, with an intent for the addresses to begin operational use within 12 months, by meeting one of the following criteria:

- *Having a previously justified IPv4 end-user assignment from ARIN or one of its predecessor registries, or;*

---

2. RIPE recently eliminated the multihoming requirement for assignment of PI space to organizations. In order to obtain address space directly, a larger enterprise may also choose to become a LIR itself (by becoming a member of RIPE and paying the associated fees).

- *Currently being IPv6 Multihomed or immediately becoming IPv6 Multihomed and using an assigned valid global AS number, or;*
- *By having a network that makes active use of a minimum of 2,000 IPv6 addresses within 12 months, or;*
- *By having a network that makes active use of a minimum of 200 /64 subnets within 12 months, or;*
- *By providing a reasonable technical justification indicating why IPv6 addresses from an ISP or other LIR are unsuitable.*

One other justification that ARIN will consider in allocating a PI prefix is if future renumbering would impact more than 2,000 individuals.

Everything You Didn't Realize You Wanted to Know About RIR Policy

No phrase in English (or any other language for that matter) consistently fails to stir the imagination like "governance, regulation, and policy."[3]

But when we're dealing with any shared resource, as we are with IP addresses, at least a modicum of regulation is necessary. If we want continued access to address resources, we'll need to familiarize ourselves with such regulation.

Fortunately, the RIR policy that we'll need to know (or at least be aware of) is relatively brief and refreshingly sane.

For one thing, if you are in North America (excepting Mexico, whose number resources are handled by LACNIC), you'll hopefully be pleased to know that the regional Internet registry ARIN has traditionally formulated its policies with the primary goal of facilitating network operations by making sure that organizations get the address resources that they need.

The bible for all things policy-related at ARIN is the Number Resource Policy Manual (NRPM).[4]

In it, ARIN outlines its overall principles and goals, as well as the ones specific to IPv6. Its general principles actually provide some insight into why address planning principles are what they are, as well as some hints as to what we'll need to consider in maintaining our own address plan. (If you think about it, the RIRs have pretty big address plans they need to maintain). These principles include:

---

3. If your imagination *is* stirred by the phrase, I humbly beg your pardon and offer my regrets that I won't be able to attend your next get-together.

4. Each RIR has its own equivalent of the NRPM available through its website.

Registration

Registration helps ensure *uniqueness* of allocated resources. If every address block is properly registered and documented, the possibility of accidental overlapping assignments is greatly reduced, if not entirely eliminated. Additionally, registration provides a basic measure of accountability if illegal or unethical activities are originating from the networks registered to a particular party. Registration also provides a way to contact the adminstrators responsible for networks numbered into a particular registered range. This can help facilitate coordination of routing policy and troubleshooting between different organizations and autonomous systems.

Conservation

According to the ARIN NRPM, the principle of conservation "guarantees sustainability of the Internet through efficient utilization of unique number resources" and that "conservation…requires that Internet number resources be efficiently distributed to those organizations who have a technical need for them in support of operational networks."

 Remember our discussion of *efficiency*? If we were casually reading the above paragraph without the context of that discussion we might, in our habit of IPv4 thinking, conclude that ARIN is defining efficiency in a way that merely encourages the conservation of host addresses. But *support of operational networks* is a big part of ARIN's DNA and their policies relating to IPv6 allocation express this. Recall also that the *sustainability of the Internet* is at least partly about conservation of router resources and the efficiency of the global routing table (the same is true, of course, for smaller networks). Incidentally, that's the next principle.

Routability

ARIN also fundamentally concerns itself with whether or not the IP address prefixes it allocates will be routed in a scalable fashion. Continued access to IP address (and AS number) resources for a given assignee (allocatee?) is premised on their good faith adherence to community standards in how address prefixes are routed on the Internet.

Stewardship

This just means that ARIN will apply the above principles in administering Internet number resources. Their stated goal is "distribute unique number resources to entities building and operating networks thereby facilitating the growth and sustainability of the Internet for the benefit of all." Sometimes this goal involves trade-offs between these principles (and resulting modification of policy), but ARIN works hard to involve the community of Internet operators in these decisions with a maximum of transparency.[5]

It's beyond the scope of this book to explore the differences between policies at the RIRs. I encourage you to visit the website of the registry for your region to learn more about how their specific guidelines may affect your IPv6 address request.

Out-of-Region Announcements

The simplest definition of an *out-of-region* announcement is PI space from one of the RIRs being announced through a network egress point within the geographical region of a different RIR.

For reasons of policy, RIRs have either explicitly or implicitly discouraged this practice. It was traditionally seen as a violation of the remit that RIRs have to manage the number resources of their particular geographic region.

The policy seemed to make more sense when those number resources were limited (or exhausted) as they were in IPv4. But prohibiting out-of-region announcements results in organizations with global networks having to announce at least one prefix for each geographic region.

In another example of the shift to efficiency through aggregation not address conservation that IPv6 enables, the current policy (as least where ARIN is concerned) is to favor allowing out-of-region announcements. A global organization free to announce an ARIN allocation within other regions (as opposed to at least one prefix per region) should result in fewer global routing table entries.

You may recall that in the preface, I mentioned my own first experience with obtaining IPv6 addresses. Working for a service provider with a presence in North America, Europe, and Asia-Pacific suggested to us at the time that we would need IPv6 address space from each associated RIR.

After receiving conflicting information as to how RIR policy was likely to evolve, we decided to make sure that we had an IPv6 allocation from each RIR. It may be prudent for any organization doing business in multiple regions to secure an IPv6 allocation from each associated RIR to number into, in case the policy should change (or for maximum routing policy flexibility in case of contingencies).

---

5. Participation in ARIN policy discussions through their Public Policy Mailing List (PPML) is open to anyone. It's a great way to get involved in the Internet community (and an equally great way to obliquely learn about the operational concerns around address resources that impact network administrators).

Measuring IPv6 Address Consumption

At the beginning of the book, we looked at a specific example of how immaterial host address consumption is when there are 18 quintillion addresses available in the smallest subnet typically assigned. Thus, we've attempted to grow the definition of *efficiency* beyond mere address conservation to durably include broader operational concerns (e.g., minimizing routing convergence time and routing table size, increasing manageability of ACLs and security policy, increasing human-readability of IPv6 subnets, avoiding renumbering, etc.).

That said, an effective (and sanctioned) way to measure the utilization of IPv6 is something we'll need in our tool belt. At first, it can help us determine the initial size of the allocation we'll need. Later, we can use it to monitor utilization and plan additional assignments.

The metric often used by allocating agencies is called the Host-Density (HD) Ratio:[6]

$$HD = \frac{log(number\ of\ allocated\ objects)}{log(number\ of\ allocatable\ objects)}$$

This equation produces a value between 0 and 1 that is then represented as a percentage.

So that's the formal method. But it's simpler and easier to just remember the figure 75%. That's the percentage of utilization threshold set by ARIN when considering if anything larger than a /56 is fully utilized. Anything smaller than a /56 is considered fully utilized immediately upon assignment. And although ARIN sets the boundary for the requirement to determine utilization at a /56, they typically allocate at least a /48 to any requesting organization.

The 75% threshold is somewhat arbitrary because it assumes that if you're below it, you have sufficient headroom for additional growth, but if you're above it, you'll immediately need additional address space to accomodate growth (and avoid renumbering). Organizations that are growing quickly (such as service providers) might consider using a lower threshold value, say 60%, to provide additional space for expansion.

Determining Initial Allocation Size

Determining the size of allocation we'll need based on the number of sites we have is the easiest way to demonstrate our 75% threshold in action.

---

6. See RFC 3194, *The Host-Density Ratio for Address Assignment Efficiency: An update on the H ratio* (*http://bit.ly/rfc-3194*).

Let's say my enterprise is smallish and has only five sites: a headquarters office, three branch offices, and a data center.

Five sites would need at least 5 /48s. Three additional bits would provide 8 /48 subnets. So a /45 would suffice for our immediate addressing needs.

Five subnets out of an available eight puts us at 62.5% utilization, below our 75% threshold. But recall from the previous chapter that as a best practice we should dedicate an entire additional /48 for infrastructure. This takes us right up to our 75% threshold, which should trigger the next largest allocation, or a /44.[7]

Since a /44 has 16 /48s, any request for up to eleven sites will yield a /44 from ARIN.[8] Twelve sites up to the 75% threshold for the next nibble boundary, or 191 sites, would result in a /40 being allocated. Table 6-1 displays the next two increments.

Table 6-1. Allocation size per site count

Number of sites	ARIN allocation
1-12	/44
13-192	/40
193-3,072	/36
3,073-49,152	/32

It's unlikely that any enterprise will have more than 49,151 physical (or even logical) sites so a /32 would prove sufficient in most scenarios.

So the 75% threshold is suitable as a generic guideline for measuring utilization during both the address planning and management phases.

During the planning phase, it can be used to determine if a particular prefix allocation will be sufficient for the number of subnets needed for a particular function or location. It can also be used to anticipate the allocation one is likely to receive from a RIR, based on the address plan and subsequent allocation request.

During the operational phase, it can be used as a threshold to trigger assignment of additional subnets (preferred) or renumbering (worst case). As we mentioned, the rate of subnet assignment may vary between and within organizations. If the rate of growth is slow, a higher threshold may be acceptable (e.g., 80%), whereas if it's fast, you may want to lower it (e.g., 65%).

---

7. Since ARIN only allocates along nibble boundaries as a matter of policy, this is the allocation we would have received anyway!

8. Chances are if you're only requesting IPv6 address space for a single site, you'll be getting an allocation from your ISP.

Many contemporary IP address management (IPAM) tools offer capacity planning features and reporting functionality that can help you track IP utilization more closely. We'll cover IPAM technologies and best practices in Chapter 8.

Navigating the IPv6 Address Request Process

Since you'll either be getting an IPv6 allocation from your ISP or a RIR, it's probably a good idea to explore the process in either case a bit. Chances are you (or someone in your organization) has at least some familiarity with it already (based on the IP addresses you've already requested and received). As a result, you may not have to complete all the steps associated with requesting address resources.

RIR Allocation Request

We'll need some guidelines for procedure and policy when it comes to getting IPv6 addresses from a RIR. As we've done for the bulk of this chapter, we'll continue to pick on ARIN to provide these. The steps are as follows:

- Meet the requirements for an End-User Initial Assignment
- Register an Organizational Identifier (Org ID)
- Register Points of Contact (POC)
- Complete and submit an allocation request
- Verify your request
- Provide additional information (optional)
- Certification of request by a company officer
- Acknowledge request approval
- Pay the fees
- Sign the Registration Services Agreement
- Receive your assignment

Please excuse a minor curmudgeonly outburst: ARIN makes this whole process as painless as possible these days by offering a handy web interface to complete the registration and request process. In *my* day, we had to submit everything through email. In the snow. Uphill. Both ways.

Let's take a look at a few screen shots of the webpages from ARIN's site associated with the most critical step, i.e., *Complete and submit an allocation request*. This walkthrough will be for an *End-user IPv6 Request*, something an enterprise that wanted PI space would make.[9]

First, after logging into ARIN Online, you'll be directed to the main screen. From there, select *Manage & Request Resources* from the left column (Figure 6-4).

Figure 6-4. ARIN online portal start page

Next, the *Number Resources* page lists your POC(s) and Org-ID(s). In the Org-ID box, under *Actions*, click on the *Request Resources* link (Figure 6-5).

---

9. If you're making a request from ARIN for an ISP allocation, the process is similar. Where possible, modify the screen selections accordingly.

Figure 6-5. ARIN Number Resources page

The next page is the *Resource Requests* page. Under *Resource Type*, select *End-user IPv6 Request* (Figure 6-6).

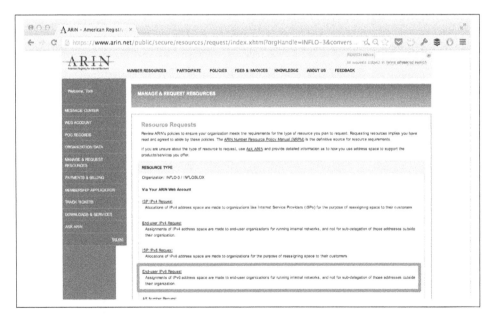

Figure 6-6. ARIN Resource Requests page

From there, the *End-user IPv6 Assignment Request Form* page comes up (Figure 6-7).

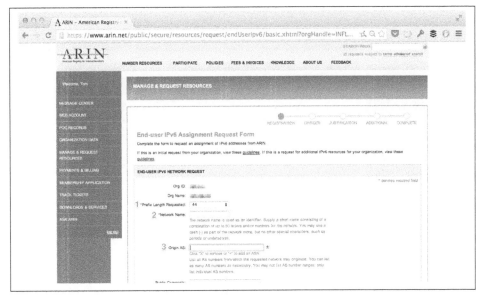

Figure 6-7. ARIN End-user IPv6 Assignment Request Form page

The field for step 1 asks for the prefix length requested. This field allows any value from 40 to 48 (as well as *Unknown/Other*). Depending on your organization's size and estimated or actual address plan requirements, it's possible that you may want to request a prefix larger than a /40 (e.g., a /36 or /32). You'll have an opportunity to make such a request and justify it on later screens.

The field for step 2 requires a network name. This name will be used as a text label (of up to 50 letters) for the assigned address prefix. You could choose a name that is administratively or operationally relevant if you like. Organizations often use their name along with a number corresponding to the assignment order, e.g., *GLOBOCORP-IPv6-1*.

The field for step 3 is optional, but requests entry of the ASN that the requested prefix will originate from. For most PI assignments, this will be the ASN of the requesting organization. More rarely, a PI request that will originate through one or more upstream ISPs could be used here.

The next page requests corporation officer info (Figure 6-8). All resource requests through ARIN require that an officer of the requesting organization attest to the accuracy of the info submitted for the request. The steps for fields 4, 5, and 6 ask for the officer's name, title, and email address respectively.

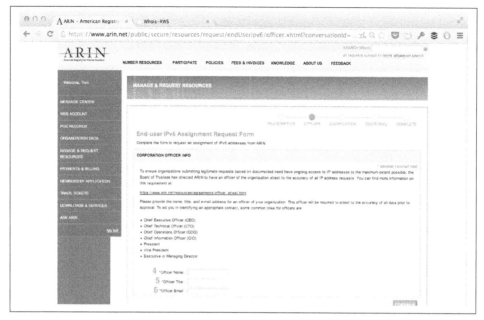

Figure 6-8. ARIN Corporation Officer Info page

Incidentally, if you don't already have executive or management buy-in for your IPv6 adoption initiative (as dicussed in Chapter 3), this requirement may provide an excellent excuse to line up some facetime with high-level management to make the case for the organization to adopt IPv6.

Next we proceed to the first of three *justification* sections (Figure 6-9) for our request.

The checkbox for step 7 asks if you've been issued any IPv4 addresses on or after December 22, 1997. If you've already received an ARIN end-user allocation of IPv4, this helps justify one for IPv6.

Step 8 asks for an optional list of *upstream providers and peers*. Here you may list the upstream networks that you purchase IP transit from or that you peer with at exchange points (or directly), e.g., "Level 3," "ASN3356," "6939," etc.

The next page continues the justification portion of the request (Figure 6-10).

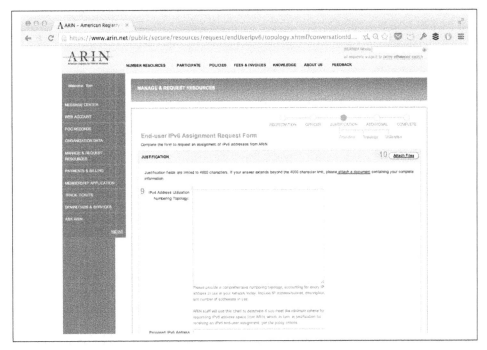

Figure 6-9. ARIN Justification page

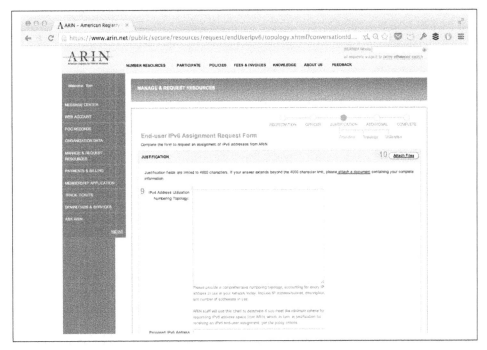

Figure 6-10. ARIN Justification page 2

The field for step 9 asks for an *IPv4 Address Utilization Numbering Topology*. Yes, you read that correctly: *IPv4*. ARIN uses this information to help validate the IPv6 allocation request.

 That ARIN wants to see your IPv4 address utilization and topology should *not* be interpreted to mean that you should be correlating your existing IPv4 address plan to your shiny new IPv6 one. The IPv6 address planning principles and best practices we're covering in this book are better suited to creating the right plan.

Field 9 (along with field 11, covered next) is limited to 4,000 words. If you need more than that, you'll need to upload a file using the button identified by 10 in the above graphic.

Field 11 (Figure 6-11) is arguably the most critical part of the end-user allocation request. This is where you'll outline your proposed IPv6 numbering scheme. As mentioned, this is the part of the request process that creates a bit of a catch-22: it's difficult to accurately gauge how much address space we'll need without a finished plan, yet it's equally difficult to decisively design a complete plan without knowing how much address space we'll be starting with.

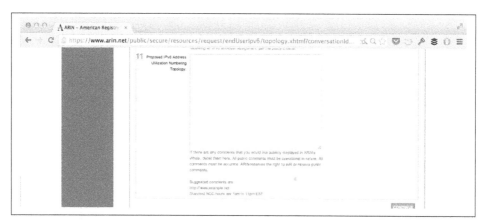

Figure 6-11. ARIN Justification, page 2 (lower half)

To best complete this field, we'll need to make some very general assumptions based on the concepts and principles we learned in the last chapter. From these, we can build a *plan outline* that contains enough information to complete our RIR (or ISP request) and get our IPv6 addresses.

A *plan outline* is a high-level outline of a (typically) forthcoming complete and operational IPv6 address plan that is produced to qualify for, and obtain, an IPv6 allocation.

The simplest estimate on which to base our request comes from:

1. The number of sites in our organization
2. The number of subnets we'll need per site

Recall from Table 6-1 that up to 75% of our total number of sites will dictate the allocation we receive. Keep in mind also that the 75% threshold triggers an allocation with an additional 4 bits of end-user /48 networks. As a result, for the purposes of estimating whether a particular allocation will be sufficient, our confidence in the estimate might be understood as inversely proportional to how close we get, without going over, to 75%.

For example, where our number of sites puts us greatly under the 75% mark for any of the rows in Table 6-1, we should have more confidence that our allocation will be sufficient to base our operational address plan on. But as we approach the 75% threshold, recognize that going over 75% generally means that getting the next largest allocation on the nibble boundary will give us stubstantial headroom for potential operational efficiency and growth.

The pages that follow (not shown) include the last page of the justification portion of the request (with two fields to be filled out if you're requesting additional IPv6 space) followed by a page to enter any additional information (the same 4,000-character limit applies, but as before, there is the option to attach a file).

After submitting the request, a ticket number is generated along with a link to the support page (Figure 6-12).

You can log back in to check the status of your request at any time. ARIN typically responds to requests within a day or two.

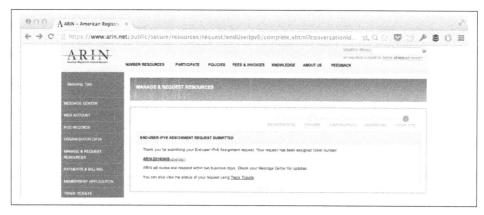

Figure 6-12. ARIN request submitted page

ISP Allocation Request

The process for requesting an IPv6 assignment from an ISP is similar to the one for requesting an allocation from a RIR.

Since a request from an organization to an ISP for an assignment would typically be for a PA assignment, an ISP might make certain assumptions about the organization's topology and size. In any case, the ISP will typically require you to fill out a service request form that includes information about your actual topology and IPv6 requirements, info such as:

1. Will you need an IPv6 prefix?
2. Is your network multihomed?
   a. If so, what is your AS number?
   b. Prefixes you plan to announce

You'll probably be using an existing IPv4 connection and adding IPv6 to it in a dual-stack configuration. Otherwise, additional information, such as the circuit type for the IPv6 connection and any settings associated with it, will need to be clarified.

It should go without saying that you need to verify that your ISP or IP transit provider supports IPv6. If you haven't done this yet, you should do it right away. Some organizations adopting IPv6 report difficulty ordering IPv6 connectivity because not all ISPs or IP transit providers have adopted IPv6 yet themselves. If your existing provider doesn't support IPv6 within a timeframe acceptable to your IPv6 adoption plans, you'll need to begin to research the requirements and costs of other providers that can provide IPv6 connectivity.

Summary

I've attempted in this chapter to demonstrate that getting IPv6 addresses is a perfectly straightforward process, as long as you know what type of allocation you'll need and where to get it.

Though policies for obtaining IPv6 addresses may vary from slightly from region to region, one thing remains consistent: the bare fact of IPv4 exhaustion means that the RIRs have a vested interest in facilitating IPv6 adoption. This means that any request for IPv6 address space backed up by an address plan that has demonstrated need based on operational best practice *as the requestor defines it* stands a good chance of seeing that request fulfilled.

Of course, not every organization requires (or should receive) a PI allocation. Organizations with a single ISP or limited to one site may conclude that a PA allocation is perfectly suitable for their current and future operational needs and rate of growth.[10]

---

10. Some single-homed organizations may be concerned about a greater likelihood of having to renumber. This could be a consequence of changing ISPs or the frequent internal reconfiguration of the network. With such a concern, the deployment of ULA with NPTv6 (a configuration that is less desirable for most networks due to greater operational overhead than GUA) may be an option.

## CHAPTER 7

Creating an IPv6 Addressing Plan

Introduction

In this chapter, we'll take advantage of the topics we learned in Chapters 4 through 6 to walk through building from scratch a couple of sample IPv6 address plans for a (thank $DEITY) fictional company.

We'll learn effective entry points into our address plan design that depend on whether we want to focus first on the part of our plan *within a site* or the part of the plan *between sites*.

Along the way, we'll explore in depth methods for mapping the network topology into the address plan—how, thanks to the typically large size of an IPv6 address allocation, subnets identifying function and location can be derived from the available bits (bits that were in short supply in IPv4).

Finally, we'll look at some of the address planning considerations for network topologies that extend the traditional enterprise network in the form of data centers, cloud deployments, and sensor networks.

Meet Strangelove Solutions, LLC

Strangelove Solutions LLC is a boutique software and engineering firm specializing in doomsday scenario and global catastrophic risk modeling, as well as deluxe mineshaft estates, for the discerning (and well-heeled) doomsday prepper.

They have a number of offices in North America, including their headquarters campus in Damascus, Arkansas, and sales offices in Faro, North Carolina and Yuba City, California (Figure 7-1).

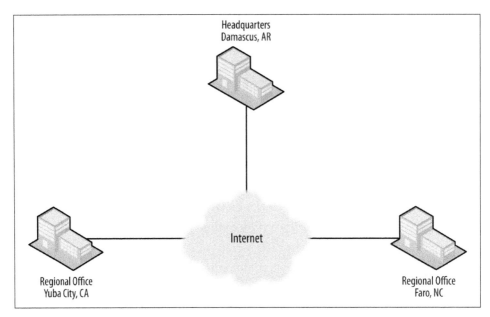

Figure 7-1. Strangelove Solutions inter-site topology

The headquarters campus also includes a data center (Figure 7-2).

The design of the network is fairly typical for an enterprise and includes the following modules:

- Edge
- Campus
- Data center
- Lab
- Infrastructure

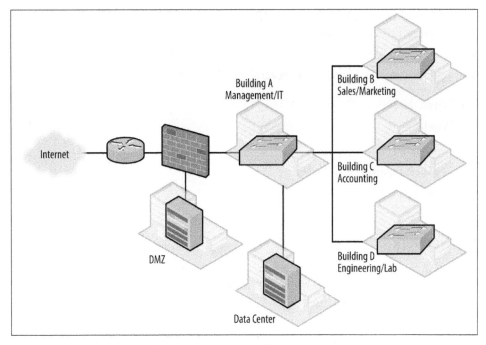

Figure 7-2. Strangelove Solutions intra-site topology

Edge Network

The enterprise edge is located in building A and consists of a head-end router with a single WAN link from their ISP. Behind that, a firewall has segments to the DMZ and to the campus network.

Segments or elements configured in the edge network include:

- Internet connectivity (WAN to ISP)
- Firewall
  - IDS
  - DMZ
    - Corporate DNS, email, web
    - VPN for remote access

Campus Network

The campus network consists of a modified campus access-distribution configuration: a distribution switch connects to the data center and has fiber runs to switches in buildings B, C, and D, and terminates VLANs and layer 3 for them. Building A houses the management and IT departments with around 200 employees total. It also houses the data center. Buildings B, C, and D each have around 50 employees.

The campus network incorporates several VLANs including:

- Wired data
- Wireless
  - Internal
  - Guest (spans the HQ site)
- VoIP

Lab Network

The lab in building D is used for research and software validation and is operated by engineering. Layer 3/VLAN termination is provided by a distribution switch in that building's primary wiring closet.

The lab network includes:

- Virtual environments
- Sensor test networks

Data Center Network

The data center network uses a hybrid design that includes both a fairly typical collapsed core with top-of-rack switches to servers, along with a small SDN proof-of-concept network.

The data center network includes:

- Storage network
- Private cloud
- SDN components

Infrastructure

As with our inter-site design, device numbering and network management comprise functions that span the headquarters site. They include such elements as:

- Loopback and management interfaces

- Point-to-point interfaces
- Out-of-band networks for lab and data center
- Guest wireless networks

Where to Start: Topology or Plan?

So now that we have a better picture of the network we need to design an address plan for, where do we begin?

Recall from Chapter 5 that, at their most essential, addressing plans in IPv6 are primarily about defining and assigning blocks of subnets based on the structure of the network or the organization.

This fundamental concept provides at least two possible entry points into creating a design for our (thankfully) fictional company:[1]

- Derive an IPv6 address plan structure from an existing topology
- Or map a generic address plan structure onto a topology

Another way to think of this is that the former is more of a *bottom-up* approach, while the latter is a *top-down* one.

Keep in mind that it's perfectly acceptable and actually quite common to use both methods interchangeably at different stages of the address plan design. Initially, however, it's helpful to pick one or the other to get started.

And, of course, over time the address plan and actual topology will interact and influence each other. For instance, using IP address management practices and tools to track subnet utilization will result in additional IPv6 space being allocated (and already-allocated space being reclaimed). This process will inevitably impact network planning and deployment, which will result in changes to the network topology.[2]

Mapping Topology to Plan Between Sites

Which of these two entry points should we use for our sample design? Well in Chapter 5, we made a distinction between inter-site and intra-site architecture—something we've reflected in Strangelove LLC's simple network diagrams shown previously.

Since there's only one instance of inter-site topology, it might make the most sense to derive the initial part of our IPv6 address plan structure from that first entry point. In

---

1. Though if you're bullish on the luxury doomsday prep vertical, I'm not here to judge!

2. We'll cover IP address management in more detail in the next chapter.

other words, we'll use the number of sites Strangelove LLC has to create an inter-site address plan structure.

Recall also from Chapter 5 that a *site* is a logical concept. It's an entity within our network topology that has well-defined and well-understood boundaries. These boundaries are most typically based on location, but could also be based on function (i.e., an application or group of users that share a common security or QoS requirement).

The actual bit boundary of the /48 is where all of the subnets at a particular location would be *rolled up* (i.e., aggregated or summarized) into that single prefix.

In a similar fashion, the bit boundary of the /48 can be used to enforce QoS or security policy for a function, as we've described previously.

With three sites (in this case, and as is typical, the sites are *locations*), Strangelove LLC would appear to need at least 3 /48s.

But keep in mind we've also got a data center at HQ. Strangelove's somewhat eccentric (i.e., insane) management team has decided that the risk of nuclear catastrophe is greater at their Damascus, Arkansas headquarters. They've tentatively decided to move the existing data center to one of their regional offices. For maximum portability, the data center should get its own /48.

Strangelove LLC is also designing a private cloud service (aka, "the Mushroom Cloud") that they hope to integrate with a secure public cloud offering in the near future. It seems prudent to allocate an additional /48 for whatever the cloud architecture ends up looking like.

Finally, connectivity between sites is currently provided by MPLS VPN, and the associated inter-site infrastructure will get a /48 as well.

Here's a summary of Strangelove LLC's inter-site topology for which /48 allocations are suggested:

- HQ
- Regional office (Faro)
- Regional office (Yuba City)
- Data-center
- Cloud architecture
- Infrastructure

So even though there are only three main sites, a total of 6 /48s will be needed. And while 3 bits would apparently provide enough (i.e., 8) /48s, you're hopefully on-board with the best practice of allocation along nibble boundaries from our earlier reading.

Thus, a /44 would be the minimum allocation size we should assume when deriving our inter-site address plan structure from our actual topology.

At this point, Strangelove LLC hasn't requested a PI allocation from the RIR, so for the purposes of planning and illustration, we'll use a /44 from the documentation range.[3] Figure 7-3 shows this placeholder /44 prefix along with the allocations described above.

Prefix: 2001:db8:def::/44			

End-user Location	Subnet (CIDR)	Hextet	Description
	/48	:def0::/48	Infrastructure
	/48	:def1::/48	HQ
	/48	:def2::/48	Faro
	/48	:def3::/48	Yuba City
	/48	:def4::/48	Data center
	/48	:def5::/48	Cloud integration
	/48	:def6::/48	future use
	/48	:def7::/48	future use
/44	/48	:def8::/48	future use
	/48	:def9::/48	future use
	/48	:defa::/48	future use
	/48	:defb::/48	future use
	/48	:defc::/48	future use
	/48	:defd::/48	future use
	/48	:defe::/48	future use
	/48	:deff::/48	future use

Figure 7-3. Strangelove LLC inter-site allocations

Mapping Plan to Topology Within Sites

As for the second design entry point (mapping a generic address plan structure onto a topology), such an approach seems to be more applicable where there are multiple, similar topologies, and we want to use our address plan to try to make overall address management and operations between sites as consistent as possible.

So what might a *generic address plan structure* look like? Well, based on our fundamental address plan design concept, it needn't be much more initially complicated than groups of subnets hierarchically arranged.

As stated, we'll focus on the inter-site portion of the plan, i.e., the 16 bits between a /48 and /64. To keep things as simple as possible, we'll use one of the subnetting hierarchies from Figure 4-1.

The first of those subnetting hierarchies gives us the most predictable allocation of the available address space as it allocates sequentially on the next available nibble boundary: e.g., /48, /52, /56, /60, and /64.

---

3. RFC 3849, *IPv6 Address Prefix Reserved for Documentation* (*http://bit.ly/rfc-3849*).

Or to put it another way:

- Each /48 provides 16 /52s
- Each /52 provides 16 /56s
- Each /56 provides 16 /60s
- Each /60 provides 16 /64s

Figure 7-4 shows the relationships between the allocations.

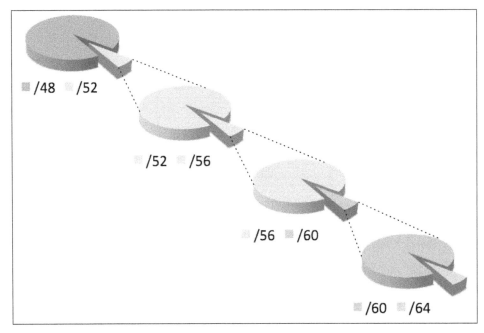

Figure 7-4. /48 to /64 in sequential nibbles

With no more than 16 elements or descriptors per level of hierarchy, this choice is also the most manageably (or, perhaps, least unmanageably) displayed as a worksheet excerpt. (Figure 7-5).

Figure 7-5 worksheet:

Site	CIDR	Subnet	Description	Element	CIDR	Subnet	Description	Element	CIDR	Subnet	Description	Element	CIDR	Subnet	Description
	/52	:0000::/52	reserved		/56	:1000::/56	reserved		/60	:1100::/60	reserved		/64	:1110::/64	reserved
	/52	:1000::/52			/56	:1100::/56			/60	:1110::/60			/64	:1111::/64	
	/52	:2000::/52			/56	:1200::/56			/60	:1120::/60			/64	:1112::/64	
	/52	:3000::/52			/56	:1300::/56			/60	:1130::/60			/64	:1113::/64	
	/52	:4000::/52			/56	:1400::/56			/60	:1140::/60			/64	:1114::/64	
	/52	:5000::/52			/56	:1500::/56			/60	:1150::/60			/64	:1115::/64	
	/52	:6000::/52			/56	:1600::/56			/60	:1160::/60			/64	:1116::/64	
/48	/52	:7000::/52		/52	/56	:1700::/56		/56	/60	:1170::/60		/60	/64	:1117::/64	
	/52	:8000::/52			/56	:1800::/56			/60	:1180::/60			/64	:1118::/64	
	/52	:9000::/52			/56	:1900::/56			/60	:1190::/60			/64	:1119::/64	
	/52	:a000::/52			/56	:1a00::/56			/60	:11a0::/60			/64	:111a::/64	
	/52	:b000::/52			/56	:1b00::/56			/60	:11b0::/60			/64	:111b::/64	
	/52	:c000::/52			/56	:1c00::/56			/60	:11c0::/60			/64	:111c::/64	
	/52	:d000::/52			/56	:1d00::/56			/60	:11d0::/60			/64	:111d::/64	
	/52	:e000::/52			/56	:1e00::/56			/60	:11e0::/60			/64	:111e::/64	
	/52	:f000::/52	reserved		/56	:1f00::/56	reserved		/60	:11f0::/60	reserved		/64	:111f::/64	reserved

Prefix: (blank)

Figure 7-5. Address Plan Worksheet excerpt

To begin to populate this worksheet using our example organization, we'll refer back to Figure 7-2 to help determine the appropriate hierarchy levels.

It makes the most sense to assign the first level of hierarchy to the primary modules within the site. (The sole exception would be the data center for which we have already set aside a /48.)

We reserve the 0/52 subnet and assign 2001:db8:def1:1000::/52 to the campus network. The edge, infrastructure, and lab networks get the next three subnets: i.e., :2000::/52, :3000::/52, and :4000::/52 (Figure 7-6).

Prefix: 2001:db8:def1::/48

Site	CIDR	Subnet	Description	Element	CIDR	Subnet	Description	Element	CIDR	Subnet	Description	Element	CIDR	Subnet	Description
	/52	:0000::/52	reserved		/56	:1000::/56	reserved		/60	:1100::/60	reserved		/64	:1110::/64	reserved
	/52	:1000::/52	Campus		/56	:1100::/56			/60	:1110::/60			/64	:1111::/64	
	/52	:2000::/52	Edge		/56	:1200::/56			/60	:1120::/60			/64	:1112::/64	
	/52	:3000::/52	Infrastructure		/56	:1300::/56			/60	:1130::/60			/64	:1113::/64	
	/52	:4000::/52	Lab		/56	:1400::/56			/60	:1140::/60			/64	:1114::/64	
	/52	:5000::/52			/56	:1500::/56			/60	:1150::/60			/64	:1115::/64	
	/52	:6000::/52			/56	:1600::/56			/60	:1160::/60			/64	:1116::/64	
/48	/52	:7000::/52		/52	/56	:1700::/56		/56	/60	:1170::/60		/60	/64	:1117::/64	
	/52	:8000::/52			/56	:1800::/56			/60	:1180::/60			/64	:1118::/64	
	/52	:9000::/52			/56	:1900::/56			/60	:1190::/60			/64	:1119::/64	
	/52	:a000::/52			/56	:1a00::/56			/60	:11a0::/60			/64	:111a::/64	
	/52	:b000::/52			/56	:1b00::/56			/60	:11b0::/60			/64	:111b::/64	
	/52	:c000::/52			/56	:1c00::/56			/60	:11c0::/60			/64	:111c::/64	
	/52	:d000::/52			/56	:1d00::/56			/60	:11d0::/60			/64	:111d::/64	
	/52	:e000::/52			/56	:1e00::/56			/60	:11e0::/60			/64	:111e::/64	
	/52	:f000::/52	reserved		/56	:1f00::/56	reserved		/60	:11f0::/60	reserved		/64	:111f::/64	reserved

Figure 7-6. Intra-site worksheet, level 1

As the color coding suggests, the next column of our worksheet corresponds only to the campus prefix we just assigned in column 1 (2001:db8:def1:1000::/52). The campus network comprises (among other attributes) four buildings. For level 2 of the intra-site hierarchy, each building will receive a /56 (Figure 7-7).

Prefix: 2001:db8:def1::/48

Site	CIDR	Subnet	Description	Element	CIDR	Subnet	Description	Element	CIDR	Subnet	Description	Element	CIDR	Subnet	Description
	/52	:0000::/52	reserved		/56	:1000::/56	reserved		/60	:1100::/60	reserved		/64	:1110::/64	reserved
	/52	:1000::/52	Campus		/56	:1100::/56	Building A		/60	:1110::/60			/64	:1111::/64	
	/52	:2000::/52	Edge		/56	:1200::/56	Building B		/60	:1120::/60			/64	:1112::/64	
	/52	:3000::/52	Infrastructure		/56	:1300::/56	Building C		/60	:1130::/60			/64	:1113::/64	
	/52	:4000::/52	Lab		/56	:1400::/56	Building D		/60	:1140::/60			/64	:1114::/64	
	/52	:5000::/52			/56	:1500::/56			/60	:1150::/60			/64	:1115::/64	
	/52	:6000::/52			/56	:1600::/56			/60	:1160::/60			/64	:1116::/64	
/48	/52	:7000::/52		/52	/56	:1700::/56		/56	/60	:1170::/60		/60	/64	:1117::/64	
	/52	:8000::/52			/56	:1800::/56			/60	:1180::/60			/64	:1118::/64	
	/52	:9000::/52			/56	:1900::/56			/60	:1190::/60			/64	:1119::/64	
	/52	:a000::/52			/56	:1a00::/56			/60	:11a0::/60			/64	:111a::/64	
	/52	:b000::/52			/56	:1b00::/56			/60	:11b0::/60			/64	:111b::/64	
	/52	:c000::/52			/56	:1c00::/56			/60	:11c0::/60			/64	:111c::/64	
	/52	:d000::/52			/56	:1d00::/56			/60	:11d0::/60			/64	:111d::/64	
	/52	:e000::/52			/56	:1e00::/56			/60	:11e0::/60			/64	:111e::/64	
	/52	:f000::/52	reserved		/56	:1f00::/56	reserved		/60	:11f0::/60	reserved		/64	:111f::/64	reserved

Figure 7-7. Intra-site worksheet, level 2

We again select the first subnet (corresponding to building A) to populate the next column in our worksheet. Building A has two organizational functions: Management and IT. Each will receive a /60 (Figure 7-8).

Prefix: 2001:db8:def1::/48

Site	CIDR	Subnet	Description	Element	CIDR	Subnet	Description	Element	CIDR	Subnet	Description	Element	CIDR	Subnet	Description
	/52	:0000::/52	reserved		/56	:1000::/56	reserved		/60	:1100::/60	reserved		/64	:1110::/64	reserved
	/52	:1000::/52	Campus		/56	:1100::/56	Building A		/60	:1110::/60	Management		/64	:1111::/64	
	/52	:2000::/52	Edge		/56	:1200::/56	Building B		/60	:1120::/60	IT		/64	:1112::/64	
	/52	:3000::/52	Infrastructure		/56	:1300::/56	Building C		/60	:1130::/60			/64	:1113::/64	
	/52	:4000::/52	Lab		/56	:1400::/56	Building D		/60	:1140::/60			/64	:1114::/64	
	/52	:5000::/52			/56	:1500::/56			/60	:1150::/60			/64	:1115::/64	
	/52	:6000::/52			/56	:1600::/56			/60	:1160::/60			/64	:1116::/64	
/48	/52	:7000::/52		/52	/56	:1700::/56		/56	/60	:1170::/60		/60	/64	:1117::/64	
	/52	:8000::/52			/56	:1800::/56			/60	:1180::/60			/64	:1118::/64	
	/52	:9000::/52			/56	:1900::/56			/60	:1190::/60			/64	:1119::/64	
	/52	:a000::/52			/56	:1a00::/56			/60	:11a0::/60			/64	:111a::/64	
	/52	:b000::/52			/56	:1b00::/56			/60	:11b0::/60			/64	:111b::/64	
	/52	:c000::/52			/56	:1c00::/56			/60	:11c0::/60			/64	:111c::/64	
	/52	:d000::/52			/56	:1d00::/56			/60	:11d0::/60			/64	:111d::/64	
	/52	:e000::/52			/56	:1e00::/56			/60	:11e0::/60			/64	:111e::/64	
	/52	:f000::/52	reserved		/56	:1f00::/56	reserved		/60	:11f0::/60	reserved		/64	:111f::/64	reserved

Figure 7-8. Intra-site worksheet, level 3

In the final column, each /60 is subnetted to provide /64s for interface assignments, corresponding to VLANs in this case (Figure 7-9).

Prefix: 2001:db8:def1::/48

Site	CIDR	Subnet	Description	Element	CIDR	Subnet	Description	Element	CIDR	Subnet	Description	Element	CIDR	Subnet	Description
/48	/52	:0000::/52	reserved	/52	/56	:1000::/56	reserved	/56	/60	:1100::/60	reserved	/60	/64	:1110::/64	reserved
	/52	:1000::/52	Campus		/56	:1100::/56	Building A		/60	:1110::/60	Management		/64	:1111::/64	Wired data
	/52	:2000::/52	Edge		/56	:1200::/56	Building B		/60	:1120::/60	IT		/64	:1112::/64	Wireless
	/52	:3000::/52	Infrastructure		/56	:1300::/56	Building C		/60	:1130::/60			/64	:1113::/64	VoIP
	/52	:4000::/52	Lab		/56	:1400::/56	Building D		/60	:1140::/60			/64	:1114::/64	
	/52	:5000::/52			/56	:1500::/56			/60	:1150::/60			/64	:1115::/64	
	/52	:6000::/52			/56	:1600::/56			/60	:1160::/60			/64	:1116::/64	
	/52	:7000::/52			/56	:1700::/56			/60	:1170::/60			/64	:1117::/64	
	/52	:8000::/52		/52	/56	:1800::/56		/56	/60	:1180::/60		/60	/64	:1118::/64	
	/52	:9000::/52			/56	:1900::/56			/60	:1190::/60			/64	:1119::/64	
	/52	:a000::/52			/56	:1a00::/56			/60	:11a0::/60			/64	:111a::/64	
	/52	:b000::/52			/56	:1b00::/56			/60	:11b0::/60			/64	:111b::/64	
	/52	:c000::/52			/56	:1c00::/56			/60	:11c0::/60			/64	:111c::/64	
	/52	:d000::/52			/56	:1d00::/56			/60	:11d0::/60			/64	:111d::/64	
	/52	:e000::/52			/56	:1e00::/56			/60	:11e0::/60			/64	:111e::/64	
	/52	:f000::/52	reserved		/56	:1f00::/56	reserved		/60	:11f0::/60	reserved		/64	:111f::/64	reserved

Figure 7-9. Intra-site worksheet, level 4

We've only included one subsequent level of hierarchy and requisite column for the campus /52: i.e., Campus → Building A → Management/IT → Wired, Wireless, VoIP.

In a fully documented plan, we would need a column for each subsequent level of hierarchy. For example, the /56 we designated for building B would have 16 /60s, corresponding to the organizational roles associated with it, i.e., marketing and sales. Each of these /60s would in turn have 16 /64s available for VLAN definition.

As you can observe, even given the extra tidiness that nibble boundaries provide, we're still confronted with the challenge of how to manageably represent our available and used allocations (something we'll cover in more detail in the next chapter).

Zero Subnets Have a Problem

The first subnet of a group of IPv6 subnets is always enumerated with a *0*. In the instance where the prefix contains consecutive zeros that allow for prefix zero compression, presentation inconsistency results.

For instance, as we saw in Chapter 4 (under "Visualizing Hierarchy"), numerating /52 subnets for 2001:db8:1::/48 gives us:

```
2001:db8:1::/52 (or, expanded for clarity, 2001:db8:1:0000::/52)
2001:db8:1:1000::/52
2001:db8:1:2000::/52
2001:db8:1:3000::/52
...
2001:db8:1:F000::/52
```

As evident, by the rules of zero compression, the first subnet can legally be expressed in its (pardon my French) *smooshed* form.

This can potentially confuse and cause problems for operational personnel, especially if they're not paying close attention to the CIDR notation, since the number of characters in the prefixes for both the parent /48 and the first /52 of the enumerated group is the same:

```
2001:db8:1::/48
2001:db8:1::/52
```

One way to prevent this confusion is to avoid assigning the zero subnet:

```
2001:db8:1::/52 (reserved)
2001:db8:1:1000::/52 (first assigned)
2001:db8:1:2000::/52
2001:db8:1:3000::/52

...

2001:db8:1:F000::/52
```

Where we adhere to the nibble boundary, this approach has the added benefit of having the first subnet we assign to an element be numbered *1*. Since this conforms to the way normals typically enumerate elements (e.g., 1,2,3,…n), it can provide for less confusion and more consistent operations and fault isolation.

Function and Location Assignment Revisited

We've now spent a fair amount of time observing how IPv6 subnets can be grouped together according to some standard concepts and practices. These steps allow us to arrange and assign subnets in ways that are logical and consistent with our network topology. We're able to reliably do this because IPv6 provides us with enough bits in any typical allocation (especially as compared with IPv4).

Another advantage of this logical and consistent structure is that we can map it on to our network topology in a way that best facilitates administration and operation of the network by enabling one or both of the following:

1. Prefix summarization

2. Security or QoS policy enforcement

As we discussed briefly in Chapter 5, this is usually accomplished by assigning our groups of prefixes to *locations* or *functions* within the network topology.

A *location* typically corresponds to *a part of the network whose address prefixes will be summarized at the boundary of that part*. This promotes operational efficiency in providing a summarized prefix in the routing table, potentially reducing convergence time and preserving router resources.

Site Versus Location

At this point, you may be asking yourself "Well just what the heck is the difference between a site and a location anyway?" It's a fair question because the distinction can be subtle (or nonexistent).

The simplest answer is that while a site is a /48 (well, almost always a /48—see below) and always on a nibble boundary, locations can correspond to any size prefix in the network.

And to *really* confuse things, recall that a site doesn't *have* to be a /48. Since a site is ultimately defined according to the addressing and operational needs of the requesting organization, it could be larger or smaller. As mentioned, some ISPs are defining a site as a home user's cable modem and assigning it a /56. (Will 256 /64s will be sufficient addressing for a single home network? Time will tell!)

If that's too abstract for your liking, it's perfectly appropriate to think of a *site* as an enterprise campus with a building on that campus as a *location*.[4]

Even where routing resources are abundant and convergence time is not an issue, mapping location into the address plan provides administrative logic that helps facilitate operations. As we saw with our loopback address example, even addresses within a single subnet can be logically encoded with location information that can help operational personnel locate and remediate resources on the network.

IPv6 subnet assignments according to *function* may correspond to *roles that have different security or QoS requirements* and that may span locations. This allows administrators to more easily define, deploy, and modify security or QoS policy. As a result, the overall number of ACL entries can be potentially reduced and ACL maintenance can be easier to accomplish.

Because there is no subnet mask in IPv6, any ultra-granular ACLs we might have configured in IPv4 (e.g., using wildcard subnet masks to identify groups of addresses for special QoS or security policy treatment) don't have an equivalent in IPv6. On the other hand, in IPv6, there should never be a shortage of unique subnets to deploy for special QoS or security policy treatment.

---

4. Any floors or departments might derive their subnets from whatever location subnet is assigned. In turn, subnets for functions such as wired data, wireless data, VoIP, printers, sensors, etc. would be derived from the relevant floor or department subnet.

Because the typically large scale of an IPv6 allocation allows for potentially many levels of hierarchy, either location *or* function may be mapped into any given hierarchy level within an IPv6 address plan (something that we'll show an example of below). But regardless of which is selected and used, the significance of the choice can be encoded into the address prefix in all cases. And as we learned in Chapter 5, defining subnets exclusively on nibble boundaries increases the legibility of our prefixes in relation to their function or location assignments.

Flatland

As the effect of Moore's law drives processor and memory costs ever lower, network devices subsequently become more efficient at holding and processing network state information, especially for typical LAN-sized networks. As a result, routing convergence and packet-switching performance can be accomplished with less network segmentation at layer 3.

The resulting trend is toward flatter networks, and fewer segments means fewer subnets and routes. Thus, for all but very large enterprise sites, it's unlikely that you'll be doing much intra-site aggregation or summarization. This fact would seem to favor assigning functional significance to our IPv6 address prefixes over location significance.

Enterprise IT is working to increase business agility by deploying (and integrating with) technologies like virtualization, cloud, and SDN. Support of mobile devices and applications has increased manyfold. These in turn require more sophisticated internal security models that deemphasize a simple perimeter model, leading to a more confederated (and typically more effective) security policy.

As a result, functional IPv6 prefix assignments may offer better integration into, and support of, this new environment.

Assigning Function and Location

Now let's take a look at the prefixes we've allocated for Strangelove LLC's network and observe what function or location significance they might receive.

We've already determined that each of Strangelove LLC's sites will receive a /48 (along with the /48s set aside for infrastructure, data center, and cloud integration). The entries in Figure 7-3 illustrate how the third hextet of the prefix provides location significance.

These /48s can be summarized to a /44 for their BGP announcement to upstream provider(s):[5]

---

5. We'll take a closer look at how BGP routing may effect our IPv6 address plan in Chapter 10.

```
2001:db8:def0::/48
2001:db8:def1::/48
2001:db8:def2::/48
. . .
2001:db8:deff::/48

2001:db8:def::/44
```

Of course, since we're using fewer than 8 /48s in our original address plan, we *could* summarize to a non-nibble boundary, creating two summary prefixes:

```
2001:db8:def0::/45
2001:db8:def8::/45
```

This could be useful if Strangelove Solutions LLC executes its plan for acquiring Pulowski Preservation Services, designers and manufacturers of "quality" personal fallout shelters.[6] Having eight unused, contiguous /48s (summarized into a contiguous /45) would be really handy if the merger leads to any obligatory renumbering of any newly acquired network infrastructure.

The further subnetting and assignment we've done within each site will still permit those subnets to be summarized at the site level, potentially reducing routing convergence time, as well as keeping the number of routes between sites to a minimum.

Next, we'll drill down on the headquarters site, i.e., 2001:db8:def1::/48. Referring to Figure 7-9, we can observe how mapping location and function significance to the levels of hierarchy we've defined for Strangelove LLC's network may be accomplished quite easily (and legibly thanks to our adherence to the nibble boundary).

Our first level of hierarchy includes the following network modules:

- Campus
- Edge
- Infrastructure
- Lab

Based on the fact that these modules represent both separate layer 3 network locations, as well as unique roles, they could be assigned either functional or locational significance. And though the modules are equally sized and will be summarized to the next level, they also have differing security requirements in relation to each other and the Internet. As a result, the ability to more easily determine security policy and simplify ACL entries may be facilitated by assigning functional significance to this group of subnets.

---

6. I think I know what you're thinking, but Vault-Tec's market capitalization is simply too large for a minor player like Strangelove Solutions, LLC.

In general, which one we assign depends on whether we'd need to be able to summarize a given group of prefixes up to the next level of hierarchy or whether any particular subnet might span multiple locations and require a more elaborate security policy and ACL configuration at the primary hierarchy level.

As a result of assigning functional significance to our first hierarchy level, we'll represent as *Fs* (for function) the first four bits (and the first hex character) of the fourth hextet.

```
2001:db8:def1:[FFFF XXXX XXXX XXXX]::/52
```

Thus, the individual /52s for each module could be assigned across multiple locations within the site while still allowing for a centralized firewalling.

Our second level of network hierarchy in our plan includes the campus buildings:

- Building A
- Building B
- Building C
- Building D

These buildings all share a /56 assignment and though not independently administered, the networks for these buildings (and any buildings added later) can be summarized up to the /52. As a result, we'll represent the second four bits as *Ls* (for location).

```
2001:db8:def1:[FFFF LLLL XXXX XXXX]::/56
```

Additional layers of hierarchy can be assigned function or location significance in the same fashion.

 Where functional significance is assigned at the top layer of hierarchy in order to facilitate security policy, it is usually not possible to assign location significance in order to aggregate subnets at a lower layer of hierarchy.

Addressing the Data Center

While the network topology for the campus module is a pretty straightforward corporate LAN, the data center architecture for Strangelove LLC (along with data center architecture in general) is a little different. As a result, we'll need to come up with a plan that makes sense for it.

Let's take a closer look at the data center topology (Figure 7-10).

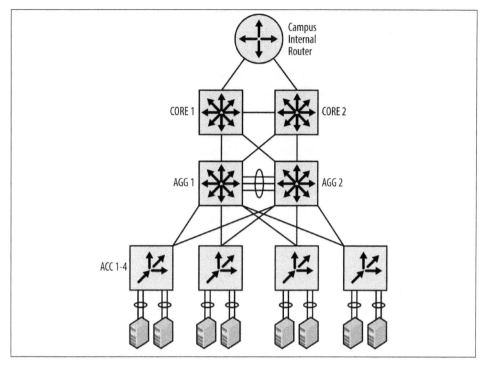

Figure 7-10. Strangelove LLC data center: topology and address plan

Strangelove LLC has what it thinks is a pretty standard data center architecture.

The campus core router feeds in to two core switches trunked together. Two aggregation layer switches are fully meshed with the core switches. This aggregation layer terminates connections from top-of-rack switches.

The top-of-rack switches connect up to servers via NIC-teaming. Functions provided by the servers include web, storage, and database. All of the links are 10GbE.

We've allocated 2001:db8:def4::/48 specifically for the data center, so as with our overall campus address plan, we'll focus on assigning the 16 bits between the /48 site-level boundary and the /64 interface-level boundary.

The topology within the data center has a few characteristics that will help guide our address planning for it.

The first of these is that the topology is relatively flat from a layer 3 perspective. Since we'll need little if any summarization below the core level, it makes sense to reserve whatever number of initial bits we'll need for functional significance.

As for the number of bits we'll need for our first level of hierarchy, the data center currently supports three primary applications (i.e., web, storage, and database services), but may add additional services in the future.

In addition, each service cluster is separated at layer 3 to support a possible multi-tenancy architecture. The number of clusters per service has been projected not to exceed 24 for the foreseeable future.

So to determine the number of bits needed for our first level of hierarchy, let's multiply the total number of existing and planned services requiring support times the number of existing and planned service clusters.

$Services_{(e+p)} \times Clusters_{(e+p)} = 8 \times 24 = 192$

Solving for $2^x = 192$, where x = number of bits needed, we easily see that x is between 7 and 8 (since $2^7 = 128$ and $2^8 = 256$). Since we can't split bits, we'll go ahead and round up to 8.

So 8 bits required for our first level of hierarchy for the data center /48 would provide 256 /56s (which gives us 32 clusters per service).

Since we're not worried about summarization below the /48 level and have selected functional assignment, we could assign /56s per service per cluster in any order. While this would require the least amount of planning (and eventually consume the highest possible quantity of available subnets), it might also make any security or QoS policy ACLs longer than necessary (e.g., a single entry per /56 for a maximum of 256 entries).

However, if we group our /56s according to their services, we can make our plan easier to administer.

For example, since we know we may have up to 24 clusters per service, it makes sense to leave enough bits between services to support sequential assignment of clusters per service.

Again, since 24 isn't on a power-of-2 network boundary (much less a nibble boundary), we'll need to round up to 32.

Since we know we have three existing services (with plans for no more than five additional services for a total of eight), we could sparsely allocate the first 3 bits required to define these services. This would ensure that any services we define later would have as many as 32 /56 subnets to sequentially number into.[7]

Recall that sparse allocation is equivalent to bitwise counting up of the left-most bits for the group of bits being allocated; in this case, the next 3 bits of 2001:db8:def4::/48. Table 7-1 has three columns: the first showing the group number; the second, the bitwise

---

7. Well, technically 31, as we'll avoid using the *0* subnet to keep our cluster numbering lined up with the actual prefix number.

counting up of the first 3 bits (to provide eight groups total); the third, showing the hexadecimal equivalent.

Table 7-1. Sparse allocation of service groups

Group #	Bits	Hex
1	0000XXXX	:0000::/56
2	0010XXXX	:2000::/56
3	0100XXXX	:4000::/56
4	0110XXXX	:6000::/56
5	1000XXXX	:8000::/56
6	1010XXXX	:a000::/56
7	1100XXXX	:c000::/56
8	1110XXXX	:e000::/56

The /56s in each group can be sequentially assigned.

We'll use 255 of the 256 /64s per /56 for VLAN assignment within each cluster (again, tossing out the *0* prefix for numbering consistency).

Summary

The purpose of this chapter was to get comfortable with the process of how the IPv6 address planning principles and methods we learned in earlier chapters are applied in order to create an actual IPv6 address plan.

Hopefully, at this point, you're beginning to see that for all of IPv6 additional complexities, it has many facets, especially those related to address planning, that are actually quite simple, both to learn and apply.

The ultimate goal, of course, is to instill the critical knowledge and confidence necessary to create (or perhaps effectively revise) an IPv6 address plan for your organization.

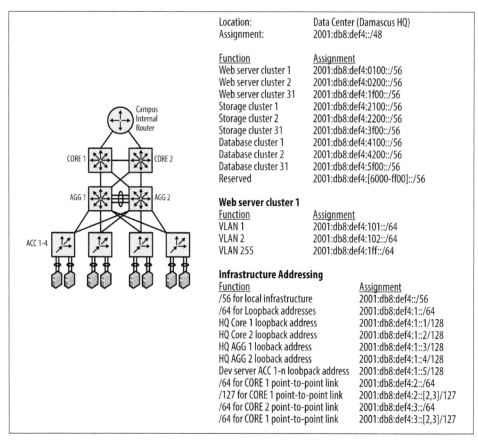

Location:	Data Center (Damascus HQ)
Assignment:	2001:db8:def4::/48

Function	Assignment
Web server cluster 1	2001:db8:def4:0100::/56
Web server cluster 2	2001:db8:def4:0200::/56
Web server cluster 31	2001:db8:def4:1f00::/56
Storage cluster 1	2001:db8:def4:2100::/56
Storage cluster 2	2001:db8:def4:2200::/56
Storage cluster 31	2001:db8:def4:3f00::/56
Database cluster 1	2001:db8:def4:4100::/56
Database cluster 2	2001:db8:def4:4200::/56
Database cluster 31	2001:db8:def4:5f00::/56
Reserved	2001:db8:def4:[6000-ff00]::/56

Web server cluster 1

Function	Assignment
VLAN 1	2001:db8:def4:101::/64
VLAN 2	2001:db8:def4:102::/64
VLAN 255	2001:db8:def4:1ff::/64

Infrastructure Addressing

Function	Assignment
/56 for local infrastructure	2001:db8:def4::/56
/64 for Loopback addresses	2001:db8:def4:1::/64
HQ Core 1 loopback address	2001:db8:def4:1::1/128
HQ Core 2 loopback address	2001:db8:def4:1::2/128
HQ AGG 1 looback address	2001:db8:def4:1::3/128
HQ AGG 2 looback address	2001:db8:def4:1::4/128
Dev server ACC 1-n loopback address	2001:db8:def4:1::5/128
/64 for CORE 1 point-to-point link	2001:db8:def4:2::/64
/127 for CORE 1 point-to-point link	2001:db8:def4:2::[2,3]/127
/64 for CORE 2 point-to-point link	2001:db8:def4:3::/64
/64 for CORE 1 point-to-point link	2001:db8:def4:3::[2,3]/127

Figure 7-11. Strangelove LLC data center: topology and address plan

PART III
Maintenance

The next three chapters explore topics related to maintaining and future-proofing your IPv6 address plan. Chapter 8 covers working with IPAM and DDI, two practices critical to the management of IPv6 networks and addressing plans. Chapter 9 will discuss dealing with network and Internet growth and change (and how they are likely to impact your address plan). Chapter 10 looks at the routing concepts you'll need to keep in mind to keep the IPv6 addresses of your plan reachable.

## CHAPTER 8

Working with IPAM and DDI

Introduction

As computer networks grow and become more complex, better tools and methods are needed to manage their resources. This is especially true as we enter the next stage of the evolution of the Internet and networking technology. Mobile devices, the Internet of Things, and cloud and virtualization architectures all require more efficient methods of provisioning and tracking basic network data like host addresses and names. These methods work best when they move beyond the traditional labor and opex-intensive processes that rely on manual changes or scripting (the latter usually only slightly more scalable than the former). Automation and orchestration of host and node provisioning become critical elements in enabling improvements in business agility, SLA enforcement, and reduction in IT costs in traditional networks (and the minimum requirement for many next-generation networks).

At first glance, IPv6 would appear to greatly complicate this picture. The larger address space, as well as the more complex address representation, would seem to necessitate more complex management requirements. And in the immediate term, managing IPv6 addresses does indeed introduce additional complexity.

But as mentioned, in the medium to long term, IPv6 is likely to facilitate improved provisioning and address management practices, helping realize the promise of automation, even in the hyper-scale environments of emerging networks and the applications they support.

In this chapter, we'll be focusing on tools that are available today to help effectively manage your IPv6 address plan and begin to build practices that will provide a foundation for the provisioning and management requirements of tomrrow's networks.

We'll introduce current IPAM methods and tools (and the concepts they apply, including how they differ from IPv4 to IPv6), and then expand our discussion to include DDI

(DNS, DHCP, and IPAM) functionality that exists to facilitate provisioning of hosts and nodes through better management of address assignment, tracking, host naming, etc. (You might think of DDI as IPAM on steroids.)

Finally, we'll examine the likely future of IPAM and DDI in the context of managing the address and naming data for emerging networks like SDN, cloud and virtualization, IoT, and mobile.

IP Address Management

Let's begin our discussion of IPAM with a basic definition:

IP Address Management (or *IPAM*) is the collection of practices and tools required by an organization to effectively manage their IP address resources. It includes allocating, administering, reporting, and tracking of IP addresses along with the associated network devices and associated data (such as DNS and DHCP).[1]

IPAM as a Cornerstone of Network Management

Before we dig in to what IPAM practices and tools are composed of, let's examine some of the concepts that IPAM is based on.

At its most basic, IPAM (along with DNS and DHCP) is merely one facet of network management as a whole. But if you consider the role it plays in keeping devices properly addressed (and users online with access to the services and applications they rely on), it becomes more evident that effective IP address management is critical to effective overall management of networks.

Far too often, in many organizations, IPAM as a formal element of network management is given short shrift or overlooked entirely. Instead of being approached with the same administrative rigor and operational zeal as, say, keeping routers and switches online, it is relegated to ad-hoc processes (nonstandardized scripting) and inadequate tools (e.g., spreadsheets or text files).

The proof of this lies in a simple test: let's suppose you were asked to go generate a report showing how your address space is allocated or assigned along with perhaps what hosts are currently online and at what addresses, how quickly and easily could you produce one?

Or to put it slightly differently: if your manager came to you tomorrow and tasked you with integrating the network of a new merger or acquisition, how much time and energy would you need to spend accounting for what IP space is currently allocated? Or where

---

1. Though not strictly IP addresses, BGP ASNs are often included as part of IPAM practice and in some IPAM tools.

---

and how much additional space you might need? Or even what is the most proper allocation to assign any new space from?

At the least, of course, you'd muddle through. But the inordinate energy required by many organizations to track the basic yet essential resource of IP addressing creates an inevitable opportunity cost in the form of cycles that could (and should) be better applied to other IT tasks and projects. Ultimately, there can be little if any business agility without the requisite agility in the IT network and organization. Big bets on cloud, virtualization, and SDN are all proof-positive of this.

Why More Than 1.8×10^{19} Addresses Aren't a Substitute for Proper IPAM

Perhaps you're thinking the vast scale of IPv6 eliminates (or lessens) the importance of IPAM. After all, the persistent struggle in IPv4 to find a few more addresses or another contiguous subnet is merely a function of the scarcity of individual public IPv4 addresses (or subnets of private ones). When the next project or department head sidles up with their proverbial bowl emptied of IP addresses or prefixes and asks "Please, sir, I want more" wouldn't we be able to just slop another /64 or /48 into it, harrumph, and say "There. Go away."

There are at least a couple of reasons why this isn't the case.

For one thing, remember that we're still going to need IPv4 addresses for the foreseeable future. In fact, managing IPv4 space can become more critical than ever for some organizations as they adopt IPv6.

For example, how quickly are you using up your remaining IPv4 resources and will you have enough addresses to keep up with the demands of legacy or new projects? What about continuing or emerging trends, like the flood of mobile devices connecting to the network?

Without an effective IPAM practice and proper IPAM tools in place, it will be much more difficult and time-consuming to generate capacity reports and track consumption of IPv4 addresses in order to determine where and when IPv6 deployment might be mandatory.

Regardless of how we might have tracked (or failed to track) IPv4, ad-hoc and primitive IPAM methods that might marginally work with the legacy protocol are entirely unsuitable for IPv6.

We've demonstrated that, despite its potential length and its use of hexadecimal, the presentation of an IPv6 address needn't automatically be unwieldy and thus more prone to transcription error. But the fact remains that any hosts or nodes utilizing addresses that require EUI-64 presentation or privacy extensions are indeed vulnerable to such errors, especially in the host ID of the address.

To get some idea of the potential for transcription errors, take a look at Table 8-1. It depicts a short sample list of IPv6 addresses, derived from either EUI-64 or temporary address algorithms.

Table 8-1. A sample list of EUI-64/temporary IPv6 addresses

Host	IPv6 address
1	2001:db8:abba:2112:13e9:5aff:fe39:bbe7/64
2	2001:db8:abba:2112:23e5:3cff:fe07:1f1a/64
3	2001:db8:abba:2112:c93d:32ff:fe2f:1196/64
4	2001:db8:abba:2112:6b27:73ff:fe68:51a0/64
5	2001:db8:abba:2112:40d5:97ff:fee5:6846/64
6	2001:db8:abba:2112:4b39:2aff:fee1:2bc7/64
7	2001:db8:abba:2112:34cd:d7ff:fe31:d85b/64
8	2001:db8:abba:2112:08a8:8bff:fe23:db50/64
9	2001:db8:abba:2112:9ab3:12ff:fed1:c1af/64
10	2001:db8:abba:2112:3a53:d6ff:fe7e:4f46/64

IPAM Policy

Like security policy, IPAM lends itself well to the application of a *policy cycle*. At its most essential, a policy cycle is a process whereby the application and effectiveness of an administrative policy is tested against the environment the policy applies to, and then updated and validated at regular intervals.

For instance, in IP address management, following the design of the address plan (i.e., policy formulation) and the allocation and assignment of addresses (i.e., policy application), continuous monitoring of the state of the network addressing through IPAM-focused tools and software allows the original plan to be kept current, inventory tracked, and capacity planned (policy enforcement and update) and any failures to be isolated, summarization maintained, etc. (policy validation and monitoring). Figure 8-1 illustrates this process cycle.

With the right tools in place, the policy in the form of an address plan can be reviewed and validated at any time through reporting that accounts for the current allocation and assignment of addresses.

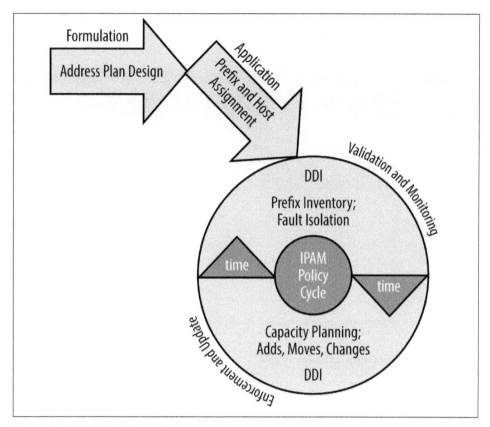

Figure 8-1. IPAM policy cycle

IPAM Features

There are a number of IPAM providers, but the tasks performed by their software and tools are generally similar. Here's a list of possible features along with a brief description for each. An assessment of the overall quality of an IPAM system can be based on how many of these features are implemented (as well as the general depth and ease-of-use of said features).

Later in the chapter, we'll take a look at what some of these features actually look like when configured in an actual IPAM system.

Display of IPv6 address space

There are different formats for displaying the IPv6 address space under management, and a good IPAM system will offer more than one view. Common views are a graphical map of the network space (Figure 8-2), a *list*, or a *table* view.

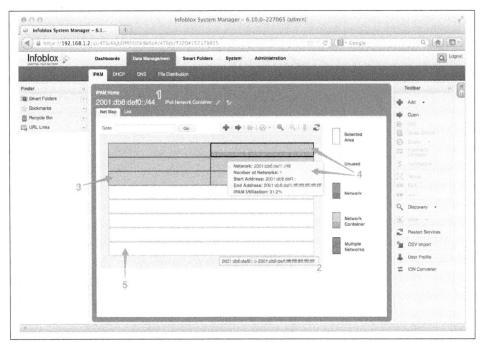

Figure 8-2. IPv6 net map, Infoblox IPAM

The parent network (aka, *supernet* or *network container*) is identified by the red box marked *1* with the value `2001:db8:def0::/44`. This is the level of hierarchy the net map illustrates and contains.

The box marked *2* shows the entire range of addresses possible at this level of hiearchy:

```
2001:db8:def0:0000:0000:0000:0000:0000 to 2001:db8:deff:ffff:ffff:ffff:ffff:ffff
```

The arrow labeled *3* points to a network container, similar in role to the formal definition of an allocation: additional subnets within it will be assigned later. Note that the arrow is pointing to the fifth network container on the network map, which would correspond to the subnet `2001:db8:def4::/48`.

4 is pointing to the second network container, as well as a mouse-over box that shows some relevant detail for that allocation. This information includes the network (`2001:db8:def1::/48`); the number of networks the block contains (1 block); the start address (`2001:db8:def1::` or `2001:db8:def1:0000:0000:0000:0000:0000`); the end address (`2001:db8:def1:ffff:ffff:ffff:ffff:ffff`); and finally, the percentage of IPAM utilization for that container—currently at 31.2% because we've allocated and assigned some subnets within this block. The black dots within the block represent these.

Finally, *5* points to the entirety of the unallocated space in our top-level allocation. Since we've only allocated 6 of the available 16 /48s, this leaves 10 /48s unallocated. Note that the unallocated space doesn't correspond to the two most logical ways we'd be likely to represent it—either as 10 individual /48s or as networks aggregated to the greatest extent possible (i.e., `2001:db8:def6::/46` and `2001:db8:def8::/45`).

A list or table view presents the defined subnets as, well, a list or table (Figure 8-3).

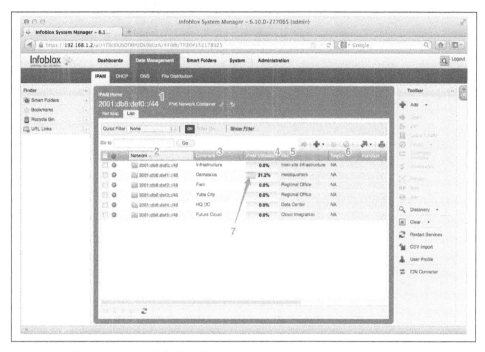

Figure 8-3. IPv6 list view, Infoblox IPAM

Once again, the parent network (aka, *supernet* or *network container*) is identified by the red box marked *1* with the value `2001:db8:def0::/44`. This is the level of hierarchy the list illustrates and contains.

The column titled *Network* (indicated by the number *2*) lists the 6 /48 prefixes we've defined from our parent allocation.

The next column, *Comment* (*3*), offers the site descriptions corresponding to each prefix.

IPAM Utilization (*4*), shows the number of subnets defined within that network container as a percentage.

Site (*5*), provides a descriptor for the generic type of site (e.g., Headquarters Regional Office, etc.). These *extensible attributes*, as they are referred to in the Infoblox IPAM system, offer a way of finding, grouping, and filtering IPAM elements and objects based on common or user-defined classes. Column 6, *Region*, is another of these attributes—in this case, *NA* for North America.

Another format for displaying IPv6 networks is the *tree* (or *outline*) view (Figure 8-4).

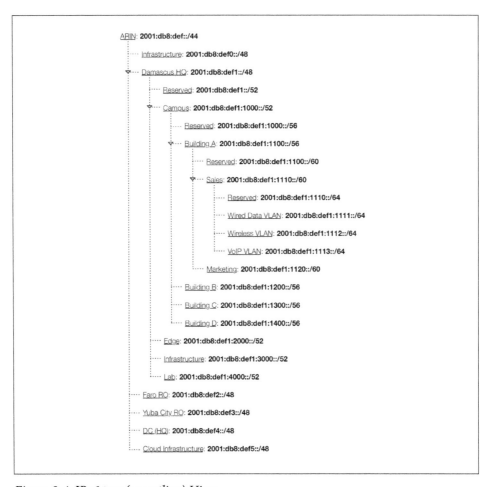

Figure 8-4. IPv6 tree (or outline) View

This view is effective at immediately conveying the network hierarchy, as well as the relationship between the various hierarchy levels.

Network aggregation

The ability to combine smaller prefixes into larger ones, for example:

```
2001:db8:abba:2000::/52
2001:db8:abba:3000::/52
```

```
can be aggregated to:
```

```
2001:db8:abba:2000::/51
```

Network splitting

The ability to split a larger prefix into two or more smaller prefixes is typically supported. For example:

```
2001:db8:abba:2000::/51

can be subnetted to:

2001:db8:abba:2000::/52
2001:db8:abba:3000::/52

or

2001:db8:abba:2000::/51

can be subnetted to:

2001:db8:abba:2000::/53
2001:db8:abba:2800::/53
2001:db8:abba:3000::/53
2001:db8:abba:3800::/53
```

 Network resizing is a common task in IPv4 address management, due to the need to *right-size* subnet assignments in order to conserve address space. Because of the astronomical number of hosts in a typical IPv6 prefix assignment, network resizing is not generally used.

Measuring consumption of IPv6 address resources

An IPAM system should offer the ability to measure and track the consumption of available IPv6 address resources—but measured in subnets rather than hosts. Recall that we're generally not concerned with tracking host address consumption in IPv6. This, in combination with reporting features, allows for better capacity planning and overall network management.

Reporting

A critical benefit of an IPAM system is the ability to generate reports that capture IPv6 network and subnet inventories for use in IT planning and strategy. Any major network numbering tasks or projects brought about by organizational change can be more effectively managed given the data that an IPAM system can provide. Address and capacity planning that reports provide can be correlated with existing or planned architectures to determine if any need for additional addressing exists.

IPv6 address plan design

An IPAM system certainly seems like a logical setting in which to build an IPv6 address plan. Application of address planning principles and best practices can be combined with the IPAM system's ability to display allocations and assignments according to organizational hierarchy, both within and between sites. Initial planning can be iterated before deployment begins, making the ultimately deployed plan much more ideal and ensuring that the overall allocation size is the right one (i.e., in most cases, large enough).

RIR registration updating
Since more end-user organizations and enterprises are obtaining IPv6 allocations directly from the RIRs, they'll need to abide by the same rules and regulatory requirements that ISPs and LIRs do. In most cases, this additional administrative burden is very light since organizations outside of ISPs seldom assign networks from their own allocation to businesses or entities under independent management. These kinds of assignments require updates to the Shared Whois Project or the Referral Whois database and having an IPAM system that can track, and even push, updates can be useful.

Policy compliance
An IPAM system tracking address resource can make it easier to validate that new or ongoing addressing assignments will comply with existing security, SLA, or routing policy requirements (such as integration with firewall and QoS ACLs, as well as routing subnet aggregation).

Integration with DNS and DHCPv6
Integrated management of DNS and DHCPv6 is always present in IPAM tools that are part of a larger DDI system. We'll cover this in more detail in the next section.

Example: Using IPAM Software

Let's take a look at how one DDI vendor accomplishes three basic IPAM tasks using their web interface.[2] This example is provided by Infoblox vNIOS software (version 6.10.0). The three tasks are:

1. Adding an IPv6 prefix (in this case a site /48)
2. Splitting the IPv6 prefix into /52s for assignment
3. Creating reverse-mapped DNS zones for the prefixes

---

2. This is not intended to be a *how-to* guide for using Infoblox IPAM, but rather to illustrate how one version of IPAM software handles IPv6 management.

Adding an IPv6 Prefix

After logging into the vNIOS web interface, users are presented with an IPAM tasks dashboard (Figure 8-5).

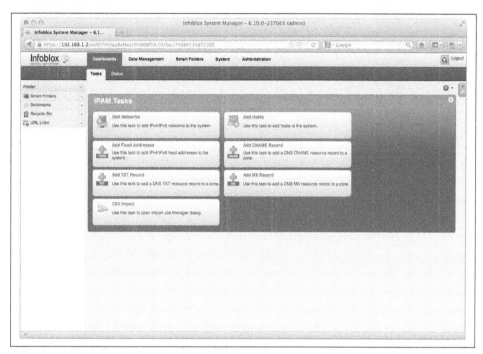

Figure 8-5. Infoblox vNIOS IPAM Tasks dashboard

Several common, predefined tasks are offered. We simply want to add an IPv6 network. After selecting the *Add Networks* link, a wizard opens (Figure 8-6).

On this screen, we first select the protocol (1), and then set the number of bits in the network ID (2), before finally entering the allocated prefix (3); in this case, 2001:db8:2112::/48.

After a few additional steps, the network appears in the main IPAM Data Management screen (Figure 8-7).

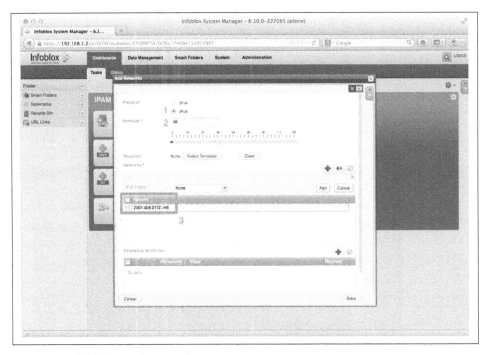

Figure 8-6. Add Networks wizard

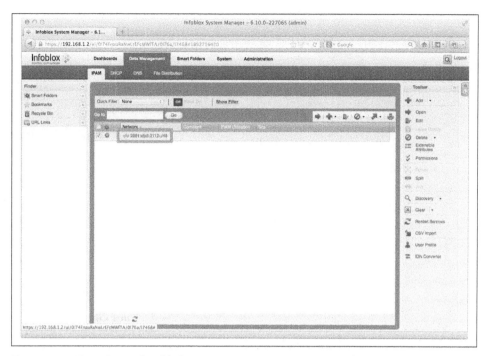

Figure 8-7. IPv6 Network added

Splitting an IPv6 Prefix

After some additional design and address planning, we decide that we're going to use the next 4 bits for our first level of hierarchy. Theoretically, we could use the same procedure above to create the 16 resulting /52s, but any good IPAM program will allow us to split an allocation (provided the bits feasible for the desired subnetting are not already in use).

Also in Figure 8-7, notice that off to the right of our highlighted network, we have an option to *Split* the selected network.

Once we click on *Split*, a new wizard opens (Figure 8-8).

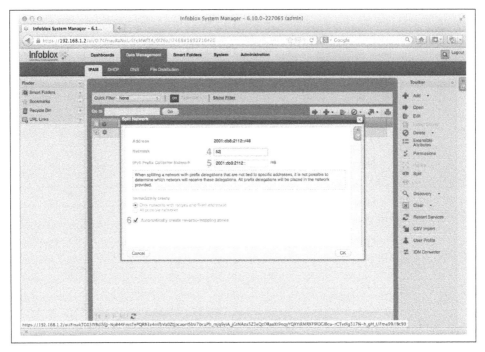

Figure 8-8. IPv6 split network

Here, we first specify the number of bits the subnets we're creating with the split function should have (4), and then enter the subnet from which the subnets are to be created (5) (still our original assignment of 2001:db8:2112::/48).

Were we to click *OK* at this point, our 16 /52s would be created—something we could easily verify (Figure 8-9).

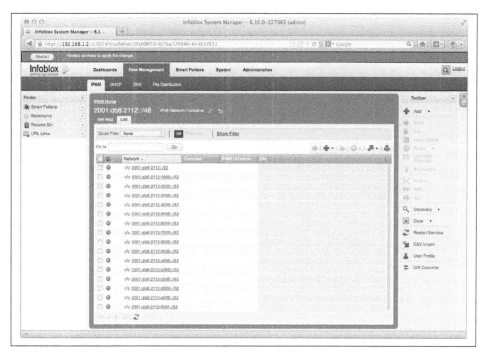

Figure 8-9. IPv6—16 newly-created /52s

Creating Reverse-Mapping DNS Zones

Instead of clicking *OK*, however, we typically would want to check the *Automatically create reverse-mapping zones* checkbox first. When checked, this does exactly what it says and creates reverse DNS zones for each new subnet.

Next, we'll verify our reverse zone files were created for each associated /52 prefix by navigating to the DNS tab in the vNIOS web interface. Here we see the individual zone entries for each generated /52 in their proper ip6.arpa format (Figure 8-10).

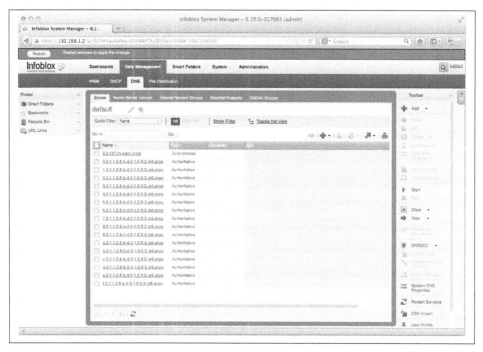

Figure 8-10. Auto-generated reverse DNS zones

We've just observed one of the key advantages of working with a DDI system. What would have been the labor-intensive creation of 16 reverse zone files is instead painlessly automated. And since the repitition (and drudgery!) associated with this type of task often leads to the introduction of errors, not to mention the requisite time required to find and fix them, additional time and effort is conserved.[3]

DDI: IPAM with 200% More Goodness

Based on the acronym, IPAM is obviously a component of DDI—yes, it's an acronym nested within an abbreviation (where will the madness end?). And as you might suspect, although all DDI includes IPAM, not all IPAM includes DNS and DHCPv6.

But some of the tasks we just listed as recommended or required for effective IPAM will only be possible where IPAM itself is integrated with DNS and DHCPv6. And while we can certainly accomplish rudimentary IPAM with legacy methods and tools, without said integration of DNS and DHCPv6 into IPAM, more complex automation and net-

---

3. Of course, such a task could also be scripted—assuming that the appropriate personnel have cultivated (or have access to) a reasonably mature scripting or devops practice.

work control tasks will only be possible through complicated scripting or API programming.

Indeed, once we start looking at best practices for IPAM policy, the integration of DNS and DHCPv6 becomes essential.

 The market view of DDI is perhaps best encapsulated by Gartner (who, incidentally, coined the DDI abbreviation in the first place): "Infrastructure and operations personnel can use DNS, DHCP and IP address management solutions to improve network availability, reduce operational expenditure, and simplify and streamline administration of critical infrastructure."[4]

One view of IPAM is that it helps provide proper *lifecycle management* of IP addresses. But since actual hosts (presumably with users running applications) are not only using but dependent on both address and name resources, DDI may be similarly understood as a critical part of the *lifecycle management* of a given host.

At a high-level, this process isn't significantly different for a host with IPv6 enabled. But the configuration of any DDI solution will require additional steps.

We've already looked at examples of how IPAM might be configured. We'll soon explore what IPv6 DNS and DHCPv6 configuration might look like using DDI. But first, let's take a look at some of the operational challenges of each.

Managing DHCPv6 and IPv6 DNS

If you've managed an enterprise network (or any network) that hosts periodically connect and disconnect from, you're already intimately familiar with how DHCP and DNS facilitate operations by automating both address and name assignment in IPv4 (as well as additional information about the network in options provided to the host by the DHCP server). In fact, it's safe to argue that the recent Bring Your Own Device (BYOD) phenomenon, driven by the explosion of personal mobile devices such as smartphones and tablets brought into the workplace, would be throw-up-your-hands-and-start-your-new-life-as-a-hermit-in-the-woods unmanageable without at least DHCP and DNS (to say nothing of IPAM or DDI).

DHCPv6 and IPv6 DNS differ enough from their counterparts in IPv4 that operational benefits, as well as challenges, are the result (with DHCPv6 arguably facing the most challenges of the two). While many of these challenges are at least partly met by the

---

4. "Gartner Market Guide for DNS, DHCP, and IP Address Management," Andrew Lerner, Lawrence Orans, 25: April 2014.

right DDI solution, protocol and operational standards are perhaps not yet mature enough to ensure that all of them will solved by a DDI solution alone.

DHCPv6 Basics

Auto-addressing in IPv6 can be accomplished using stateful DHCPv6, stateless DHCPv6 (a combination of SLAAC and DHCPv6), and plain old SLAAC. In stateful DHCPv6, the server provides an IPv6 address to the host. By comparison, in stateless DHCPv6, the host uses SLAAC to autoconfigure an address while a DHCPv6 server provides options.

With either stateful or stateless DHCPv6, the server provides additional options to the host, including DNS server and search domain information. Also, stateful and stateless DHCPv6 both rely on RAs from one or more routers to provide default gateway information. And depending on which mode is selected, deploying either requires a specific router configuration on the interface leading to the relevant link.

As far as which of these auto-addressing methods you should select, that will depend on the particulars of your deployment (and may vary, depending on what part of the network you're addressing).

In IPv4 DHCP, the only time you typically need to touch the router configuration is if you're configuring a DHCP relay helper address. In DHCPv6, however, you always have to set the proper router advertisement flags, depending on which auto-address configuration method you're using. Figure 8-11 shows the proper settings and the resulting differences in address configuration.[5]

Auto-address Configuration Method	ICMPv6 RA (Type 134)			Resulting IPv6 Addresses Configured	Additional Configuration Options (DNS servers, domain search list, TFTP, etc)
	A Flag	M Flag	O Flag		
SLAAC	1	0	0	Link-local, IPv6, Temporary IPv6	Manual (except where RFC 6106/ RDNSS supported)
Stateless DHCPv6	1	0	1	Link-local, IPv6, Temporary IPv6	DHCPv6
Stateful DHCPv6	0	1	N/R	Link-local, DHCPv6	DHCPv6

Figure 8-11. SLAAC, stateful and stateless DHCPv6 comparison

---

5. The prefix information provided by Router Advertisements include an *On-Link Flag* (or *L* flag), which is usually set by default. This flag specifies whether or not the advertised prefix is *on-link* (i.e., other nodes with IPv6 addresses in that prefix are directly reachable on the shared segment). If the L flag is not set, traffic destined to addresses in the prefix advertised in the RA must be sent to the gateway router for processing (behavior that isn't generally expected or desirable for standard DHCPv6 or SLAAC deployments).

When IPv6 is enabled on a router interface, the default flag settings are shown in Table 8-2:

Table 8-2. Default router interface RA flags

RA flag	Setting
A	1
M	0
O	0

As you can see from the above table, these settings correspond to SLAAC as the auto-address configuration method. Setting the flags for stateful DHCPv6 is relatively easy, provided you know the proper router configurations. Figure 8-12 shows the appropriate settings for Cisco IOS.

> As you might imagine, in LAN environments where some combination of stateful DHCPv6, stateless DHCPv6, and SLAAC are deployed on the same link, host address assignments and resulting host/network interaction can be unpredictable and more difficult to manage.[6] To the extent possible, choosing a single host platform and auto-addressing method per link will minimize any such operational challenges.

---

6. See the IETF Draft *DHCPv6/SLAAC Address Configuration Interaction Problem Statement* (*http://bit.ly/ dhcpv6-statement*).

Figure 8-12. Cisco RA flag configuration

Configuring DHCPv6 in DDI

Now let's take a look at configuring stateful DHCPv6, again using the Infoblox DDI solution (vNIOS software, version 6.10.0). Figure 8-13 provides a view of the DHCP configuration tab (1).

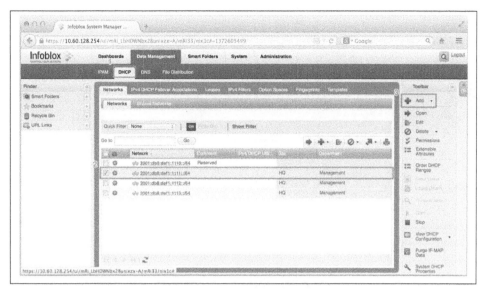

Figure 8-13. DHCPv6 configuration, network selection

The networks listed here (e.g., 2001:db8:def1:1110::/64, 2001:db8:def1:1111::/64, etc.) appear automatically based on the same networks being defined in our IPAM example earlier in the chapter. (2) indicates the network that we will select to configure a sample DHCPv6 range. Clicking on *Add* (3) opens a wizard to define this IPv6 range.

Figure 8-14 jumps to the second screen of the wizard, where we can see our selected network (4), as well as the fields to define the (inclusive) start and end addresses of our DHCPv6 range (5). You'll also notice that we have the option of doing prefix delegation (by itself or along with an address from the defined range). There are also fields here to name this particular range (and provide a comment if we need to).

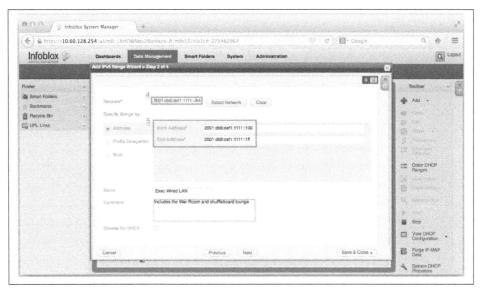

Figure 8-14. DHCPv6 configuration, range definition

After some additional steps, including restarting the DHCP service, the DHCPv6 server in Infoblox NIOS begins assigning IPv6 addresses from the defined range. Figure 8-15 shows a small sample of client leases.

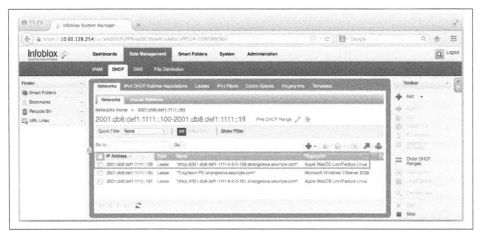

Figure 8-15. DHCPv6 configuration, acquired leases

By default, the lease information (6) includes the assigned address, the type of assign-ment (a DHCPv6 lease, in this case, as compared with, say, a fixed address), the hostname provided by the client, and the DHCP fingerprint identifying the device type and OS.

Figure 8-16 illustrates that, if we need or want to, we can get a more detailed look at the lease info.

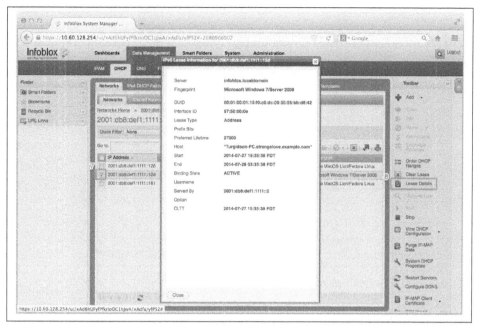

Figure 8-16. DHCPv6 configuration, lease detail

We can accomplish this by selecting the checkbox (7) next to a lease we're interested in (e.g., the address 2001:db8:def1:1111::12d) and then selecting *Lease Details* (8). The *IPv6 Lease Information* window that appears contains lots of useful info (in addition to the hostname and DHCP fingerprint from the previous screen), such as the DUID, the IAID, the preferred lifetime, lease end and start times, lease state, and the IPv6 address of the DHCPv6 server that provided the lease.

Figure 8-17 shows the screen accessed by clicking on *DNS* (9) → *Zones* → *Records*.

Here, we can see the dynamic DNS records (10) that have been generated by the DHCPv6 server and sent to the DNS server. Both the DHCPv6 server and DNS server may exist (as they do in this example) within a single instance of a virtual NIOS or physical Infoblox appliance.

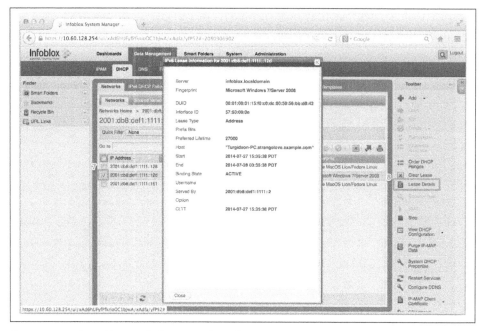

Figure 8-17. DDNS records from DHCPv6 leases

DHCPv6 Challenges

Most enterprise networks (along with any network environment where tighter control over hosts is desired) choose to run DHCPv6 instead of SLAAC. Based on our knowledge of how SLAAC operates, the reason for this choice should be evident. For one thing, as long as the router is sending appropriately configured RAs, SLAAC allows the host to autoconfigure an address and access the network.

Many IT network administrators have already encountered this scenario on their corporate LANs, given that most versions of modern OSes are installed with IPv6 on by default.

This has led to a regression in IPv6 adoption, where these administrators faced with little or no IPv6 expertise and an uncertain security environment opt to disable IPv6 altogether on host OSes.

Obviously, we want to be able to deploy IPv6 in a controlled manner and maintain the goals of our security policy. But disabling IPv6 on hosts can cause unintended consequences. On recent Microsoft Windows versions (including 7 and Server 2012), IPv6 is required to support features like Windows Server Clustering and applications like Direct Access.[7]

 We don't have to disable IPv6 on host OSes. Indeed, it's possible to reasonably secure your LAN while phasing in IPv6 by adopting some simple practices:

- Ensure that only router interfaces to links participating in phased IPv6 adoption are configured to send RAs.
- Where such interfaces are configured, make sure that the RAs have the proper flags set for the desired choice of auto-addressing (stateful/stateless DHCPv6 or SLAAC).
- Ensure that your firewall ACLs are configured to filter address ranges and ports that transition technologies like Teredo, 6to4, and ISATAP rely on.

Regarding the last practice, without a connection to an IPv6 ISP, it shouldn't be possible for hosts to use their IPv6 address to connect to the Internet. But keep in mind that older versions of Windows [TBD] have the transition technology Teredo enabled by default, which could allow certain hosts to bypass existing security checks and gain unauthorized access to the Internet. Other transition technologies like 6to4 and ISATAP may allow similar breaches. These three simple steps will instantly enhance the degree of security in place across your IPv6 adoption effort.

DUID versus MAC

One of the persistent operational challenges of working with DHCPv6 is the fact that there is no simple equivalent to the method in IPv4 DHCP of identifying a host by its 48-bit MAC address. The benefit of this method is well known to IT administrators: once hosts are uniquely identified by their layer 2 address they can be assigned a particular address, given DHCP options, or even blocked from obtaining an address at all.

By contrast, DHCPv6 standard relies on a Device Unique Identifier (DUID) for unambiguous host identification, given that there is only ever supposed to be one DUID per host.[8]

---

7. In fact, a Windows host with IPv6 disabled may be considered *out of scope* for support from Microsoft. You can learn more about this along with best practices for Windows IPv6 configuration in Ed Horley's excellent book on the subject, *Practical IPv6 for Windows Administrators*. (See Appendix C.)

8. Individual interfaces on a host are identified by an Identity Association Identifier (IAID), which when combined with the DUID creates an explicit identification for a DHCPv6 reservation.

While it is possible to construct a DUID to include link layer information like the MAC address, most hosts don't yet manageably support this. Additionally, link layer information doesn't persist in requests relayed to DHCPv6 servers on a different link.

The end result of this difference in host identication methods is that it is still more difficult to identify IPv4 and IPv6 addresses as belonging to the same host than would be preferable for easier host management in a dual-stack environment.

IPv6 DNS Considerations in DDI

From the standpoint of ease of deployment, IPv6 DNS is much less operationally complex as compared with DHCPv6. As we've already observed in the case of automatically generating reverse zones, using a DDI solution makes it even simpler.

We'll examine the very basics of IPv6 DNS. Then, as with DHCPv6 and IPAM, we'll briefly cover what configuring DNS in a DDI system looks like.

IPv6 DNS Basics

Getting IPv6 into DNS in the first place involved introducing a new record type and a new domain, respectively. They are:

- AAAA
- ip6.arpa

    AAAA
    > *Quad A* records are for forward mapping domain names to IPv6 addresses. Why are they called AAAAs? Well, recall that forward mapping a domain name to an IPv4 address requires an *A* record. And since IPv6 addresses have 4 times as many bits, a touch of pseudo-arithmetic gives us: 4xA = AAAA.[9]

A AAAA record in a standard DNS master file configuration looks like this:

```
www     IN      AAAA    2001:db8:def2:2000::1
```

ip6.arpa
> PTR records in the *ip6.arpa* domain are for, you guessed it, reverse mapping IPv6 addresses to domain names. Unlike the IPv6 address in a AAAA record, we're not allowed to compress the address in an ip6.arpa record. And as with PTR records for IPv4 addresses in in-addr.arpa zones, the address is reversed to maintain the proper delegation hierarchy within the ip6.arpa name space:

---

9. We can all look forward to the next iteration of IP, which I expect should have no fewer than 256 bits for addressing resulting in AAAAAAAA DNS records.

1.0.0.0.0.0.0.0.0.0.0.0.0.0.0.0.0.0.0.0.0.0.2.2.f.e.d.8.b.d.1.0.0.2.ip6.arpa. IN PTR www.strange-lovesolutions.com.

That's a lot of characters to account for in a single PTR record. But since every 4 bits of the 128-bit IPv6 address represents a subdomain under ip6.arpa in the namespace, we have to include all 32 hexadecimal characters to account for all 32 subdomains. (The automatic generation of these PTR records is part of the reason DDI makes IPv6 DNS much more manageable, as we observed in our earlier IPAM example with the automatic generation of ip6.arpa reverse zones).

Configuring IPv6 DNS in DDI

Once again using the Infoblox DDI solution (vNIOS 6.10.0), let's explore configuring IPv6 DNS. Figure 8-18 shows the first window of the DNS *Add Authoritative Zone* wizard.

Figure 8-18. IPv6 DNS configuration, authoritative zone wizard, type of zone

We've got the choice to add a forward-mapping authoritative zone or a reverse-mapping authoritative zone for either IPv4 or IPv6. In this example, we'll create a forward-mapping zone (1).

The domain name that we're creating the forward-mapping zone for is entered in the next screen of the wizard, Figure 8-19.

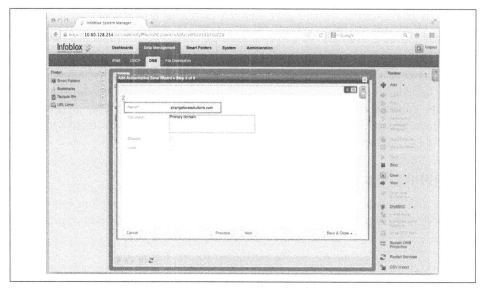

Figure 8-19. IPv6 DNS configuration, authoritative zone wizard, name

In addition to entering our domain name (2), we can enter a comment here if we'd like. (Also, note the checkboxes that allow the zone to be temporarily disabled or locked to keep others from making changes to it.)

Next up is the third screen of the wizard, Figure 8-20.

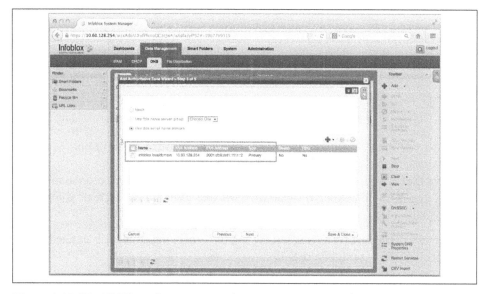

Figure 8-20. IPv6 DNS configuration, authoritative zone wizard, name server selection

Here, we define the name servers (including primary and secondaries) for our newly created zone. (3) shows the defined name server name, its IPv4 and IPv6 address, and whether it's a primary or secondary name server.

Once we finish the wizard and create the zone, Figure 8-21 displays the results.

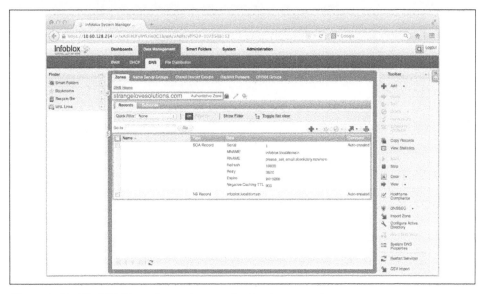

Figure 8-21. IPv6 DNS configuration, authoritative zone view

(4) indicates the name of the new authoritative zone and (5) shows details for the zone, including the start of authority (with requisite serial and TTL info) and NS record.[10]

Next, we'll add a AAAA record. Figure 8-22 is our previous screen with the pull-down menu activated to select the addition of a AAAA (6).

---

10. For our limited example, we've configured only one NS record. In a production network, you should have at least two.

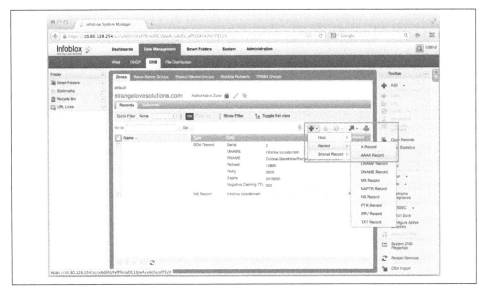

Figure 8-22. IPv6 DNS configuration, add AAAA record

The *Add AAAA* record wizard appears (Figure 8-23).

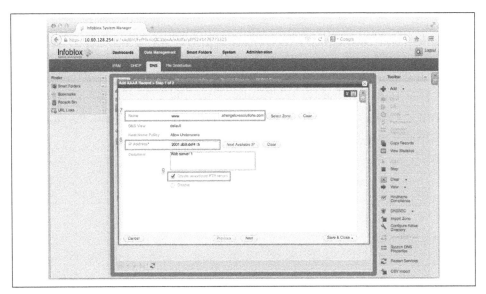

Figure 8-23. IPv6 DNS configuration, add AAAA record, detail

On this screen, we enter the forward-mapping name (in this case *www*) for the record (7), the IPv6 address (8), and check the box to automatically generate a PTR record for it (9).

Figure 8-24 displays the added record (10).

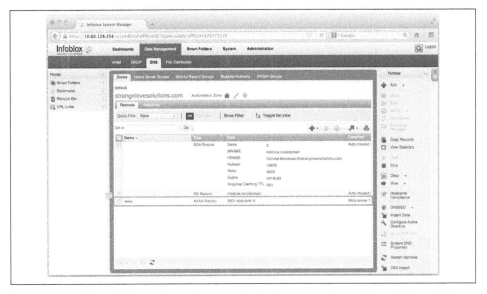

Figure 8-24. IPv6 DNS configuration, authoritative zone view with added AAAA record

Lastly, Figure 8-25 shows the records available for our ip6.arpa reverse zone. Here, we can verify the creation of the PTR record and associated information (11).

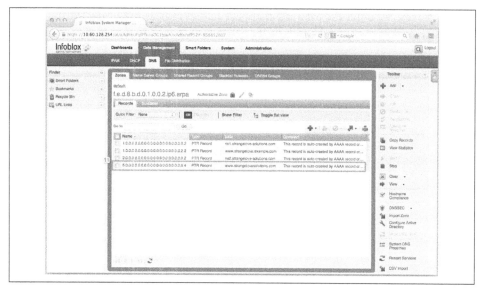

Figure 8-25. IPv6 DNS configuration, ip6.arpa zone with auto-generated PTR record

Summary

IPAM and DDI have become essential components for effectively managing larger networks—especially ones planning or running IPv6 deployments. The ability to closely track address assignments and utilization is critical for ensuring the most efficient use of the now-scarce resource that is IPv4. It's also necessary in helping establish and develop an IPAM practice for IPv6 that will facilitate address planning and grow with the organization.

These operational efficiencies are further enhanced by integration with DNS and DHCP. Beyond simply tracking address allocations, automating the process of numbering and naming of hosts on the network shortens provisioning time and helps eliminate any errors along the way. While enterprise networks will no doubt realize a reduction in operational expenses, hyper-scale deployments, like most cloud architectures, will simply not be feasible without some form of DDI (whether off the shelf or in the form of a custom-developed solution).

We explored the IPAM policy cycle and the features we should expect to see from most IPAM systems. We also looked at some examples of how to configure IPAM, as well as DHCPv6 and IPv6 DNS using Infoblox virtual NIOS. And reviewing some of the operational challenges of DHCPv6 suggests that we're going to be very busy managing dual-stack (and perhaps IPv6-only) environments.

## CHAPTER 9

Managing Growth and Change

Introduction

In the last chapter, we looked at some of the tools that DDI in general and IPAM in particular provide for the provisioning and management of address and name resources.

In this chapter, we'll explore some of the principles and best practices for managing the address plan through network and organizational growth and change.

We'll also review how best to manage network renumbering in IPv6 (something made easier by the protocol's improvements on handling multiple addresses).

Finally, we'll consider some of the address planning considerations for both next-generation networks and those transition technologies besides dual-stack that remain relevant, as well as how to deal with unplanned growth.

Renumerology: IP Renumbering Made Easy... (or Somewhat Less Painful)

No matter how thorough our address planning or how diligent our address management, we'll eventually be confronted with the requirement to renumber some or all of our network. Networks grow—and shrink—along with the businesses and organizations they support. Where growth occurs, it can be the result of corporate mergers or acquisitions, the planned deployment of new services or technologies, or just good old-fashioned network bloat as infrastucture is grafted on to work around problems as they arise. Or sometimes we have to change providers, number into a new assignment from our new provider, and out of the old one to return it.[1]

---

1. At least some of NAT's traditional appeal for organizations is that it could help prevent or delay the need to renumber.

A renumbering project could theoretically apply to any sized network. But fortunately, renumbering is more often required for a subset of the overall addressable infrastructure within an organization. Readdressing an entire medium-sized or large network is a daunting task and one that can realistically only be accomplished in several phases; that is, if we're trying to keep the network in production as we do it.[2]

For our discussion, we'll keep our renumbering scenario limited in scope.

Renumbering in IPv4 was (and is) the inevitable consequence of the interaction of two characteristics of IPv4 subnets.

Sparse allocation can be difficult or impossible with IPv4 subnets due to the lack of bits available for the network portion of the address. Because of characteristic two, we often lack an unused contiguous subnet to increase the size of the right-sized subnet we used in characteristic one; i.e., whatever subnet was contiguous at the time the interface was originally configured has already been assigned somewhere else.

As a result, if we want to add more hosts to a segment, we're stuck renumbering into a different subnet with sufficient addresses (or using a secondary subnet, which adds to both operational complexity and to the size of the routing table).

IPv6 was designed in part to reduce the necessity and frequency of network renumbering. For one thing, with 1.8x10^19 addresses per /64 it should *never* be necessary to renumber because of insufficient host addresses! But IPv6 was also designed to make renumbering as painless as possible. Recall that an IPv6 node can have as many IPv6 addresses configured from as many prefixes as may be needed or practicable.

To best understand how, we'll review the general method for IPv6 renumbering along with a closer look at the mechanisms built into the protocol to help facilitate it. But first, let's examine some renumbering preparations we can make.

---

2. In some sense, deploying dual-stack IPv6 and the eventual migration to native IPv6 is renumbering an entire network, but considering the fact that most organizations will do this over the course of years, such a project is made much more manageable as a result.

Remember that a PI allocation from a RIR is portable—i.e., announceable to any regional ISP—allowing the organization that receives and numbers into it to use it indefinitely (provided they continue to meet the RIR's policies). PA space by comparison is assigned by the ISP and must be numbered out of by the organization if they switch providers.

While it would certainly seem to make sense to an end-user organization to simply ask for PI space and reduce the possibility of having to renumber, given a change of providers, we still need to consider the effect on the global routing table that such PI allocations have. After all, every PI allocation in use is another entry in the global routing table.

For some smaller organizations and associated networks, renumbering may be eminently more manageable, reducing the need for a PI allocation and helping slow the growth rate of the global routing table.

The Lifetime and State of an Autoconfigured Address

We learned in Chapter 2 that IPv6 relies on Neighbor Discovery (ND) to allow nodes on a local segment to learn about and keep track of each other; e.g., "to discover each other's presence, to determine each other's link-layer addresses, to find routers, and to maintain reachability information about the paths to active neighbors." [3]

ND also facilitates address autoconfiguration. A critical message option of this process is the Prefix Information option. This 32-byte option is included in Router Advertisements and includes a number of fields, such as type and length, as well as one for Mobile IPv6 and two reserved for future use. But the remaining fields are most relevant to the operation of address autoconfiguration. These include:

- Prefix
- Prefix length
- On-Link flag
- Autonomous flag
- Valid Lifetime
- Preferred Lifetime

---

3. RFC 4861, *Neighbor Discovery for IP Version 6 (IPv6)* (*http://bit.ly/rfc-4861*).

The Prefix field contains the IPv6 network being advertised by the router. When combined with the prefix length field, it defines the prefix that will be combined with the node interface ID to autoconfigure an IPv6 address on that node.

The On-Link flag notifies a node whether a given prefix in the option is available on the local link or only available through the advertising router.

The Autonomous flag indicates to the node whether or not the included prefix is to be used for stateless address autoconfiguration. When set to 0, it informs the node to use the stateful method (i.e., DHCPv6).

The Valid and Preferred Lifetime fields enable a key enhancement of IPv6 protocol functionality over IPv4: the addition of the *address lifetime* concept and mechanism (and a set of address statuses associated with it).

The Valid Lifetime field is 32 bits and defines how long an address configured using the included prefix and any subsequent SLAAC address will remain valid.[4]

Similarly, the Preferred Lifetime field defines in seconds how long a prefix and SLAAC address will remain *preferred*. Once the Preferred Lifetime value exceeds the Valid Lifetime value, the address becomes invalid and may not be used to send or receive any packets. Thus, all valid addresses are also either preferred or *deprecated*. Preferred addresses can be used for any communication, while deprecated ones are not to be used for new communication (though existing communication can continue until completed). The expiration of a Valid Lifetime invalidates the address for any communication.

Either field has an infinite lifetime if set to all ones. e.g., 0xFFFFFFFF. If the Valid Lifetime is set to infinity and never expires while the Preferred Lifetime is allowed to lapse, the resulting address is permanently deprecated. Once existing sessions finish, no new sessions may be initiated from that address. (The address, however, may remain configured on the interface.)

Since IPv6 was designed to permit the configuration of as many addresses on an interface as necessary, this mechanism helps manage the preference and selection of these addresses by the host. SLAAC has five address states that we'll need to be aware of if we're renumbering any network that relies on it:[5]

Tentative address
   This is the state of a host address when it is first generated but not yet assigned to an interface because it is being validated as unique by the Duplicate Address Detection (DAD) that IPv6 Neighbor Discovery performs.[6]

---

4. Also, how long the included prefix will be used for determining on-link status.

5. RFC 4862, *IPv6 Stateless Address Autoconfiguration* (*http://bit.ly/rfc-4862*).

6. RFC 4862.

Valid address
> A live address that can be used to send and receive unicast traffic. Valid addresses can either be *preferred* or *deprecated.*

Preferred address
> A valid address whose Preferred Lifetime has not been exceeded. Preferred addresses can send and receive traffic without restriction.

Deprecated address
> A valid address whose Preferred Lifetime (but not Valid Lifetime) has been exceeded. Deprecated addresses should be used to send and receive traffic for existing sessions but not for new sessions.

Invalid address
> An address whose Valid Lifetime has expired. It cannot be used to send or receive any traffic.

Preparing to Renumber

Most of us have experienced (i.e., been traumatized by) a major network renumbering project at least once in our careers. But for those that haven't had the pleasure, let's clarify what we mean when we say *renumbering*.

> Network renumbering is essentially a reconfiguration plan and procedure in which an existing, in-use address prefix (or set of prefixes) is replaced by a new, yet-unused address prefix (or set of prefixes).

Though the old and new prefixes are typically the same size (something which should make the renumbering plan a bit easier to put together), they don't *have* to be.

An IPv6 renumbering checklist

Handling a network renumbering project is made easier—with less danger of disruption to the existing network—by using a simple checklist to remind us of all the areas of the network we'll need to configure with new prefixes, addresses, and names.

- Router and switch interfaces
  - Point-to-point links
  - LAN interfaces
  - Loopback and management
- Routing protocols
- ACLs

- Security
    - Firewalls
    - IDS/IPS
- Routing
    - BGP/WAN edge
- Auto-addressing ranges
    - DHCPv6
    - SLAAC
- Host interfaces
- DNS entries
    - AAAA
    - PTR
- Any applications using embedded addresses

Address abstraction

One approach for reducing the amount of overall reconfiguration necessary for any renumbering effort is to use names or variables instead of actual IPv6 addresses wherever possible. Two examples of this include:

1. The use of FQDNs instead of IP addresses (for things like VPN tunnel endpoints)
2. The use of variables and names in ACLs and flat text configuration files

This method can simplify network management in general in the long run and, if put into practice ahead of time, may reduce the amount of preparation required when network renumbering becomes necessary.

Address lifetimes and DNS TTLs

Whether end hosts on the network are relying on DHCPv6 or SLAAC, reconfiguration of addresses can be timed and tuned to reduce operational strain.

The Renumbering Method

Renumbering must usually occur in phases in order to keep the network up and running. However, depending on the operational agility and management practice of the IT organization, smaller- to medium-sized networks can possibly renumber using the *flag day* approach.

At the beginning of the renumbering project, the network is live using the old prefix.

The first step of renumbering (following planning, of course) is adding addresses from the new prefix to network infrastructure like routers and switches and the links that connect them. Since IPv6 has been designed to better support multiple addresses and subnets on single interfaces, this step can be accomplished without impacting production traffic using the old prefix.

The next step is to configure hosts to use addresses from the new prefix. The procedure for this will be slightly different, depending on whether you're using DHCPv6 or SLAAC.

As we've discussed, most enterprise hosts will likely be using DHCPv6. At the planned time, a unicast RECONFIGURE message from the DHCPv6 server to the hosts will trigger the necessary change of addresses. Dynamic DNS will then automatically update the hosts' AAAA and PTR records. Groups of hosts can be renumbered in stages to reduce potential operational strain and better isolate any problems that arise.

If SLAAC is in use, the procedure is a bit more involved.

First, the Valid and Preferred Lifetime settings for the existing prefix are adjusted. Neither of these timers should exceed the overall duration of the renumbering effort.

In most networks, host sessions are short-lived, so there may be little benefit in making the valid lifetime longer than the preferred lifetime for a given prefix.

However, if there are hosts on the network that maintain persistent sessions (e.g., video or real-time services), a longer valid lifetime for a prefix will provide a buffer that allows applications to continue using an address for existing sessions, even though the preferred lifetime has elapsed and the address has moved to a deprecated state.

Next, the new prefix must be added to the router or daemon configuration and advertised to the host. The updated RAs will cause the hosts to autoconfigure a new address.

At this point, host logic for address selection will determine which of the two configured addresses gets used for new sessions.[7]

Finally, once everything is stable, the old prefix and addresses can be removed from hosts, network infrastructure, and DNS.

---

7. The proper address selection logic is defined in RFC 6724, *Default Address Selection for Internet Protocol Version 6 (IPv6)* (*http://bit.ly/rfc-6724*).

And speaking of DNS, I probably can't say it any better than the IETF says it: "It is recommended that the site have an automatic and systematic procedure for updating/synchronizing its DNS records, including both forward and reverse mapping. In order to simplify the operational procedure, the network architect should combine the forward and reverse DNS updates in a single procedure. A manual on-demand updating model does not scale and increases the chance of errors."[8]

Translation: *DDI will make renumbering easier and less error-prone!*

Frequent Renumbering

If your particular network design or business requirements compel you to change prefixes and/or addresses often, there are perhaps a couple of architectural and operational practices you might want to cultivate to streamline this process as much as possible.

If you change ISPs often and are unable to secure a PI allocation for whatever reason, you might consider using ULA space along with NPTv6 (Figure 9-1).[9]

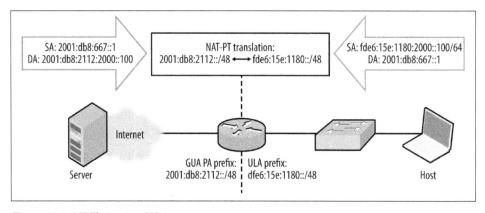

Figure 9-1. NPTv6 using ULA

In this illustration, a small enterprise is singly-homed to an ISP (and the Internet). The ISP has assigned a PA prefix to the customer, 2001:db8:2112::/48. Internally, the enterprise has deployed ULA addresses. The prefix from which these addresses are configured has been generated in the proper pseudo-random fashion to help insure that it doesn't overlap with any other ULA assignments anywhere. That way, if this enterprise

---

8. RFC 6879, *IPv6 Enterprise Network Renumbering Scenarios, Considerations, and Methods* (*http://bit.ly/ rfc-6879*).

9. RFC 6296, *IPv6-to-IPv6 Network Prefix Translation* (*http://bit.ly/rfc-6296*).

network should ever need to merge or connect to another network that is also using a ULA prefix, the probability of overlap is exceedingly unlikely. (Compare this scenario to one with an IPv4 network where the 10.0.0.0/8 network is in use.)

The host has been assigned an address from a /64 assigned from the ULA prefix, i.e., fde6:15e:1180:2000::100. The host wants to connect to a server on the IPv6 Internet offering content at the address 2001:db8:667::1. The enterprise's edge router has been configured for NPTv6, which statelessly translates any traffic from any address in the ULA prefix fde6:15e:1180::/48 to the equivalent address using the GUA prefix 2001:db8:2112::/48 (i.e., prefix translation). The process is reversed for traffic returning to the host from the server.

In a renumbering scenario compelled by the enterprise's switching to a new ISP (or the existing ISP needing to change the prefix assigned to the enterprise), the enterprise would have no need to renumber internally. Instead, they'd need only change the external routed GUA prefix on the edge router and within the NPTv6 configuration.

Also, in instances where small end sites within the network might frequently change addressing, it may be desirable to use DHCPv6 and prefix delegation for such sites— much as a broadband ISP might assign a prefixes to a customer's cable modem or home router.

Unplanned Growth

IPv6 provides tremendous advantages over IPv4 in providing addressing when unexpected or unplanned growth of the network takes place. Here are general recommendations for prefix assignment size, depending on the network element being added:

- /64s
  - New LAN segment
  - New point-to-point link
  - Any "flat" network (a single broadcast or collision domain)
  - A group of sensors
- /48s
  - New sites
  - New data centers
  - New lab environments
  - Any location or network that requires direct reachability to the Internet
- >/48
  - Networks of acquired or merged companies

If you've done your address planning correctly, you'll have IPv6 subnets in reserve at all levels of your network hierarchy. Depending on the scope and location of the network(s) and supporting infrastructure being added, the appropriate-sized subnet can be allocated.

An Address in Cloud City

I may be just an empty flesh terminal relying on technology for all my ideas, memories, and relationships. But I am confident that all of that—everything that makes me a unique human being—is still out there somewhere, safe in a theoretical storage space owned by giant multinational corporations.

— Stephen Colbert

I would bet my signed first edition of "DNS and BIND" that had I invited you to join me in a round of technology buzzword bingo covering the last few years, your first, second, and third words would be *cloud*, *cloud*, and *cloud*. But setting aside whatever hype factor might accompany this set of technologies, there can be little doubt that cloud services are dramatically reshaping the way computing resources are created and consumed, especially for enterprise IT.

In spite of this ubiquity of both the technology and the term, it might still be helpful to start our discussion with a working definition of *cloud*. The National Institute of Standards and Technology (NIST) offers a pretty serviceable one:[10]

"Cloud computing is a model for enabling ubiquitous, convenient, on demand network access to a shared pool of configurable computing resources (e.g., networks, servers, storage, applications, and services) that can be rapidly provisioned and released with minimal management effort or service provider interaction."

It should be evident from that definition that the value proposition of cloud computing (and SDN) is founded on *agility*, i.e., how quickly computer, storage, and network resources can be provisioned (as well as de-provisioned) in support of IT services and applications. The *on-demand* aspect of these offerings allows enterprises to spend only as much as is needed on cloud services to support what they actually use (instead of the danger of either underutilizing or quickly exhausting the resources of the infrastructure they already own or must acquire).

But such agility must be engineered into the cloud provider's underlying architecture, infrastructure, and operations. The necessity of pooling compute and storage resources to support the economical and rapid scaling of services to a given client means that

10. *The NIST Definition of Cloud Computing*, NIST Special Publication 800-145 (*http://bit.ly/nist-cloud-compute*).

many such clients must share access to these resources in a cloud provider's data center. Keeping these customers logically separate for routing, security, and SLA enforcement purposes requires unique addresses (as well as the ability to rapidly provision and de-provision them).

Meanwhile, these cloud solution providers face the same challenges confronting tradi-tional service providers: how to use the relatively limited space available in IPv4 to scale their offerings. Since little if any public IPv4 space is left, cloud providers would need to rely on private IPv4 addressing (and possibly NAT).

Service categories have arisen as products from this concept include:

- Software as a Service (SaaS)
- Platform as a Service (PaaS)
- Infrastructure as a Service (IaaS)

These services are generally *public* (or external to the organization) cloud offerings. *Private* (or internal) clouds are "homegrown," internal to the organization (though IT can offer the same categories of service to different business units or divisions within the organization). Some organizations have adopted a *hybrid* cloud approach, seeking benefit from the use of some combination of both private and public clouds.

We should probably also talk about what problem cloud computing was developed to solve: namely, controlling IT costs—especially capital expenditures (CAPEX) on infra-structure while simultaneously expanding the quality and quantity of technology re-sources available to the organization.

Traditional corporate networks connect to external public cloud offerings via the In-ternet. Of course, in the age of teleworkers, remote offices, and mobile device produc-tivity, connections to public cloud services are not limited to originating from corporate LANs. This is an argument for ensuring that CSPs offer their services over IPv6. As we've discussed, the broadband and mobile networks these itinerant workers rely on themselves increasingly rely on IPv6 addressing to cost-effectively solve their challenges of scale in an operationally efficient way.

The interface between the public network (or VPN) acts as a frontend to all customer traffic. Frontends often groom the arriving traffic in some way: by load-balancing it, or translating it in some way so that application or database servers on the backend with particular presentation requirements can focus on doing what they're supposed to be doing and not have to worry about modifying arriving session traffic.

In this fashion, the frontend can be used to service requests arriving over IPv6 without regard for whether the backend network and servers comprising the cloud service are IPv6 or IPv4.

But as we've discussed, the elastic provisioning requirements of cloud services suggest that IPv6 adoption promises operational efficiencies and cost savings over time.

As a result, IPv6 and cloud are becoming inextricably linked. IPv6 has attributes that better enable the rapid provisioning models cloud computing requires to deliver on its promise of economical business agility. These include:

Sufficient addressing
> This enables cloud providers to rapidly provision and deprovision any number of virtual servers.

Enhanced auto-addressing
> The provisioning of virtual servers is better facilitated by multiple auto-addressing mechanisms, including SLAAC, as well as stateful and stateless DHCPv6.

Improved management of Layer 2 to Layer 3 mapping
> ARP in IPv4 is replaced by ND in IPv6. ND's use of multicast, as compared with broadcast in IPv4, is much more efficient and preserves LAN resources.

The abundant addressing of IPv6 provides hierarchical consistency and unlimited scale. IPAM practice can be improved to enable automation and more agile service provisioning and operations.

Adopting IPv6 *and* Cloud

A fairly compelling argument can be made for an organization tackling IPv6 adoption at the same time that they take steps to adopt cloud technology. Cloud and IPv6 intiatives are contemporaenous for many organizations and as a result certain synergies can be realized by combining the two.

For instance, when shopping for cloud services, a bit of additional due diligence is in order. We should determine, of course, whether the proposed CSP supports IPv6 at all. If they don't today, when will they? And what is their take on how IPv6 fits into their overall strategy? But assuming they do support IPv6 connections from customers, does their backend support IPv6 and if not, why? Obviously, there are many other criteria for deciding on a given CSP, but perhaps we can agree that it's better to understand up front how they perceive any necessity (or lack of it) in supporting IPv6 both externally and internally.

The Internet of Things

Remember the statistic from Chapter 1? 50 billion devices connected to the Internet by 2020.[11]

And thank goodness for IPv6, or there'd be no hope of manageably getting these devices online.

But before we explore a specific instance of what address planning for these devices might look like, let's step back to look at the bigger picture.

Figure 9-2 illustrates the progression of Internet-connected device types in the past and up to the 50 billion mark while Figure 9-3 shows the number of Internet-connected devices per person over time.

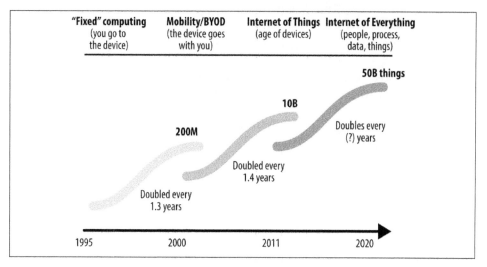

Figure 9-2. Internet-connected devices over time

11. 50 billion sounds like a large number (and it is), but it only equals slightly more than seven devices per person for the global population. It's quite easy to imagine a scenario where a person is the logical endpoint of many, many more devices than seven.

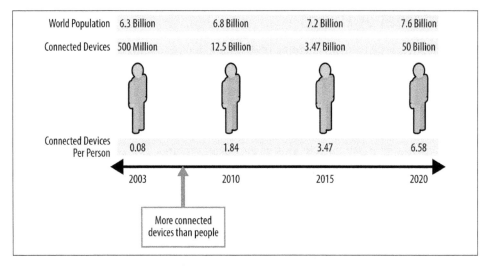

Figure 9-3. Internet-connected devices per person

Beyond the devices we're already acutely aware of (tablets, smartphones, laptops, routers, switches, etc.), what makes up the *things* in the Internet of Things?

- Utility distribution (Electric/H2O/Gas)
  - — Home meters
  - — Smart grid
  - — Smart home (lighting/HVAC)
    - — Home appliances
- Sensors
  - — Automotive
  - — Industrial
  - — Agricultural
  - — Infrastructure
  - — Medical devices
- Wearables
- Biochipped animals

At some point in the future, existing and new devices will comprise an *Internet of Everything* (IoE), potentially allowing data collected from every device to be leveraged to help solve economic, environmental, and social problems. Figure 9-4 and Figure 9-5 illustrate the relationships between the *things* in IoT and the data, people, and processes that will drive the IoE.

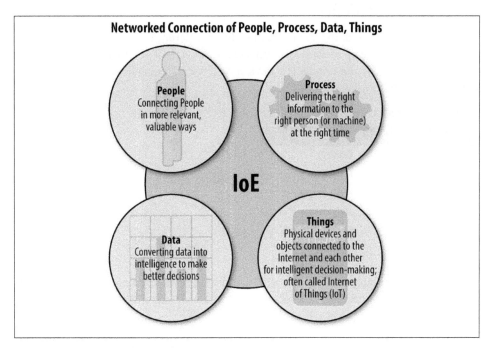

Figure 9-4. Internet of Everything

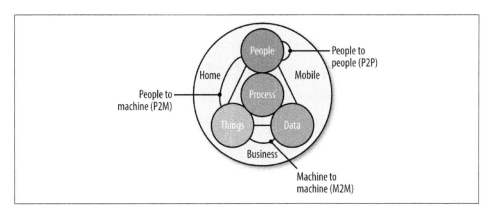

Figure 9-5. Internet of Everything

Why IPv6 for the Internet of Things? We've already mentioned the obvious reason: sufficient unique addresses for tens of billions of devices. But there are other reasons why IPv6 is critical to the success of the IoT. These reasons have to do with the unusual characteristics of many IoT devices themselves.

Characteristics of IoT Devices

As you may have guessed, IoT devices can be quite different than the fixed and mobile devices that have made up the bulk of connected Internet nodes up till now. For instance, many, if not most, of the connected devices will share the following characteristics shown in Table 9-1:

Table 9-1. Characteristics of IoT devices

Characteristic	Unit(Scale)
Low cost	Cents(50)
Low power	Milliamps(~1)
Limited memory and processing	Kilobytes(~100)
Low bandwidth	Kilobytes/second(~100)
Lossy wireless	Megahertz(<1000)
Small packet size	Bytes(~100)

These limits to available power, bandwidth, and processing capability drive the standards and protocols required to connect such devices and lead to the need to reduce their complexity (thus reducing cost).

Part of the complexity of IoT deployments is that there are competing standards and propietary technologies attempting to make the best of the strict "scale down" engineering requirements stemming from IoT device characteristics.

For instance, several low-power wireless standards exist, as shown in Table 9-2:

Table 9-2. Low-power wireless standards

Name	Standard
ZigBee	802.15.4
Bluetooth "Smart"	Part of Bluetooth 4.0
Z-Wave	G.9959
DECT ULE	ETSI 300-175

IPv6 in particular, and IP in general is one way to help accomplish this. Engineers focused on IoT are fond of calling IP the *integration protocol* for the promise it holds in stitching together different lower layer protocols.

This is the focus of the IETF 6LoWPAN effort. The associated standards introduce methods to *scale IPv6 down* in order to work within the IoT device constraints (Table 9-3).

Table 9-3. 6LoWPAN standards

Standard	Purpose
RFC 4944 (*http://bit.ly/rfc-4944*)	Basic encapsulation for 802.15.4 links
RFC 6282 (*http://bit.ly/rfc-6282*)	Stateless header compression
RFC 6775 (*http://bit.ly/rfc-6775*)	Neighbor discovery/address registration

With IPv6 successfully scaled down to work in constrained device networks of various types, routing for these networks can also be standardized. This approach reduces the so-called *Internet of Gateways* problem where silos created by various IoT device network solutions end up using different layer 3 protocols, requiring translation and reducing scalability.

Routing standardization is provided by RPL (pronounced "ripple"), or routing protocol for low-power and lossy networks. The limited bandwidth and low rates of packet delivery in LLNs create requirements to support multiple modes of traffic flow: exclusively between endpoints (point-to-point), as well as between endpoints and a central control point (multipoint-to-point) and vice-versa (point-to-multipoint).

Figure 9-6 shows an example of an LLN topology applied in the form of a simple last-mile smart grid infrastructure with redundancy.

The LLN itself is indicated as a Neighborhood Area Network (NAN), perhaps a radio mesh of smart meters. But it could also be any collection of constrained devices requiring interconnectivity and communication to a central system.

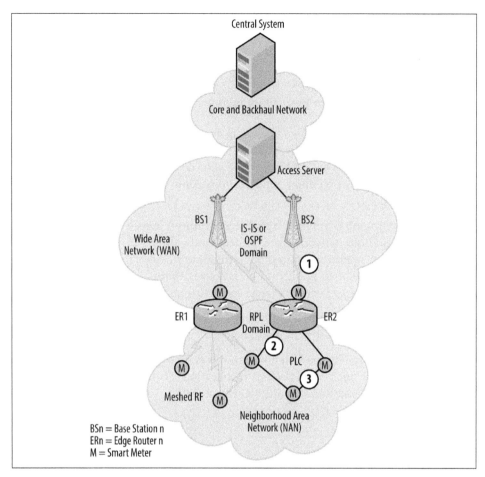

Figure 9-6. Last-mile smart grid infrastructure

IPv6 Address Planning for IoT Deployments

Though IoT networks, such as smart grids for utilities, may ultimately consist of several million devices, for ease of management and maximum scalability, subnets of no more than a few thousand nodes may be desirable. These subnets may logically terminate at edge routers, which will also likely be the interface to the WAN or LAN, the routing protocol redistribution point (if RPL is in use), and the location (or gateway to) the required auto-addressing configuration components.

It's very likely that an organization's device network architecture will be consistent and repeatable for discrete locations providing the same application set. Because of this, an IoT deployment often follows the same design practice that is common for ISPs and data-center deployments: a cookie-cutter architecture consisting of well-defined infrastructure modules with configurations standardized (except those configuration elements unique to that module).

Such uniform architectures lend themselves well to a similarly uniform address planning approach.

 This generalized topology imagines that most, if not all, device networks will be stub networks connected to a distribution and/or core layer to provide more operationally familiar routing (e.g., OSPF or IS-IS) with sub-second convergence times. In other words, any required communication between devices within these stub networks would necessarily be carried through the distribution or core layer. RPL provides true distance vector routing with a minimum of control traffic more suitable for an LLN. This may permit the construction of more complex topologies supporting communication between many thousands of devices.

Three Suggestions for IoT IPv6 Address Assignments

1. Assigning a default subnet size of a /64 to the device network (e.g., the NAN in the above illustration). A /64 assignment would usually preclude any prefix delegation within the constrained network. But the feasibility of successfully incorporating PD given the processing limits of IoT devices is probably low.

2. Using prefix delegation to assign a /56 or /60 to the device network gateways (e.g., in the previous illustration, PD to the border routers in the WANs directly connected to the NANs).

3. Setting aside a /48 per region, per device network application. A /48 guarantees portability on the Internet if needed but is still large enough to provide sufficient /64 subnets for the application the device network is providing across a given region.

Summary

The practice of renumbering needn't always remain the laborious and costly process it has frequently been in the past. As we've learned, IPv6 provides mechanisms that make it more manageable. And in fact, the resulting evolution of renumbering practice should happen concurrently with leveraging IPv6 to provide addressing and address management for the new network environments such as cloud, IoT, and SDN—environments that will prove critical to scaling the next phase of the Internet.

## CHAPTER 10

Keeping Your IPv6 Addresses Reachable

> A name indicates what we seek. An address indicates where it is. A route
> indicates how we get there.
>
> — Jon Postel

Introduction

There wouldn't be much point to the whole exercise of creating and managing a great IPv6 address plan if we didn't also implement policies and practices that keep those addresses reachable.

Routing on our internal networks and across the Internet requires some considerations unique to IPv6. We'll review the IPv6 versions of the routing protocols familiar to us from IPv4 with special attention to the differences that will help us keep our IPv6 addresses live.

Many enterprises (especially small to medium-sized organizations) have traditionally relied on PA IPv4 space from an ISP. They may be opting for an IPv6 PI allocation directly from a RIR for the first time. The practices to keep those IPv6 prefixes externally reachable and optimally routed may be less familiar to them.

We'll also examine the impact of IPv6 routing table size on memory that may affect the overall reachability of our networks.

Routing with IPv6

Just as with IPv4, you'll be relying on a routing protocol to get traffic between sites or within sites. Thankfully, for the sake of preserving our copious amounts of free time (CAFT), we don't have to learn any new routing protocols exclusive to IPv6. That is, the IGPs and EGPs we know and (as long as we've configured them correctly and they're behaving) love from IPv4 have all been enhanced to support IPv6.

These include:

- IGPs
  - RIPng
  - EIGRP for IPv6, *IPv6 Implementation Guide, Cisco IOS Release 15.2M&T—Implementing EIGRP for IPv6 (http://bit.ly/cisco-guide).*
  - OSPFv3[1]
  - IS-IS for IPv6[2]
- EGPs
  - MP-BGP[3]

Figure 10-1 provides a comparison between the IPv4 protocols and the newer IPv6 versions.

		Address Family	Type	Port/ Protocol Used	Multicast Address(es)	Authentication	Administrative Distance	RFC(s)	Notes
Interior Gateway Protocols (IGPs)	RIPv2	IPv4	Distance vector	UDP 520	224.0.0.9	Plain text, MD5	120	2453	
	RIPng	IPv6	Distance vector	UDP 521	ff02::9	None	120	2080	
	EIGRP	IPv4	Distance vector (hybrid)	IP 88	224.0.0.10	MD5	Internal: 90 External: 170	Proprietary (Cisco)	Auto-summarization, split-horizon enabled
	EIGRP for IPv6	IPv6	Distance vector (hybrid)	IP 88	ff02::a	MD5	Internal: 90 External: 170	Proprietary (Cisco)	Auto-summarization, split-horizon disabled (multiple interface prefixes possible)
	OSPFv2	IPv4	Link state	IP 89	All routers: 224.0.0.5 DR, BDR: 224.0.0.6	MD5	110	2328	Configured per subnet
	OSPFv3	IPv6	Link state	IP 89	All routers: ff02::5 DR, BDR: ff02::6	IPSec (AH)	110	5340	Configured per link; single or multi-topology mode
	IS-IS	IPv4	Link state	n/a	n/a	Plain text, MD5	115	1142	
	IS-IS for IPv6	IPv6	Link state	n/a	n/a	None	115	5308	Single or multi-topology mode
Exterior Gateway Protocols (EGPs)	BGP	IPv4	Path vector	TCP 179	n/a	MD5	Internal: 200 External: 20	4271	
	MP-BGP	IPv6	Path vector	TCP 179	n/a	MD5	Internal: 200 External: 20	2858	Multi-protocol (NLRI can be carried over IPv4 or IPv6)

Figure 10-1. Routing Protocols Comparison, IPv4 to IPv6

---

1. RFC 5340, *OSPF for IPv6 (http://bit.ly/rfc-5340).*

2. RFC 5308, *Routing IPv6 with IS-IS (http://bit.ly/rfc-5308).*

3. RFC 4760, *Multiprotocol Extensions for BGP-4 (http://bit.ly/rfc-4760).*

We'll leave any exhaustive exploration of these protocols to other, more worthy texts. But to explore some of their important operational considerations, we'll need to at least briefly review them.

Selecting Your IPv6 Routing Protocol(s)

If you haven't already been through this exercise and selected your IPv6 routing protocols (or even if you have and want to validate your choice), how do you go about choosing? Since we have at our disposal all the same routing protocols as in IPv4, one path forward is simply to select the one(s) we're currently using.

As we'll see, this approach is perfectly valid, but shouldn't be made without examining some of the other considerations that should inform our choices based on how they may impact our operations.

But first, let's look at the primary benefit of using the routing protocol (or protocols) we're already using.

Operational Continuity

Using the same routing protocol(s) in IPv6 that we're currently using in IPv4 has the powerful benefit of providing operational continuity. Since you and your colleagues are probably intimately familiar with how to keep whatever protocol you're using today up and routing packets, you'll be taking advantage of some institutional knowledge that should lead to (in theory at least) better and faster fault isolation and route optimization.

Even if we choose to run the same routing protocol for IPv6, there may be additional considerations (and gotchas).

Distance Vector and Link State Routing Protocols

Before getting into the difference between topology modes, let's briefly review how dynamic routing protocols accomplish tracking network paths and routing packets. The most widely deployed routing protocols generally fall into one of two classes (or, in one case, a combination of both):

- Distance vector
- Link state

Of course, the goal of either of these types of routing protocols is to converge (and reconverge) quickly enough to create a stable, loop-free topology that gets packets from where they are to where they need to be in the network.

A distance vector protocol relies on each routing node sharing its entire routing table with all of its directly connected neighbors. The *distance* in distance vector is a measurement of the cost (often, the number of hops) to reach a destination, and the *vector* is via which next-hop router. Routers running a distance vector protocol pass along a routing table from one neighbor to another, i.e., "routing by rumor."

RIP and EIGRP are examples of distance vector routing protocols.

By contrast, a node in a link state protocol knows about its directly connected links and shares these link states with its immediate neighbor nodes. Each node uses that information to build and maintain a link state database and calculate the shortest path to any given destination for a packet or flow. The reliability of this route information is generally much greater than its equivalent in a distance vector protocol because no router is sharing more than what it knows about directly and every node has calculated a complete picture of the network.

OSPF and IS-IS are examples of link state protocols.

 One significant variation of the distance vector protocol is known as the *path vector* protocol. A path vector protocol associates each destination prefix with a particular path through the network. This path is formed by the chain of autonomous system numbers that would be traversed by a packet to reach the destination prefix. The path vector algorithm analyzes each path and removes any destination prefix with a path that contains the same ASN two or more times (implying a loop in the topology). BGP is an example of a path vector protocol.

EIGRP is primarily a distance vector protocol, but shares some features with link state protocols, such as neighbor state tracking and triggered updates (versus periodically sending the entire routing table). This provides for much faster convergence and a more reliable picture of the network.

All of 'Em

Years ago I worked for a large ISP that had several smaller ISPs as customers. One ISP customer in particular always seemed to be suffering outages and, as a result, initiated many calls to our NOC for emergency help. During one such troubleshooting session with this customer, I asked him what routing protocol or protocols he was running. "All of 'em," he replied (which, at the time and in his case meant RIP, OSPF, EIGRP, IS-IS, and BGP). My laugh was cut short by the realization that he was serious (and that this fact of his, um, network *configuration* was likely the source of his many, many outages). If only he'd been an early adopter of IPv6: he could have tried running no fewer than 10 routing processes!

Dual-Stack…but Not Necessarily Dual Topology

When it comes to choosing the IGP we're going to use in a dual-stack environment, there's an additional consideration that may not be immediately obvious. It's based on the fact that two of our IGPs (as well as our EGP) provide a way to either share or isolate elements of the topology and (any associated router processes) according to what address family they belong to, i.e., IPv4 or IPv6.

Most current implementations of router and switch code available from Vitamin C, J, and B (i.e., Cisco, Juniper, and Brocade) vendors offer these options. Such options vary in scope and implementation, depending on the routing protocol in question, so let's review each.

IS-IS for IPv6: Single-topology or Multi-topology Mode

IS-IS for IPv6 offers a choice of single-topology or dual-topology mode.

In single-topology mode, routers participating in IS-IS share a single link state database. Thus, the IS-IS process in this case bases its best path selection for both IPv4 and IPv6 routes on a single shortest path first (SPF) calculation for that database.

 Keep in mind that this means anywhere you've configured an interface for IPv4, you'll need to configure the same interface for IPv6 (and vice versa).

Because of this, the two protocols are sometimes said to *share the same fate*. Link-state changes that might normally only affect one protocol can cause an SPF recalculation and network reconvergence that affects both the IPv4 and IPv6 network.

By comparison, a router configured for IS-IS multitopology mode performs a separate SPF calculation for each protocol, isolating reconvergence and eliminating fate-sharing —at least as a consequence of routing protocol configuration and activity. After all, routers can still lose power! Because of this isolation, having disjointed sets of interfaces configured for IPv4 and IPv6 is perfectly fine.

So if you're using IS-IS, which mode should you choose? Beyond the criterion of operational consistency that we already mentioned, the above described behavior has at least two consequences to consider:

- Router resource preservation
- Isolation and fault tolerance

Since single-topology mode maintains and performs SPF calculations on a single link state database, both router memory and CPU are conserved. Therefore, if the availability of these router resources in your dual-stack network is scarce, it might conceivably be necessary to run IS-IS in this mode.

By contrast, because mutlitopology uses two separate link state databases, each with its own SPF calculations, isolation and fault tolerance for each address protocol is better accomplished.

 My recommendation is to run multitopology mode wherever possible. Any interruption to the production IPv4 network during the initial deployment of IPv6 can result in delays and setbacks to its adoption. By running multi-topology mode, the inevitable misconfiguration of IPv6 as it's deployed in routing infrastructure will ideally only affect IPv6 traffic (and vice versa once IPv4 is officially the *legacy protocol* on your network).

OSPFv3 Address Families

The version of OSPF we're likely most familiar with is version 2. This has traditionally been the IGP of choice among larger enterprises, especially where the greatest degree of interoperability between different vendors is desired.[4]

Version 3 of OSPF relies on the same basic link-state algorithms, but its link-state advertisements (LSAs) and packet formatting have been updated to accommodate the larger address size. It also leverages the IPv6 link-local address to form adjacencies. And since it's per link instead of per subnet (and since IPv6 is designed to permit configuration of multiple IPv6 addresses and subnets per interface), a single link can support more than one instance of it.

For our discussion, the most important feature of OSPFv3 is that it allows for multiple address families. Let's look at an example of this with an OSPFv3 configuration (Figure 10-2)—in the syntax of our favorite Vitamin C vendor.

4. As a result of such wide deployment, there is a tremendous amount of collected operational wisdom on how OSPF behaves in production that can be leveraged by engineers and operational staff.

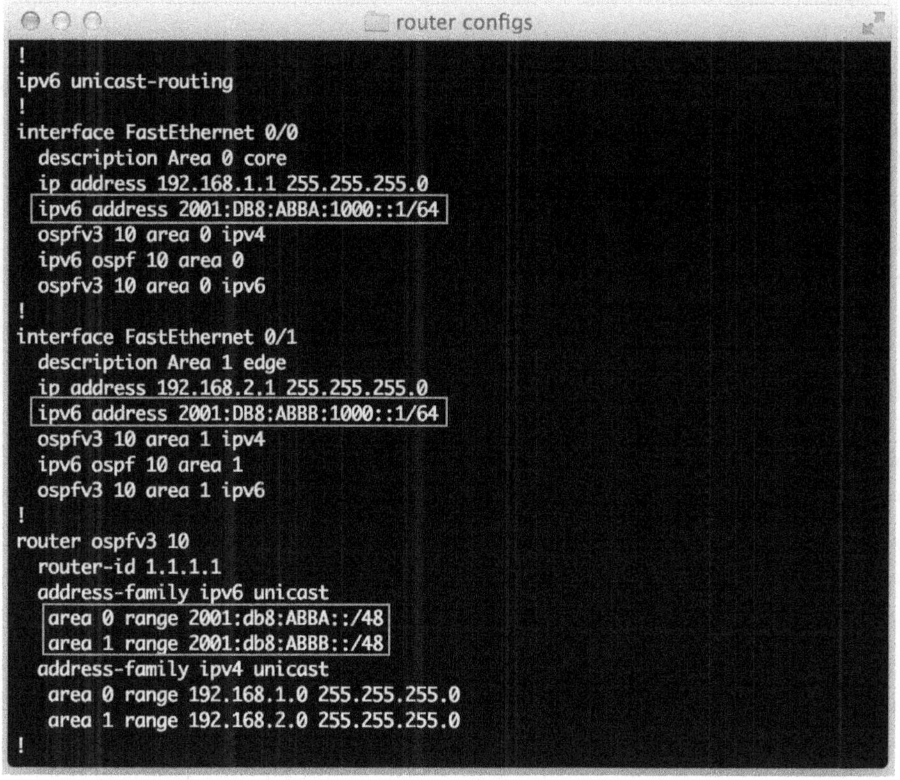

```
● ○ ○                          🗀 router configs
!
ipv6 unicast-routing
!
interface FastEthernet 0/0
  description Area 0 core
  ip address 192.168.1.1 255.255.255.0
  ipv6 address 2001:DB8:ABBA:1000::1/64
  ospfv3 10 area 0 ipv4
  ipv6 ospf 10 area 0
  ospfv3 10 area 0 ipv6
!
interface FastEthernet 0/1
  description Area 1 edge
  ip address 192.168.2.1 255.255.255.0
  ipv6 address 2001:DB8:ABBB:1000::1/64
  ospfv3 10 area 1 ipv4
  ipv6 ospf 10 area 1
  ospfv3 10 area 1 ipv6
!
router ospfv3 10
  router-id 1.1.1.1
  address-family ipv6 unicast
   area 0 range 2001:db8:ABBA::/48
   area 1 range 2001:db8:ABBB::/48
  address-family ipv4 unicast
   area 0 range 192.168.1.0 255.255.255.0
   area 1 range 192.168.2.0 255.255.255.0
!
```

Figure 10-2. OSPFv3 router config example

Similar to IS-IS for IPv6 single-topology mode, all routers running a particular OSPFv3 process share a link-state database and SPF calculation. Thus, where maximum isolation and fault tolerance is desired, it's perhaps preferable to run OSPFv2 for IPv4 and OSPFv3 for IPv6.[5]

---

5. RFC 5838, *Support of Address Families in OSPFv3* (*http://bit.ly/rfc-5838*).

MP-BGP

MP-BGP, or Multi-Protocol BGP, is an extension to BGP that allows BGP to carry Network Layer Reachability Information (NLRI, i.e., IP prefixes being advertised by a BGP peer) for multiple routed prototols—most importantly for our discussion, IPv6 *and* IPv4.[6]

MP-BGP shares configuration syntax with OSPFv3 in the form of *address families*. Because MP-BGP extenstions allow for multiple network protocol types, it is possible to send and receive IPv4 *and* IPv6 NLRI to and from a given peer over a single peering session of either protocol.

But the configuration preferred in nearly all cases is a peering session each for IPv4 and IPv6 to a given peer. As with our IGPs, it's usually better to have isolation and fault tolerance than to, in the case of MP-BGP, save a few lines of configuration (as well as preserve a negligible amount of memory and CPU).

Figure 10-3 shows an example of an MP-BGP router config with the preferred configuration (separate peering sessions to the same external router and AS for IPv4 and IPv6).

---

6. The extensions in MP-BGP also allow for carrying NLRI for MPLS VPN and multicast.

```
● ○ ○                    🔲 router configs                          ⬏
router bgp 64511
 bgp router-id 1.1.1.1
 no bgp default ipv4-unicast
 neighbor 192.2.0.1 remote-as 64496
 neighbor 192.2.0.1 soft-reconfiguration inbound
 neighbor 192.2.0.1 description eBGP with ISP64496
 neighbor 192.2.0.1 password bgpwith64496
 neighbor 192.2.0.1 ttl-security hops 2
 neighbor 2001:DB8:2112::2 remote-as 64496
 neighbor 2001:DB8:2112::2 soft-reconfiguration inbound
 neighbor 2001:DB8:2112::2 description eBGP with ISP64496
 neighbor 2001:DB8:2112::2 password bgpwith64496
 neighbor 2001:DB8:2112::2 maximum-prefix [1|20000]
 neighbor 2001:DB8:2112::2 ttl-security hops 2
 !
 address-family ipv4 unicast
 network 1.1.0.0/16
 neighbor 192.2.0.1 default-originate
 neighbor 192.2.0.1 prefix-list bogons-v4 in
 neighbor 192.2.0.1 prefix-list announce-v4 out
 exit-address-family
 !
 address-family ipv6 unicast
 network 2001:DB8:ABBA::/48
 neighbor 2001:DB8:2112::2 activate
 neighbor 2001:DB8:2112::2 prefix-list bogons-v6 in
 neighbor 2001:DB8:2112::2 prefix-list announce-v6 out
 exit-address-family
 !
 ipv4 route 1.1.0.0/16 Null0
 ipv4 prefix-list announce-v4 description Our allowed IPv4 routing announcements
 ipv4 prefix-list announce-v6 seq 5 permit 1.1.0.0/16
 ipv4 prefix-list announce-v6 seq 10 deny 0.0.0.0 le 32
 !
 ipv6 route 2001:DB8:ABBA::/48 Null0
 ipv6 prefix-list announce-v6 description Our allowed IPv6 routing announcements
 ipv6 prefix-list announce-v6 seq 5 permit 2001:DB8:ABBA::/48
 ipv6 prefix-list announce-v6 seq 10 deny ::/0 le 128
 !
```

Figure 10-3. MP-BGP router config example

Routing Table Size and TCAM Space

Routing protocols provide a picture of the current network to all the connected and participating routers (as well as the hosts attached to them). The more complete and up-to-date this picture, the more flexibility an engineer may have to shape routing policy to improve network performance, lower costs, and reduce or eliminate outages (and successfully sleep through the night without getting called by the NOC!).

How this picture of the network is created and applied to routing and packet switching has changed (and improved) greatly over the years. As we'll see, there is at least one aspect of IPv6 adoption that is problematic as a result of the current practice. But first, let's briefly review how we got here.

RIB versus FIB

A RIB, or routing information base, is essentially the routing table on a router. A router could have a number of ways of determining what networks are reachable to it, including the ones that are added as static routes, the ones that are directly connected, or the ones that are learned via a dynamic interior gateway protocol (IGP) like OSPF or EIGRP. Since every valid destination network is paired with at least one next hop or outgoing interface, routers must have some mechanism for determining the availability and desirability of one or more of these exit points. Most routing protocols provide this, but BGP, as well as some static routes, can have a next hop that is not directly reachable. This requires that the router perform a recursive lookup for these "remote" next hops. Because of this, it's not always possible to directly switch a packet without at least one recursive lookup.

Very early routers would look up the destination for each packet in the routing table and send it on its way.

Obviously, this process was very CPU- and memory-intensive and generally inefficient —especially for more modestly sized networks with a small number of unique destinations. *Fast switching* was created to increase the performance and efficiency of routing by caching the results of a recursive lookup so that ensuing packets to those same destinations wouldn't need to be processed by the router CPU but could be *fast-switched* instead. This was accomplished by copying the RIB to a forwarding information base (FIB) that didn't rely on process switching but could be pushed down to the port, along with the any cached next-hops, for fast packet switching.

FIBs are stored at the port level in something called ternary content addressable memory, or TCAM (alternately spelled $$$). Because TCAM is expensive, it is usually limited in size, meaning the number of supported FIB entries is subsequently limited as well. This means that the picture of the network on a given port might risk being incomplete if all the routes needed to complete that picture won't fit because of limited memory.

Complicating this is the continued growth of the IPv4 routing table, which now contains over 512,000 IPv4 prefixes (Figure 10-4).[7] As the impact of IPv4 exhaustion begins to be felt, more organizations will be looking for ways to sell some of their existing

---

7. As of Tuesday, August 12th, 2014: "The Internet Just Broke Under Its Own Weight…". (*http://bit.ly/internet-crash*)

---

allocations. This will result in more /24s being carved out for deployment along with the precipitous increase in routing table size this results in.

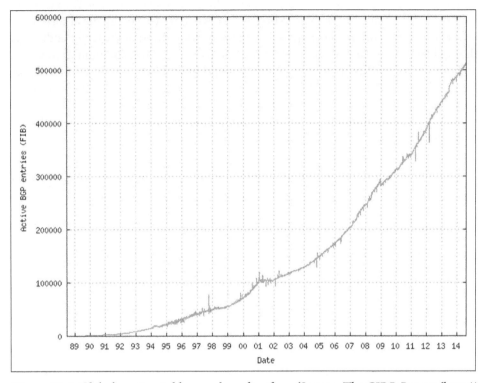

Figure 10-4. Global routing table, number of prefixes (Source: The CIDR Report (http:// www.cidr-report.org/))

Enter IPv6. One consequence of the adoption of IPv6 is a four-times increase over IPv4 in the amount of TCAM required for an IPv6 address entry, e.g., 32 bits for an IPv4 address, 128 bits for an IPv6 address. But wait, couldn't some memory be conserved by reserving only 64 bits of addressing for IPv6, given that we generally don't keep track of networks for routing for those prefixes smaller than a /64 in prefix size? Don't forget that we still have to accommodate networks for point-to-point links and loopback interfaces. Also, it's possible that some future IPv6 network architecture or configuration might rely on a network smaller than a /64, yet not one of the well-known exceptions to the *no subnets smaller than a /64* rule.

Since most ports are doing double duty supporting dual-stack, this has resulted in the necessity of creating profiles for the TCAM available on a given port. Such profiles require the engineer to pre-partition the available TCAM, allocating some TCAM for IPv4 routes and some for IPv6. If the architecture requires a higher degree of routing visibility and policy granularity for a particular interface (e.g., one of two or more egress ports to the Internet), a larger amount of TCAM may be needed.

As mentioned, the DFZ for IPv4 contains more than 512,000 routes. The IPv6 Internet routing table contains more than 18,000, which, when mutliplied by the at-least-two-times factor based on the bits required by the network portion of the larger address, is the equivalent of no fewer than 36,000 IPv4 prefixes. 512K is a common TCAM size and obviously insufficient to hold all DFZ IPv4 prefixes, much less the combined prefixes for both the IPv4 and IPv6 global routing table. For example, 512,000 IPv4 routes + 18,000(x2) IPv6 routes = 548K routes. As TCAM must be partitioned according to the rules of binary arithmetic, a profile for 512K of TCAM might provide 384K for IPv4 and 128K for IPv6.

While the current IPv6 global routing table would consume only half of the available partition, the IPv4 partition would be at 132% utilization, resulting in the unreachability of some significant portion of the IPv4 global routing table.

Increasing the TCAM size to, say, 1M provides both adequate memory for current IPv4 and IPv6 global routing tables, as well as additional memory overhead to accommodate the inevitable growth of the IPv4 and IPv6 routing tables. But with the greater expense of additional TCAM, you'll need to verify that the enhanced egress traffic control (with the more complex routing policy associated with it) is justified by the existing network architecture. For example, an enterprise would need to be multihomed to at least two providers to take advantage of such policies (and the extra visibility receiving the full routing table for both address families affords).

Mars Needs IP Address Blocks

A big part of keeping your IPv6 addresses reachable on the Internet is keeping your routing table free of *Martians*, *bogons*, and *fullbogons*. And by the way, keep in mind that all bogons are now Martians but not fullbogons.

Wait, what?!

Don't panic! In case you didn't know, all of these are merely somewhat whimsical idioms for bad (i.e., bogus) IP addresses and prefixes. So what's the difference between them (and what's the etymology of these somewhat silly terms)?

Martian

A Martian is any reserved or private address block.[8] We're likely most familiar with these from IPv4 as private addresses defined in RFC 1918.[9]

IPv6 Martians can be found in RFC 5156, *Special-Use IPv6 Addresses* (*http://bit.ly/ rfc-5156*), some prefixes of which we reviewed in Chapter 2. Table 10-1 shows the full list.[10]

Table 10-1. IPv6 Martians

Address(es)	Description	RFC
::1/128	Node-Scoped Unicast, loopback address	4291
::/128	Node-Scoped Unicast, unspecified address	4291
::ffff:0:0/96	IPv4-mapped addresses	4291
::/96	IPv4-compatible addresses (deprecated)	4291
fe80::/10	Link-Scoped Unicast	4291
fc00::/7	Unique-Local addresses (ULA)	4193
2001:0002::/48	Reserved for IPv6 Benchmarking	5180
2001:db8::/32	Documentation prefix	3849
100::/64	Remotely Triggered Black Hole addresses	6666
2001:10::/28	Overlay Rouf Cryptographic Hash IDentifiers (ORCHID)	4843
fec0::/10	Site-Local Unicast (deprecated)	3879
ff00::/8	Multicast	4291.[a]
5f00::/8	First 6bone allocation	1897
3ffe::/16	Second 6bone allocation	2471

[a] ff0e:/16 is globally scoped and may be permitted on the Internet.

Bogons

A bogon includes not only all Martians but also space that hasn't been allocated by IANA yet to a RIR. A bogon list can be generated by reviewing both IANA's updated list of reserved and allocated prefixes, as well as the combination of lists of prefixes not yet assigned by IANA to the RIRs. However, Team Cymru maintains a list of

---

8. Nothing should ever originate from the Red Planet!

9. We may be less familiar with the other two RFCs that define Martians in IPv4—RFC 5735 (*http://bit.ly/ rfc-5735*) (i.e., *Special Use IPv4 Addresses*) includes all the other reserved addresses along with those already defined as private in RFC 1918. Meanwhile, RFC 6598 (*http://bit.ly/rfc-6598*) (i.e., *IANA-Reserved IPv4 Prefix for Shared Address Space*) more recently defined a /10 of IPv4 addresses to share among those providers deploying CGN. Feel free to look up these additional ranges, as we won't clutter up our beautiful IPv6 address planning book with more IPv4 addresses than necessary!

10. Not all address ranges in RFC 5156 are Martians. For example, the Teredo prefix (2001::/32) and 6to4 prefix (2002::/16) may be advertised on the Internet where these services are offered.

bogons and fullbogons (explained below) that can be retrieved manually or automatically using an Internet routing registry (IRR).[11]

Fullbogons

A fullbogon is a concept (and accompanying list) invented by Team Cymru after they realized that the existing bogon lists were not granular enough, given that they didn't also contain allocations from IANA to the RIRs that had not yet been assigned to ISPs or end-users.

Attack of the Bogons!

At this point, you may be asking yourself (if you don't already know from bitter experience), what's so bad about bogons anyway?

Black-hat hackers and assorted reprobates use bogons to provide spoofed source addresses to enable denial-of-service (DoS) and distributed denial-of-service (DDoS) attacks. Any Internet routability of bogon prefixes makes such malicious efforts easier.

The miscreants responsible for these attacks would like nothing better than to have a new network protocol at their disposal—especially one for which operational and security standards are still maturing, leaving potential paths of exploit open and available.

It's incumbent on all of us deploying IPv6 for the first time to make sure that we maintain (or even improve) our security policy and enforcement in IPv6.

What this means in the context of our current topic is making sure that you properly filter bogons (preferably inbound and outbound) at your Internet edge.

Bogon Etymology

So how does a peculiar little word like *bogon* come into existence anyway?

Well, according to programmer, hacker, and sys/netadmin lore, *bogons* are the quanta of the property of being bogus (i.e., bogusness, or *bogosity* if you prefer). Further clarification for the ESL set: *bogus* has traditionally meant fake or counterfeit, but according to some American slang has come to mean undesirable or useless (i.e., "suckiness") in slang. Network folks have apparently found a nice overlap of the traditional definition and the slang one in the fact that a bogon prefix is used to counterfeit packets *and* create general, shall we say, *suckage*.

---

11. *The Bogon Reference—Team Cymru (http://bit.ly/cymru-bogons)*. Team Cymru Research NFP describes itself as "a specialized Internet security research firm and 501(c)3 non-profit dedicated to making the Internet more secure…Team Cymru helps organizations identify and eradicate problems in their networks, providing insight that improves lives."

Filtering Bogons

So how do we go about filtering bogons in IPv6? Before we look at the specifics, let's briefly review the general architecture and configuration to which such filtering is applied.

Unless you're running a service provider network with lots of peers and IP transit connections to the Internet, chances are you are connected to one or two (a few at the most) ISPs.

Those among us running singly-homed networks probably needn't worry about edge filtering because, in all but the most unusual cases, they wouldn't be running BGP. Instead, they would typically have static routes for both Internet ingress and egress. Incoming traffic would be routed to their network by a route on the ISP side. Outgoing traffic would be routed by a default route to the Internet.

However, where a network is dual- or multihomed and using BGP to share routes with two or more upstream ISPs, proper prefix filtering is a must.

Figure 10-5 shows an enterprise network customer multihomed to two providers.

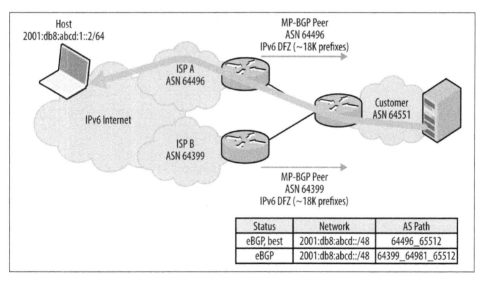

Figure 10-5. Egress route optimization, multihomed network

Say the enterprise customer would like to be able to control outbound traffic flows and send them via ISP A *or* ISP B, depending on performance, based on the shortest path, to a particular flow's destination, e.g., in the figure's example, responding to a request for content from a host located at the address 2001:db8:abcd:1::2/64.

For traffic optimization, the customer would need to be configured, and have sufficient router memory, to receive the entire global routing table. As discussed earlier in the chapter, there are currently slightly more than 500K routes for IPv4 and more than 18K routes for IPv6. The full table allows the enterprise content server to select the best egress path, e.g., shown in the figure as the path to the host through ISP A).

In instances where basic redundancy is desired (or router memory is insufficient), the customer could instead receive a default route from each ISP and preference an outbound link, according to criteria like best performance or price (Figure 10-6).[12]

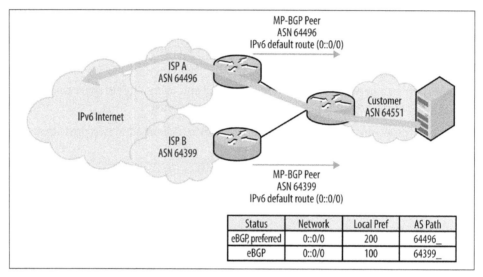

Status	Network	Local Pref	AS Path
eBGP, preferred	0::0/0	200	64496_
eBGP	0::0/0	100	64399_

Figure 10-6. Basic redundancy, multihomed IPv6 network

In either case, the customer would need to be configured to advertise its IP netblock(s) to both ISPs, providing redundancy and more optimal performance for inbound traffic.

Bogon filtering is configured for both sent and received routes on the customer's BGP sessions with each of the ISPs. If they are adhering to best practices, the ISPs will likewise be filtering the routes they send to, and receive from, the customer.[13]

Note that the provider's outbound announcement immediately becomes the customer's received routes, just as the customer's become the provider's. Thus, in an ideal world, a perfectly maintained bogon filter applied outbound on the provider's BGP configura-

---

12. The customer might also opt to receive the network prefixes of the provider's other customers along with the default route. While not requiring as much memory as the full table, this BGP policy at least ensures that egress traffic will select the provider with the shortest path to learned, more specific destination networks.

13. Belt *and* suspenders, baby!

tion and session would preclude the need for a bogon filter on the customer's inbound BGP configuration (and vice versa).

So if you trust your provider as you would your brain surgeon, feel free to leave that ingress filter off. After all, it's one less configuration you'd have to deal with. While you're at it, see if you can convince your provider that you'll keep your filters up-to-date with the latest bogons and meticulously applied so the provider can do the same. What could possibly go wrong?

Mild sarcasm aside, bad routes filtered at your provider's egress would never clutter up your link to the ISP before being dropped anyway when received by your router and filtered by what should be, in an ideal world, the exact same filter.

But as we know, in the less-than-ideal world of network operation, we can't guarantee that our ISP will never accidentally advertise bogons to us, any more than we can guarantee our ISP that some fat fingers or a security breach on our end won't result in us announcing garbage to them.

Thus, for the best security, bogon filters should be applied to our sent and received BGP routing advertisements. And the more complete and up-to-date the bogon list, the better the protection.

Table 10-2 summarizes filter sources in order of completeness.

Table 10-2. Filter sources, from least to most complete

Filter	Source
Martians	Reserved and special-use IP addresses
Bogons	Martians + IP netblocks not yet allocated to the RIRs by IANA
Fullbogons	Bogons + IP netblocks allocated to the RIRs but as yet unassigned

As you've probably inferred, the list of netblocks allocated by IANA to the RIRs, as well as the netblocks allocated to the RIRs but not yet assigned to ISPs or end-users, changes over time.

For example, since IANA handed out the last of the unallocated IPv4 netblocks back in 2011, bogons now include only martians. But the fullbogons list will continue to change. As a result, our filters need to be updated often enough to track and accommodate these changes.

Perhaps the best way to keep up with changes is to automate the whole process by peering with a bogon list maintainer (e.g., Team Cymru) or an IRR (e.g., RADb). Such a configuration is beyond the scope of this book but can be found on the Team Cymru website (*https://team-cymru.org/*).

Finally, the appropriate filtering logic for catching IPv6 bogons is a bit different than it is in IPv4. The reason is that the list of fullbogons for IPv6 is in the neighborhood of 50K prefixes,[14] and is around 20 times larger than the list for IPv4.

More than 50K entries is a whole lot of config real estate and, unless maintained automatically, an opportunity for incorrect new entries or changes with typos. As a result, it makes more sense to explicitly allow only the known valid IPv6 prefixes while implicitly denying everything else (Figure 10-7).

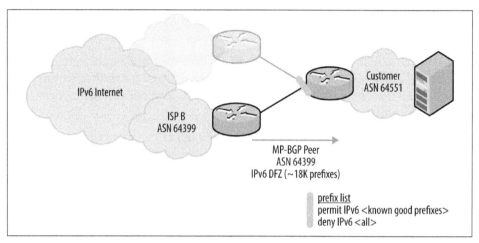

Figure 10-7. Fullbogon filtering in IPv6

This is the reverse of the filtering logic we apply in IPv4 with its more manageable fullbogon list: explicitly deny the bogons while implicitly allowing everything else (Figure 10-8).

---

14. This is more than twice as many entries as the actual IPv6 global routing table!

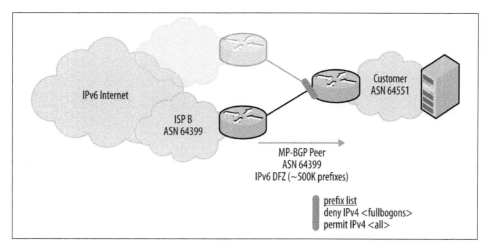

Figure 10-8. Fullbogon filtering in IPv4

Summary

In this chapter, we covered some of the critical operational aspects of keeping the pre-fixes of your IPv6 address plan reachable.

As we've learned, the routing protocols we're most familiar with from our IPv4 operational environments all have IPv6 versions. But we'll need to take care to select the right one based on balancing the need for operational continuity with the need for IPv4 production network stability. The former is arguably provided best by using the same routing protocol for IPv6 as we use for IPv4 (along with perhaps single-topology mode where available and required by any limits on router resources). Meanwhile, using a different routing protocol (or dual-topology mode) may provide better isolation and fault tolerance of both IPv4 and IPv6 networks (but especially the existing IPv4 production network).

Proper filtering of routes received from, and announced to, your ISP will also help keep your IPv6 network prefixes reachable. We covered the differences between bogon lists in the respective address families and the contrasting filtering logic required to catch them. We also need to ensure that we're not announcing garbage to our peers, even if it's just our upstream ISP.

Glossary

GENTEEL, adj. Refined, after the fashion of a gent.
Observe with care, my son, the distinction I reveal:
A gentleman is gentle and a gent genteel.
Heed not the definitions your "Unabridged" presents,
For dictionary makers are generally gents.

— Ambrose Bierce
The Devil's Dictionary (1911)

Allocation

(As compared with *assignment*) Formally, the apportionment of an IP address prefix to a RIR by IANA or to a LIR by a RIR. Informally, any allotment of an IP prefix which will be further subnetted for smaller allotments (referred to as *assignments*).

Assignment

Formally, the apportionment of an IP address prefix by an ISP to an end-user, but sometimes used interchangeably with *allocation* and/or to mean any allotted prefix.

Bogon

An invalid (i.e., *bogus*) routing prefix that should never appear in the global routing table. Perhaps the most well-known example of a bogon is RFC 1918, or private, IPv4 address space. Addresses from bogon prefixes can be used by hackers and miscreants to spoof source addresses in malicious packets and therefore should be filtered, ideally inbound and outbound, at an organization's network edge.

Bisection

An IP allocation method (preferred by service providers and RIRs) that leaves the maximum amount of space between each prefix assignment (while still providing enough prefixes of the desired subnet size for immediate use). Subsequent allocations may evenly divide the space remaining between original assignments. Bisection is better suited to allowing aggregation of current and future assignments.

Bogons

IP allocations that have not been allocated to a RIR by IANA and should never appear in the Internet routing table. Many bogons are private and reserved addresses as specified in RFCs 1918, 5735, and 6598. See also, fullbogons.

BYOD

Bring Your Own Device, the trend of employees bringing personal mobile computing devices (e.g., smartphones, tablets, etc.) into the workplace.

CAFT

Copious Amounts of Free Time, all the extra time you have to, upon heedless request, immediately drop whatever you were previously asked to accomplish and take up, with top priority, a brand new task. For example, "Yes, of course I can watch this latest video from HR on maximizing productivity: I'll do it with my Copious Amounts of Free Time."

CIDR

Classless Inter-domain Routing, allows for the division of an IP address's network and host portion along any bit boundary. (This is in contrast to classful networking that defined strict 8-bit boundaries.) The greater granularity of address assignment, subnetting, and routing offered by CIDR permitted both conservation and better aggregation of IPv4 addresses. CIDR (with CIDR notation) is used in both IPv4 and IPv6. In IPv4, CIDR is accomplished through Variable Length Subnet Masking (VLSM).

CIDR Notation

CIDR notation is a method of IP address presentation where the number of bits reserved for the network (and implying the remaining host bits) is appended to the end of the network prefix after a forward slash. For example, CIDR notation for an IPv4 address prefix with 24 bits reserved for the network (leaving 8 bits for hosts) would look like this: 192.168.10.0/24. In IPv6, a 64 bit interface prefix would be represented like this: 2001:db8:1000:abba::/64.

Classful Networks

(Also referred to as class A, B, and C networks). IPv4 prefixes characterized by either 8, 16, or 24 bits in the network portion of the address. Classful networks were used in the early days of the Internet to create hierarchical routing but were eventually deprecated in favor of network prefixes that could be any length by using VLSM and CIDR. This provided additional address space while attempting to keep in check the number of IPv4 prefixes in the global routing table.

Contiguous Subnets

Contiguous subnets are subnets of equal size that are adjacent to each other. Contiguous subnets that are divisible by factors of 2^n can be aggregated into larger blocks, or *summarized*, in order to reduce the number of entries in the routing table. By comparison, discontiguous subnets cannot be aggregated into larger blocks without rendering any intervening blocks unreachable.

Convergence

A state of agreement by all the routers participating in a dynamic routing protocol about what the network topology looks like. A network is *converged* (i.e., the routing is stable) when all routing nodes have received all updates and performed all path calcluations for every known destination and no immediate changes to the topology (outages, reconfigurations) have occurred. In networks running both IPv4 and IPv6, convergence for each address family is acheived independently (unless running in single-topology mode for IS-IS or OSPFv3 with IPv4 as an address family).

DAD

Or duplicate address detection; a component of Neighbor Discovery that verifies whether an autoconfigured address is already in use on the link. Autoconfigured IPv6 addresses are in a *tentative* state until the node sends a Neighbor Solicitation with its proposed address. If it doesn't receive a response, it assumes that no node is using the proposed address and the address is activated. Otherwise, no address is configured.

DDI

DNS, DHCP, and IP address management, a class of technology whose purpose it is to facilitate network control and automation by providing a collection of tools and practices that optimize network addressing and naming, as well as leverage the data associated with it.

DFZ

Default-free Zone (see Global Routing Table).

Deprecated Address

An autoconfigured IPv6 address whose peferred lifetime (but not valid lifetime) has elapsed. Applications should not use any deprecated address for new connections, but may use such an address for existing connections.

Dual-Stack Network

Or, dual-stack IPv6. A network architecture where IPv4 and IPv6 are configured and run in parallel on the same network infrastructure. Contrast with IPv6-only networks (e.g., where no IPv4 is configured) or IPv4 to IPv6 transition/translation where IPv4-only and IPv6-only networks communicate through transition technologies (see below).

EGP

Exterior Gateway Protocol is a routing protocol optimized for routing between autonomous systems (AS), i.e., networks that are under one administrative authority. For example, BGP is the exterior gateway protocol of the Internet.

Fullbogon

The set of bogons (see above) plus any IP space that has been allocated to a RIR by IANA but is not yet assigned to an ISP or end-user. Like bogons, fullbogons should never appear in the global routing table.

Global Routing Table

(aka the DFZ) is the routing table of all prefixes currently being announced on the Internet via BGP. It's called the default-free zone because, ideally, it never contains a default route (i.e., a route to 0.0.0.0/0 or 0::0/0). Since IPv4 and IPv6 constitute separate address families, there is one DFZ for each. As of the time of this writing, the IPv4 DFZ numbered just over 500,000 prefixes while the IPv6 DFZ was in the neighborhood of 18,000 (roughly 3.6% the size of the IPv4 table).

IGP

Interior Gateway Protocol, a routing protocol optimized for routing with an autonomous system (a network under one administrative authority). Examples of IGPs for IPv6 include OSPFv3, IPv6 IS-IS, and (Cisco-proprietary) EIGRP for IPv6.

IPAM

IP Address Management is the collection of practices and tools utilized by an organization to effectively manage both IPv4 and IPv6 address resources. IPAM software tracks IP addresses and, in some cases, can correlate them to DHCP(v6) and DNS; technology collectively referred to as DDI (i.e., DNS, DHCP, and IP Address Management). Though formal IPAM tools have in the past been considered optional by some organizations with lightweight addressing requirements, it is largely considered a necessity in effectively tracking IPv6, given the larger address space and more complex representation.

IPv6-Only

A nirvana-like network configuration and topology in which only IPv6 addresses are used and IPv4 addresses are but a strange and fading memory, like 53-byte ATM cells or thick ethernet vampire taps.

ISP

Internet Service Provider, an LIR.

Invalid Address

An autoconfigured IPv6 address whose valid lifetime has elapsed. Invalid addresses may not be used for any connections.

LIR

Local Internet Registry, an ISP.

ND

Neighbor Discovery is a required protocol used in IPv6 on a local link to perform various tasks, including discovering neighboring nodes, facilitating host address autoconfiguration, determining link layer addresses of other nodes (layer 2 to layer 3 mapping, replacing ARP in IPv4), detecting duplicate addresses, and discovering routers and DNS servers. ND relies on five ICMPv6 packet types to accomplish these tasks: Router Solicitation, Router Advertisement, Neighbor Solicitation, Neighbor Advertisement, Redirect.

Native IPv6

An IPv6 network that doesn't need to rely on any IPv4 in order to function.

PA Allocation

Provider assigned allocation (sometimes referred to as a *provider aggregateable allocation*) is an allocation of IP addresses (either IPv4 or IPv6) to an end-user organization from an ISP or LIR. PA allocations are not portable (i.e., cannot be announced via another ISP or provider) and must be numbered out of and returned if service with the allocating ISP is terminated.

PI Allocation

Provider independent allocation. IP addresses (either IPv4 or IPv6) are allocated and registered to an end-user organization from a RIR. PI allocations are portable, meaning any connecting ISP should receive and reannounce them. Since PI allocations are registered directly to the end-user organization, renumbering when switching ISPs is avoided.

Preferred Address

One of two address states (the other being *deprecated*) of a *valid* auto-assigned IPv6 address. Preferred addresses are addresses whose configured preferred lifetime has not elapsed. They are unrestricted and can be used by applications for any communication, new or existing (contrast with deprecated address).

Privacy Extensions

(aka IPv6 Privacy or Temporary Addresses) is a method whereby the interface identifier (the right-most 64 bits) of an autoconfigured IPv6 address is randomized to obscure the identity of the node originating any traffic.

RA

Router Advertisement is an ICMPv6 packet of type 133 that contains fields that instruct the host what form of auto-addressing (if any) it is to support (stateful or stateless DHCPv6 or SLAAC). It also contains IPv6 prefix information that a host will use to self-configure if SLAAC is the configured mechanism. Finally, it instructs the host about the available gateway(s) to use.

RIR

Regional Internet Registry (or Registries) are the geographically regional organizations responsible for managing and allocating Internet number resources like IPv4 and IPv6 addresses and Autonomous System Numbers (ASNs). These numbers are allocated to them by the Internet Assigned Numbers Authority (IANA). There are five RIRs: ARIN, RIPE, APNIC, LACNIC, and AFRINIC (see separate entries).

SDN

Software Defined Networking is a recent networking architecture designed around the decoupling of an openly programmable network control plane from a forwarding (data) plane that is abstractly programmed using protocols like OpenFlow. Such an abstraction is usually isolated inside a router or switch for the primary purpose of supporting legacy protocols that often have limited flexibility in dynamically improving network performance or enhancing functionality.

SLAAC

Stateless Address Autoconfiguration is a method that nodes (i.e., hosts) use to auto-configure addresses in IPv6. SLAAC relies on ND Router Advertisements via ICMPv6 to receive prefix information and complete the address configuration process. SLAAC is used less frequently than DHCPv6 in enterprise environments where greater control of hosts is desired.

Single-Stack IPv6

Also referred to as *IPv6-only*; a network that exclusively runs IPv6. In contrast to a dual-stack network that runs both IPv4 and IPv6.

Stateful DHCPv6

Autoconfiguration of a host IPv6 address by a DHCPv6 server. Hosts must still obtain their default gateway information via router advertisement (RA).

Stateless DHCPv6

Autoconfiguration of a host IPv6 address by SLAAC with other configuration settings (DNS servers, domain search list, etc.) provided by a DHCPv6 server.

TCAM

Ternary Content Addressable Memory is specialized memory used by routers to store routing tables for fast lookups. TCAM can be configurable to allow for both IPv4 and IPv6 routes to be stored and the additional expense of TCAM may limit the number of routes available to either address family based on a preconfigured profile.

TCAM Profile

A router or switch configuration that logically partitions port or interface TCAM to provide FIB space for both IPv4 and IPv6 prefixes.

Transition Technology

Alternately referred to as a *translation technology*, any solution with one or more interfaces that translates packets between IPv4 and IPv6, allowing an IPv4 endpoint to communicate with an IPv6 endpoint. Transition technologies were ostensibly designed to ease the *transition* between IPv4 and IPv6. Transition technologies include DNS64/NAT64, 464XLAT, DS-Lite, and MAP-E and MAP-T.

VLSM

Variable Length Subnet Masking is a method of creating subnets of an arbitrary length from a prefix by using a variable length bit mask (as compared to a fixed mask of 8, 16 or 24 bits, used for defining *classful* addressing prefixes of a subsequently fixed size, e.g., class A, B, and C networks). CIDR notation indicates the the number of bits in the chosen mask and provides a more human-readable format for determining the size of a given subnet.

Valid Address

An autoconfigured IPv6 address whose valid lifetime has not elapsed. Valid addresses can be either preferred or deprecated (see above).

Planning Worksheets

Use the following worksheets to help apply some of the principles and methods from the book to your own addressing plan.

Note: Soft copies of these worksheets are available at *www.ipv6.works.*

IPv6 Address Plan Worksheet			
Description	Value	Notes	
Company name:			Intersite Planning
IPv6 Prefix from RIR (or ISP):			
# of region(s):		(by RIR: e.g., NA, LATAM, EMEA, APAC, AFRICA)	
# of countries:			
# of subregions:			
# of sites:			
Predicted growth per region:		Sites added per year	
Location(s) with Internet:			
Prefix from RIR (or ISP):			
Hierarchy Level 0:		e.g., /32	
Level 1:		e.g., /36	
Level 2:		e.g., /40	
Level 3:		e.g., /44	
Level 4:		e.g., /48	
# of locations:			Intrasite Planning
# of functions:			
# of departments:			
# of VLANs:			
# of interfaces:			
Predicted growth per site:		Locations or functions added per year	
Site prefix		e.g., /48	
Hierarchy Level 0:		e.g., /48	
Level 1:		e.g., /52	
Level 2:		e.g., /56	
Level 3:		e.g., /60	
Level 4:		e.g., /64	

Figure A-1. IPv6 Address planning worksheet

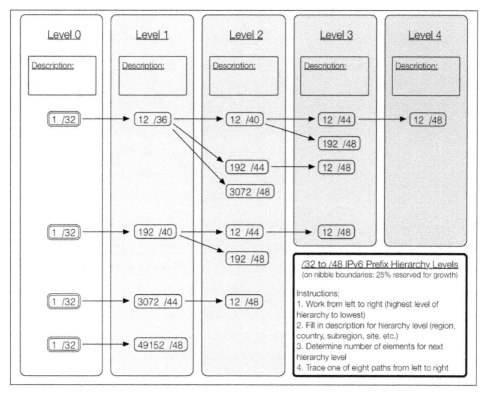

Figure A-2. Intersite (/32 to /48) hierarchy planner

Site	CIDR	Subnet	Description	Element	CIDR	Subnet	Description	Element	CIDR	Subnet	Description	Element	CIDR	Subnet	Description
	/36	:0000::/36	reserved		/40	:1000::/40	reserved		/44	:1100::/44	reserved		/48	:1110::/48	reserved
	/36	:1000::/36			/40	:1100::/40			/44	:1110::/44			/48	:1111::/48	
	/36	:2000::/36			/40	:1200::/40			/44	:1120::/44			/48	:1112::/48	
	/36	:3000::/36			/40	:1300::/40			/44	:1130::/44			/48	:1113::/48	
	/36	:4000::/36			/40	:1400::/40			/44	:1140::/44			/48	:1114::/48	
	/36	:5000::/36			/40	:1500::/40			/44	:1150::/44			/48	:1115::/48	
	/36	:6000::/36			/40	:1600::/40			/44	:1160::/44			/48	:1116::/48	
/32	/36	:7000::/36		/36	/40	:1700::/40		/40	/44	:1170::/44		/44	/48	:1117::/48	
	/36	:8000::/36			/40	:1800::/40			/44	:1180::/44			/48	:1118::/48	
	/36	:9000::/36			/40	:1900::/40			/44	:1190::/44			/48	:1119::/48	
	/36	:a000::/36			/40	:1a00::/40			/44	:11a0::/44			/48	:111a::/48	
	/36	:b000::/36			/40	:1b00::/40			/44	:11b0::/44			/48	:111b::/48	
	/36	:c000::/36			/40	:1c00::/40			/44	:11c0::/44			/48	:111c::/48	
	/36	:d000::/36			/40	:1d00::/40			/44	:11d0::/44			/48	:111d::/48	
	/36	:e000::/36			/40	:1e00::/40			/44	:11e0::/44			/48	:111e::/48	
	/36	:f000::/36	reserved		/40	:1f00::/40	reserved		/44	:11f0::/44	reserved		/48	:111f::/48	reserved

Prefix from RIR (or ISP):

Figure A-3. Intersite subnet chart

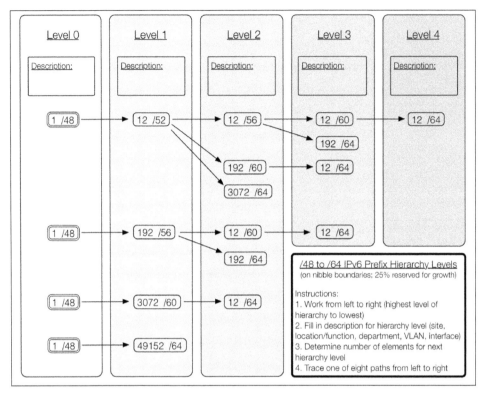

Figure A-4. Intrasite (/48 to /64) Hierarchy Planner

Site Prefix: _____

Site	CIDR	Subnet	Description	Element	CIDR	Subnet	Description	Element	CIDR	Subnet	Description	Element	CIDR	Subnet	Description
	/52	:0000::/52	reserved		/56	:1000::/56	reserved		/60	:1100::/60	reserved		/64	:1110::/64	reserved
	/52	:1000::/52			/56	:1100::/56			/60	:1110::/60			/64	:1111::/64	
	/52	:2000::/52			/56	:1200::/56			/60	:1120::/60			/64	:1112::/64	
	/52	:3000::/52			/56	:1300::/56			/60	:1130::/60			/64	:1113::/64	
	/52	:4000::/52			/56	:1400::/56			/60	:1140::/60			/64	:1114::/64	
	/52	:5000::/52			/56	:1500::/56			/60	:1150::/60			/64	:1115::/64	
	/52	:6000::/52			/56	:1600::/56			/60	:1160::/60			/64	:1116::/64	
/48	/52	:7000::/52		/52	/56	:1700::/56		/56	/60	:1170::/60		/60	/64	:1117::/64	
	/52	:8000::/52			/56	:1800::/56			/60	:1180::/60			/64	:1118::/64	
	/52	:9000::/52			/56	:1900::/56			/60	:1190::/60			/64	:1119::/64	
	/52	:a000::/52			/56	:1a00::/56			/60	:11a0::/60			/64	:111a::/64	
	/52	:b000::/52			/56	:1b00::/56			/60	:11b0::/60			/64	:111b::/64	
	/52	:c000::/52			/56	:1c00::/56			/60	:11c0::/60			/64	:111c::/64	
	/52	:d000::/52			/56	:1d00::/56			/60	:11d0::/60			/64	:111d::/64	
	/52	:e000::/52			/56	:1e00::/56			/60	:11e0::/60			/64	:111e::/64	
	/52	:f000::/52	reserved		/56	:1f00::/56	reserved		/60	:11f0::/60	reserved		/64	:111f::/64	reserved

Figure A-5. Intrasite Subnet Chart

IPv6 Prefix Maps

These prefix maps may help you more quickly visualize two of the different subnetting methods presented in Chapter 4. Figure B-1 illustrates the basic format of the prefix maps that follow: Incrementing the leftmost bits (Figure B-2) or the rightmost bits (Figure B-3) of a prefix.

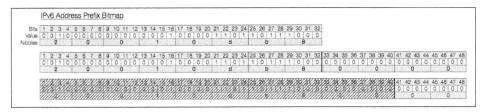

Figure B-1. IPv6 Address prefix bitmap

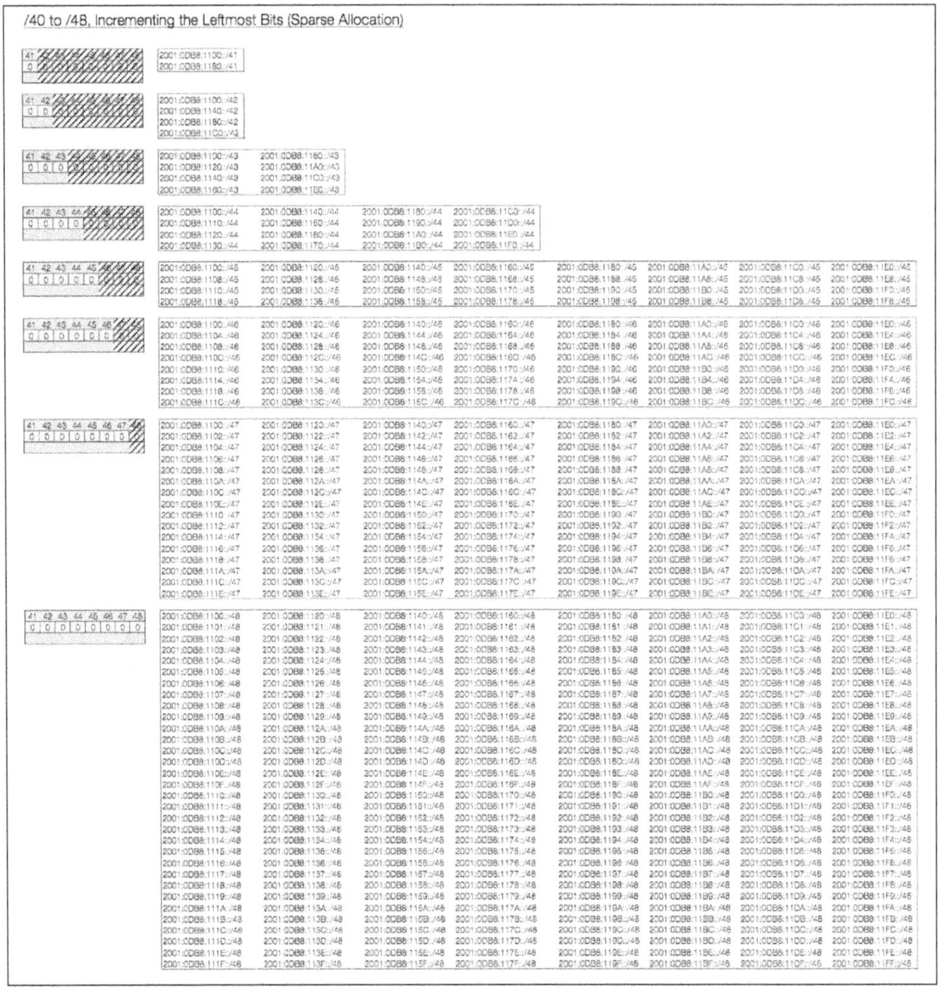

Figure B-2. /40 to /48, Incrementing the leftmost bits (sparse allocation)

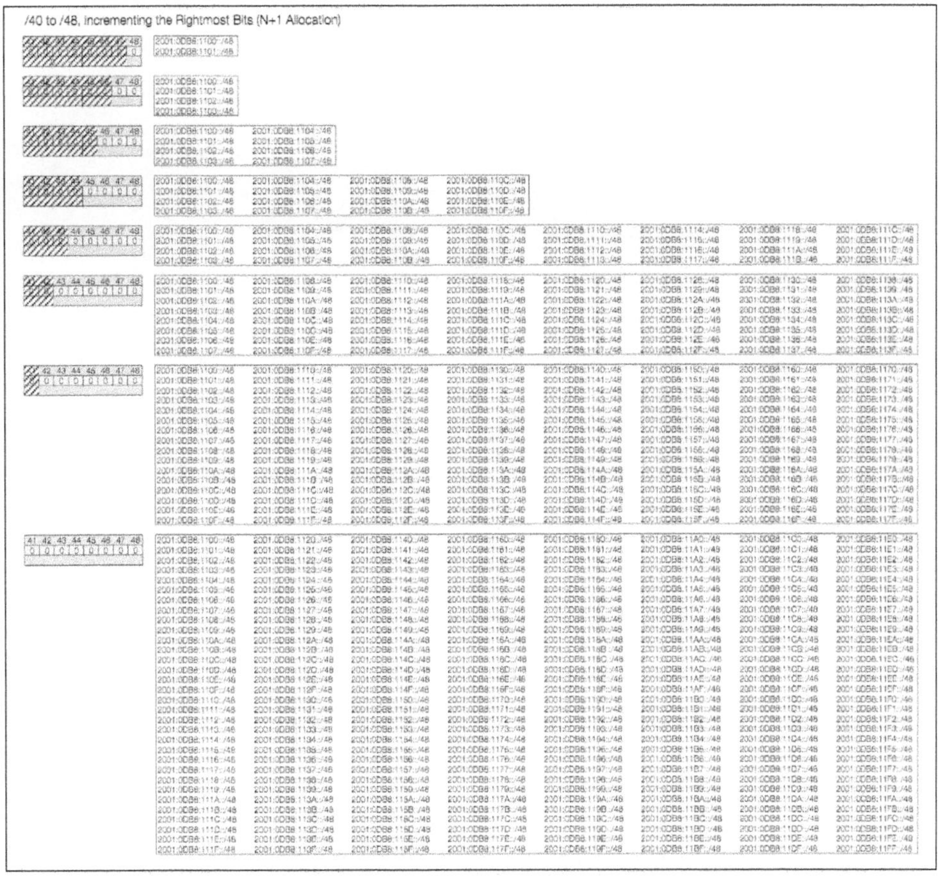

/40 to /48, Incrementing the Rightmost Bits (N+1 Allocation)

Figure B-3. /40 to /48, Incrementing the rightmost bits (N+1 allocation)

Recommended Reading

Davies, Joseph. *Understanding IPv6: Your Essential Guide to IPv6 on Windows Networks* (*http://bit.ly/understand-ipv6*), 3rd ed. Microsoft Press, 2012.

Grossetete, Patrick; Popoviciu, Ciprian; Wettling, Fred. *Global IPv6 Strategies: From Business Analysis to Operational Planning* (*http://bit.ly/globalipv6*). Cisco Press, 2008.

Grundemann, Chris, et al. *Best Current Operational Practice (BCOP)—IPv6 Subnetting* (*http://bit.ly/bcop-ipv6*). 2012.

Hagen, Silvia. *IPv6 Essentials* (*http://bit.ly/ipv6-3e*), 3rd ed. O'Reilly, 2014.

Hagen, Silvia. *Planning for IPv6* (*http://bit.ly/planning-ipv6*). O'Reilly, 2011.

Hogg, Scott; Vyncke, Eric. *IPv6 Security* (*http://bit.ly/ipv6-security*). Cisco Press, 2008.

Horley, Ed. *Practical IPv6 for Windows Administrators* (*http://bit.ly/prac-ipv6-wa*). Apress, 2013.

Liu, Cricket. *DNS and BIND on IPv6* (*http://bit.ly/dns-bind*). O'Reilly, 2011.

McFarland, Shannon; Sambi, Muninder; et al. *IPv6 for Enterprise Networks* (*http://bit.ly/ipv6-enterprise*). Cisco Press, 2011.

Rooney, Timothy. *IP Address Management Principles and Practices* (*http://bit.ly/ipa-mpp*). John Wiley & Sons, Inc., 2011.

SURFnet/RIPE NCC. *Preparing an IPv6 Addressing Plan* (*http://bit.ly/prep-ipv6*), 2nd ed. 2013.

Index

We'd like to hear your suggestions for improving our indexes. Send email to index@oreilly.com.

MP-BGP, 224
multi-homed organizations
    bogon filtering and, 231
Multi-Protocol BGP, 224
multicast addresses, 28
multicast scopes, 28
multihomed organizations, 123
multiprotocol networks, 8

N

N+1 allocations, 111
National Institute of Standards and Technology
    (NIST), 206
Neighbor Discovery (ND), 2, 32
    cache exhaustion, 34
neighborhood area network (NAN), 213
Network Address Translation (NAT), 2, 35–39
    address exhaustion and, 10–13
    addressing and, 35–39
    deficiencies of, 62
    end-to-end model of Internet and, 35
    for ISPs, 37
    IPv4 and, 35–39
    performance and, 36
    reliance on, and internal IPv6 adoption, 62
    security and, 36
network containers, 170
Network Control Protocol, 6
Network Layer Reachability Information
    (NLRI), 224
networks
    consolidating after mergers/acquisitions, 27
    design principles of, 12
    IPAM and, 166
    multiprotocol, 8
    resizing, 173
    segmentation, 73
    splitting, 173
    testing under load, 55
nibble boundaries, 75
non-nibble subnetting, 81–83
    defining from left-most bits, 84
    defining from middle bits, 85–86
    defining from right-most bits, 84
    with ipv6gen, 87
Number Resource Policy Manual (NRPM), 127
numeric subnets, 86

O

Orans, Lawrence, 181
OSPFv3 Address Families, 222
out-of-region announcements, 129

P

packet flow for CGN networks, 37
packet headers, 32
parent networks, 170
path vector protocol, 220
performance
    N+1 allocations and, 112
    NAT and, 36
    routing efficiency and, 72–75
    summarization and, 74
ping-pong attack, 34
plan outline, 139
Platform as a Service (PaaS), 207
point-to-point link subnets, 33
policy
    compliance, 174
    cycles, 168
Practical IPv6 for Windows Administrators
    (Horley), 189
Prefix Information message option (RAs), 199
prefixes
    adding, 175
    legibility of, 76
    splitting, 177
privacy extensions, 35
private Class A networks, 11
private cloud services, 207
Production Loopback Addresses example, 39–
    43
properly-sized initial IPv6 allocation, 92
provider assigned (PA)
    allocations, 123
    GUA, 28
provider independent (PI) allocations, 123
    disadvantages of, 124
Provider Independent (PI) allocations
    renumbering projects and, 199
provider independent (PI) GUA, 28
PTR DNS records, 190
public cloud services, 207

About the Author

Tom Coffeen is currently the Chief IPv6 Evangelist at Infoblox, where he is focused on helping customers deploy IPv6 and enhancing Infoblox's IPv6 product strategy. He can also often be found speaking at IPv6 and network engineering conferences around the world. Prior to Infoblox, Tom was the VP of Network Architecture at the global CDN and service provider Limelight Networks, where he managed their deployment of IPv6 beginning in 2008. He's been professionally designing, building, managing, breaking, fixing, and occasionally destroying computer networks since 1997. Before 1997, Tom worked as a recording artist, session guitarist, audio engineer, and producer for various bands including Machines of Loving Grace, Grievous Angels, and Beats the Hell Out of Me. (He still makes records occasionally.) A native of Phoenix, Arizona, Tom now lives in San Francisco with his partner, Eva, and their elderly cattle dog, Wojciehowicz.

Colophon

The animal on the cover of *IPv6 Address Planning* is the Pander's ground jay (*Podoces panderi*), also known as a chough thrush, grey ground jay, or Turkestan ground jay. These birds are members of the *Corvidae* family, which includes crows and jays. They can be found in central Asia, particularly the countries of Kazakhstan, Turkmenistan, and Uzbekistan.

They are small birds with slim, slightly curved beaks and sand-colored plumage. Their tails are black, and they also have a large black spot on their breast. Pander's ground jays live in desert habitats with plenty of bushes for cover, but will also forage near human settlements.

As their common name suggests, ground jays spend most of their time on the ground, and are indeed more adept at running than flying. Their beaks are well adapted for digging and probing the earth as they forage for a diet of insects, seeds, and plant matter.

Birds of the *Corvidae* family are very intelligent, with a brain-to-body mass ratio equal to that of great apes (and only slightly lower than humans).

Many of the animals on O'Reilly covers are endangered; all of them are important to the world. To learn more about how you can help, go to *animals.oreilly.com*.

The cover image is from *Riverside Natural History*. The cover fonts are URW Typewriter and Guardian Sans. The text font is Adobe Minion Pro; the heading font is Adobe Myriad Condensed; and the code font is Dalton Maag's Ubuntu Mono.

Get even more for your money.

Join the O'Reilly Community, and register the O'Reilly books you own. It's free, and you'll get:

- $4.99 ebook upgrade offer
- 40% upgrade offer on O'Reilly print books
- Membership discounts on books and events
- Free lifetime updates to ebooks and videos
- Multiple ebook formats, DRM FREE
- Participation in the O'Reilly community
- Newsletters
- Account management
- 100% Satisfaction Guarantee

Signing up is easy:

1. Go to: oreilly.com/go/register
2. Create an O'Reilly login.
3. Provide your address.
4. Register your books.

Note: English-language books only

To order books online:
oreilly.com/store

For questions about products or an order:
orders@oreilly.com

To sign up to get topic-specific email announcements and/or news about upcoming books, conferences, special offers, and new technologies:
elists@oreilly.com

For technical questions about book content:
booktech@oreilly.com

To submit new book proposals to our editors:
proposals@oreilly.com

O'Reilly books are available in multiple DRM-free ebook formats. For more information:
oreilly.com/ebooks

O'REILLY®

©2014 O'Reilly Media, Inc. O'Reilly logo is a registered trademark of O'Reilly Media, Inc. 14373

Have it your way.

O'Reilly eBooks

- Lifetime access to the book when you buy through oreilly.com

- Provided in up to four, DRM-free file formats, for use on the devices of your choice: PDF, .epub, Kindle-compatible .mobi, and Android .apk

- Fully searchable, with copy-and-paste, and print functionality

- We also alert you when we've updated the files with corrections and additions.

oreilly.com/ebooks/

Safari Books Online

- Access the contents and quickly search over 7000 books on technology, business, and certification guides

- Learn from expert video tutorials, and explore thousands of hours of video on technology and design topics

- Download whole books or chapters in PDF format, at no extra cost, to print or read on the go

- Early access to books as they're being written

- Interact directly with authors of upcoming books

- Save up to 35% on O'Reilly print books

See the complete Safari Library at safari.oreilly.com

©2014 O'Reilly Media, Inc. O'Reilly logo is a registered trademark of O'Reilly Media, Inc. 14373

www.ingramcontent.com/pod-product-compliance
Ingram Content Group UK Ltd.
Pitfield, Milton Keynes, MK11 3LW, UK
UKHW011705140325
456236UK00008B/113